THE CZECHS UNDER NAZI RULE

EAST CENTRAL EUROPEAN STUDIES
OF COLUMBIA UNIVERSITY

THE CZECHS
UNDER
NAZI RULE

*THE FAILURE OF
NATIONAL RESISTANCE, 1939–1942*

By VOJTECH MASTNY

COLUMBIA UNIVERSITY PRESS
New York

Copyright © 1971 Columbia University Press
ISBN: 0–231–03303–6
Library of Congress Catalog Card Number: 72–132065
Printed in the United States of America
10 9 8 7 6 5 4 3 2

EAST CENTRAL EUROPEAN STUDIES
OF COLUMBIA UNIVERSITY

THE East Central European Studies comprise scholarly books prepared at Columbia University and published under the auspices of the Institute on East Central Europe of Columbia University. The faculty of the Institute on East Central Europe, while not assuming responsibility for the material presented or the conclusions reached by the authors, believe that these studies contribute substantially to knowledge of the area and should serve to stimulate further inquiry and research.

To My Parents

ACKNOWLEDGMENTS

THIS STUDY, begun as a doctoral dissertation at Columbia University, owes much to the encouragement of Fritz Stern, who originally sponsored and guided it. In pursuing it, I had not only the advantage of benefiting from his expert advice but also the privilege of earning his invaluable friendship. Among my present colleagues at Columbia University Alexander Dallin, Istvan Deak, Lewis J. Edinger, and Christoph M. Kimmich contributed decisively in shaping my work by comment and criticism.

I gratefully acknowledge three grants from the Foreign Area Fellowship Program which enabled me to conduct research in the United States, West Germany, Great Britain, France, and Israel in 1964–1967. The librarians and archivists of the following institutions invariably showed great understanding and readiness to help: National Archives in Washington, D.C., World War II Records Division in Alexandria, Virginia, International Law Library of Columbia University in New York City, New York Public Library, Yivo Institute for Jewish Research in New York City, Institut für Zeitgeschichte in Munich, Bundesarchiv in Koblenz, Politisches Archiv des Auswärtigen Amtes in Bonn, Geheimes Staatsarchiv in West Berlin, Berlin Document Center in West Berlin, Collegium Carolinum in Munich, Bayerische Staatsbibliothek in Munich, Johann-Gottfried Herder-Institut in Marburg a.d. Lahn, Institut für Auslandsbeziehungen in Stuttgart, Institut für Weltwirtschaft of the University of Kiel, Imperial War Museum in London, Wiener Library in London, Centre de documentation juive contemporaine in Paris, Bibliothèque de documentation internationale in Paris, and Yad Vashem in Jerusalem.

Conversations and correspondence with the following persons have helped to clarify my views and correct many of my errors: Johann W. Bruegel (London), F. W. Deakin (Oxford University), Alfred Fichelle (Paris), Norman H. Gibbs (Oxford University), William E. Griffith (Massachusetts Institute of Technology), O. D. Kulka (Hebrew University), John A. Lukacs (Chestnut Hill College, Philadelphia), Otakar Odlozilik (University of Pennsylvania),

Paul Riege (Buxtehude, Lower Saxony), Paul Schmidt (Munich), Miroslav Schubert (Laguna Hills, California), and Sir John W. Wheeler-Bennett (Garsington Manor, Oxfordshire). Expert editorial assistance by Anita Feldman of Columbia University Press was invaluable in preparing my manuscript for publication.

My wife Catherine deserves the greatest amount of gratitude not only for her patience with my seemingly interminable work but also for her own contribution—as a merciless critic and a merciful proofreader.

New York City, October, 1969

CONTENTS

ABBREVIATIONS

AA	Records of the German Foreign Office (microfilm)
Alex.	World War II Records Division, Alexandria, Virginia
BA	Bundesarchiv, Coblenz
BA, MA	Bundesarchiv, Militärarchiv, Coblenz
BDC	Berlin Document Center, West Berlin
CDJC	Centre de documentation juive contemporaine, Paris
CPC	Communist Party of Czechoslovakia
CU	International Law Library, Columbia University, New York
DDI	*I documenti diplomatici italiani*
DGFP	*Documents on German Foreign Policy*
DHCSP	*Dokumenty z historie československé politiky, 1939–1943* [Documents on the History of Czechoslovak Politics]
Eich.	Records of the Eichmann Trial (mimeographed)
GSA	Geheimes Staatsarchiv, West Berlin
IfZ	Institut für Zeitgeschichte, Munich
IWM	Imperial War Museum, London
Meld. Reich	*Meldungen aus dem Reich* (mimeographed confidential news bulletin of the Security Service)
NA	National Archives, Washington, D.C.
NSDAP	Records of the German National Socialist Workers Party (microfilm)
NSM	National Solidarity movement [*Národní souručenství*, official Czech political organization]
Nur.	Documents assembled for the Nuremberg trials (mimeographed)
OKH	Records of Headquarters, German Army High Command (microfilm)
OKW	Records of Headquarters, German Armed Forces High Command (microfilm)
ON	*Obrana národa* [Nation's Defense, a resistance organization]
Propag.	Records of the Reich Ministry for Public Enlightenment and Propaganda (microfilm)
PÚ	*Politické ústředí* [Political Center, a resistance organization]
PVVZ	*Petiční výbor "Věrni zůstaneme"* [Committee of the Petition "We Remain Faithful," a resistance organization]

RFSS	Records of the Reich Leader of the SS and Chief of the German Police (microfilm)
RGB	*Reichsgesetzblatt* [Reich Law Gazette]
RSHA	Reichssicherheitshauptamt [Reich Security Head Office]
RuSHA	Rasse- und Siedlungshauptamt [Race and Settlement Head Office]
SA	Sturmabteilungen [Storm Troops]
SD	Sicherheitsdienst [Security Service]
SGV	*Sammlung der Gesetze und Verordnungen des Protektorates Böhmen und Mähren* [Law and Ordinance Collection of the Protectorate of Bohemia and Moravia]
SOE	Special Operations Executive (British agency for underground warfare)
SS	Schutzstaffel [Elite Guard, "Black Shirts"]
Trial	*Trial of the Major War Criminals* ("Blue Series")
ÚVOD	*Ústřední vedení odboje domácího* [Central Leadership of Home Resistance]
VOB	*Verordnungsblatt des Reichsprotektors in Böhmen und Mähren* [Ordinance Gazette of the Protector in Bohemia and Moravia]
WL	Wiener Library, London
Yivo	Institute for Jewish Research, New York
YV	Yad Vashem, Jerusalem

THE CZECHS UNDER NAZI RULE

INTRODUCTION

REPRESSION, treason, and revolt are as old as human history. But only the more recent age of the all-encompassing state and of politically articulate masses has produced the typically modern phenomena of terror, collaboration, and resistance. Terror, first to be applied systematically by the new power-holders during the French Revolution, later became not only a favorite device of revolutionaries but, perfected in twentieth-century totalitarian states, a "normal" method of government by already established regimes. The terms "collaboration" and "resistance" originated during World War II when, within a short period of time, a number of nations came under the domination of a foreign totalitarian power, Nazi Germany.

Terror—the use of extreme force for intimidation rather than for destruction—was an essential component of German occupation policies. But while it was the most conspicuous and the most odious of Nazi methods, the use of terror was only one among the many means by which they kept their subjects subdued. In the present study, these other methods of domination will receive equal attention.

Collaboration—if it is to be used as a scholarly term rather than a label in political polemics—presents considerable semantic problems. In the last analysis everybody collaborated in order to survive; just working and performing other normal social functions sustained the social organism which served the needs of the oppressor. In explaining political behavior, this "objective" concept of collaboration is of little use.

In a narrower sense, the notion of collaboration ought to be limited to situations where free choice existed, that is, whenever it was possible either to engage in an action likely to promote the enemy's interests, or to abstain from it. But the probable consequences of such an action were usually not immediately clear, and individuals made their decisions from a variety of motives. Only seldom did they want to serve the enemy unconditionally; more often, they hoped to trade advantages for themselves or for their own people. In this confusion of motives and objectives, collaboration assumed the many shades which make its fair evaluation so difficult.

Like collaboration, resistance was a matter of voluntary decision, regardless of its "objective" results. It was an action designed to harm the oppressor, and as such it had to be conscious and deliberate; otherwise, there would have been no basic distinction between a bad road and a man who dynamited a bridge—they both, after all, obstructed the movement of the enemy.

The resistance action obviously did not have to be violent: quiet sabotage of production in a factory may have been more effective than guerrilla warfare, and sometimes even simple refusal to fulfil orders brought similar results. Outlawed as they were, such activities are difficult to document; only if effective are they usually reported in the sources. Still, attempts—no matter how unsuccessful—were unquestionably also part of the resistance effort. On the other hand, mere hostile disposition, unless transformed into a specific action against the enemy, counted little; so-called "moral resistance" alone indicated only inability or unwillingness to act.

The underlying conflict of interests which generates collaboration and resistance has often existed as a result of internal civil strife. But it is especially marked in confrontations between nations. For this reason the history of German rule in Europe during World War II is so well suited for the study of the two antithetic responses. And yet, despite massive literature—usually written *cum ira* and *sine studio*—we know pitifully little about the real attitudes of the subject peoples at that time. Most of them could claim both famous resisters—Jean Moulin, Josip Broz (Tito), Zoia Kosmodemianskaia—and notorious collaborators—Pierre Laval, Ante Pavelić, Andrei Vlasov. But one can hardly avoid the impression that these men and their followers were exceptional rather than typical. The behavior of the overwhelming majority of other people probably did not fit easily into the clear-cut categories of either collaboration or resistance; it was a curious mixture of both. In the Protectorate of Bohemia and Moravia, which the Nazis had created in 1939 from the western parts of the former territory of Czechoslovakia, the dramatic extremes appear to have been less conspicuous than in most other occupied countries. The story of the Czechs under Nazi rule therefore seems particularly conducive to the understanding of the "intermediate" response.

Only recently have the potentialities of repression and of resistance to it become subjects of serious study.[1] Yet situations where the former can arise and the latter would be needed are by no means hypothetical; even after the defeat of Nazism, the threat to individual and national self-assertion is still very much present in the world. After the manuscript of this study had been almost completed, the very Czechs who had first suffered at Hitler's hands again became victims of a foreign occupation which dramatized the problem of collaboration and resistance. The tragic events of August 1968 have since then inspired a flood of writing with much speculation about the resemblance of the recent events to those of 1938–1945. Thinly documented and hastily made, most of the conclusions reached merely attest to the tricky nature of parallels in history.[2] Whereas a careful reader of this study will become aware of both the similarities and the differences between the Czech response to the Nazi invasion and to the Soviet invasion, the drawing of historical parallels has been purposely avoided. The sorry fate of the Czechs in recent times is not the sole subject of our investigation. Their experience raises the more consequential question of how an advanced industrial nation should or should not behave in the face of a brutal force intent upon its destruction.

[1] Cf. especially E. V. Walter, *Terror and Resistance*, and A. Roberts (ed.), *The Strategy of Civilian Defense.*

[2] Cf. V. Mastny, "Unfinished Revolution," *The New Leader*, June 23, 1969, pp. 21–24. The best evaluation of the August 1968 events is P. Windsor and A. Roberts, *Czechoslovakia 1968.* For conflicting Czechoslovak views of the resistance against Soviet occupation see the anonymous symposium, "Options in Czechoslovakia," *Studies in Comparative Communism*, II (1969), No. 2, pp. 74–89.

PART I

IN THE GERMAN ORBIT

1 THE NATIONALITY CONFLICT
BEFORE AND AFTER MUNICH

G EOGRAPHY and history determined the Czechs' position in Europe as that of a small nation in a strategically important borderland between the West and the East. Unlike the Poles, squeezed between powerful neighbors on two sides, the Czechs faced only the Germans—but on three sides. The area to their east was ethnically and politically amorphous for most of its history. This peculiar location explains both the strong impact of Western influence among the Czechs and their recurrent confrontation with the Germans.

Since the Middle Ages, the Czechs had alternately experienced independence and incorporation into a larger German-dominated political entity. Formally, they belonged to the Holy Roman Empire until its end in 1806. They were ruled by the German Habsburg dynasty from 1526 to 1918. In the nineteenth and early twentieth centuries, Germans held different opinions about the respective roles of Austria and Prussia in central Europe. Yet they agreed that the lands inhabited by the Czechs were part of the German orbit politically, economically, and culturally.[1]

Bohemia and Moravia, the western sections of present-day Czechoslovakia, have been, taken together, a distinct entity for most of their history. Only in the ninth century and again since 1918 were they politically united with Slovakia. Since the Bohemian rulers had called in German colonists in the twelfth and thirteenth centuries, Germans predominated in the border areas, called the Sudetenland. The frontier between the Sudetenland and the rest of Bohemia and Moravia has always been vague. After the Thirty Years' War, the German ethnic element advanced deep into the country's interior. German, the language of the Habsburg administration, also became the tongue of the majority of burghers and

[1] H. C. Meyer's *Mitteleuropa in German Thought and Action* traces the plans for a German-dominated central Europe from 1815 to 1945.

intellectuals. Although Czech survived among the peasant population in the countryside, much of the area assumed a German
character.[2]

Under the impact of modern nationalism, the ethnic situation in
Bohemia and Moravia changed profoundly. From the early nineteenth century, the Germans retreated gradually and steadily from
their position of leadership. Romanticism stimulated the growth
of Czech national culture. The Industrial Revolution brought the
masses of the rural population into the cities, whose character
changed from German to Czech. In the interior of the country,
compact German settlements were broken up into enclaves; the
Czechs even advanced into the Sudetenland proper. After 1866,
Austrian constitutionalism enabled them to wage a successful
political struggle for control of the local government. This drive
for self-assertion inevitably generated tension between the two
nationalities.[3] By the end of the nineteenth century, intransigent
nationalist parties dominated political life in the country. On the
German side, several movements foreshadowed the ideology of
National Socialism. Hitler later acknowledged his indebtedness to
Georg Schönerer, the proto-racist prophet of "ethnic community"
(*Volksgemeinschaft*) who commanded a following in the Sudetenland.[4] There were links between the German National Socialist
Workers' Party (DNSAP), founded by the Bohemian Germans in
the early twentieth century, and its infamous Nazi namesake two
decades later.[5]

During World War I, the two antagonistic peoples in Bohemia
and Moravia sympathized with opposing coalitions. The victory of
the Entente enabled the Czechs to settle the nationality question on
their own terms with the approval of the Versailles peacemakers.[6]

[2] A good summary of the conditions prevailing toward the end of the eighteenth
century is given in S. Harrison Thomson, *Czechoslovakia in European History*, pp.
187–96.

[3] E. Wiskemann's *Czechs and Germans*, published in 1938, is the most objective
and dispassionate account of the nationality conflict in Bohemia and Moravia.

[4] A. Hitler, *Mein Kampf*, pp. 98–99. The most recent study of Schönerer is C.
Schorske's "Politics in a New Key," in *The Responsibility of Power*, ed. by Krieger
and Stern, pp. 233–51.

[5] There is no adequate literature about the Czech nationalist movements which
would complement A. G. Whiteside's study on the Bohemian roots of German
National Socialism, *Austrian National Socialism before 1918*.

[6] The story of how the Czechs achieved the satisfaction of their maximum demands
at the Paris peace conference is told in D. Perman, *The Shaping of the Czechoslovak
State*.

Although joined with the Slovaks on the basis of parity, they dominated the newly created Czechoslovak Republic because of their numbers and organization. In 1918, the Germans of the Sudetenland unsuccessfully attempted, by demonstrations and sporadic armed resistance, to oppose incorporation into the new state. Since Czechoslovakia's political system was democratic and since the numerical superiority of the ruling nationality was none too great, the Sudeten Germans suffered no severe oppression.[7] Yet they understandably considered themselves second-class citizens in a state which was not of their making. In the depression of the thirties, which hit the light industries of the Sudetenland especially hard, the Czechoslovak Germans—rightly or wrongly— blamed the Prague government for most of their misfortune. Frustration made them eager listeners to the Nazi gospel which promised redress for all the indignities Germans everywhere were thought to have suffered as a result of the Versailles *Diktat*.[8]

Hitler's own view of the Czechs had much in common with the prejudices nurtured by the Sudeten German extremists. He had shaped it during his young days in Vienna where he witnessed the nationality conflict wrecking the Habsburg monarchy. He had hated the sight of the Czechs who were, as he later described them, "arriving penniless and dragging their worn-out shoes over the streets of the city," only to "install themselves in key positions soon afterwards."[9] For Hitler, the Austrian, dislike of the Czechs took precedence over the more typical German aversion to the Poles or to the French.

Despite Hitler's obvious desire to crush the Slav upstarts, there was no simple correlation between his emotions and Nazi policies toward the Czechs. *Mein Kampf*, the authoritative account of the Führer's goals, did not mention his views about Bohemia and Moravia or the Sudetenland. Yet his professed ambition to unite

[7] The Czechoslovak political system safeguarded the control of the state by a coalition of the strongest Czech parties. Cf. the forthcoming study of interwar Czechoslovakia by Joseph Rothschild in *Political History of East Central Europe between the Two World Wars*.

[8] In his important study, *Tschechen und Deutsche*, J. W. Bruegel emphasized the impressive contribution of the Sudeten German "loyalist" parties, especially the Social Democrats, to Czech-German reconciliation. Admirable though their efforts were, the rapid Nazification of Czechoslovakia's German minority in the thirties casts doubt upon the actual strength of the conciliatory feelings in the Sudetenland.

[9] *Hitler's Table Talk*, p. 405. Cf. *Mein Kampf*, pp. 93, 109–110, 123, and W. A. Jenks, *Vienna and the Young Hitler*.

all Germans in a new Reich necessarily implied paramount interest in a country where over three million compatriots lived. Although Hitler envisaged eastern, rather than central Europe as the area for future German colonization, Bohemia and Moravia, too, were included in the program for the Reich's expansion. Hermann Rauschning, his one-time confidant, later recorded the Führer's secret statement at a Nazi gathering in 1932: "The Bohemian-Moravian basin and the eastern districts bordering on Germany will be colonized with German peasants. The Czechs . . . we shall transplant to Siberia or the Volhynian regions, and we shall set up reserves for them in the new allied states. The Czechs must get out of Central Europe."[10] Rauschning confirmed that the Nazi leaders hoped to turn Bohemia and Moravia, along with Austria, into the "iron core" of the new Reich.[11] The old idea that the area belonged to the German orbit reappeared in a new, especially aggressive version which challenged the uneasy control the Czechs had recently established over their country.

Although the desire to control the whole of Bohemia and Moravia conformed to Nazi doctrine, ideology did not decisively determine Hitler's policies toward Czechoslovakia immediately after his seizure of power. He hoped above all to restore Germany's position as a great power, an aspiration which was not radically different from that of his Weimar predecessors.[12] His announced intention to "break the chains of Versailles" implied a covert threat to the existence of Czechoslovakia, which was itself a pro-duct of the much-resented peace settlement. Still, the Nazi regime initially continued to pursue a conciliatory policy toward the neighbor republic. In their efforts to break Germany's diplomatic

[10] H. Rauschning, *Hitler Speaks*, p. 46. Although some of Rauschning's assertions cannot be verified, others are consistent with the evidence available elsewhere. No serious doubts have been raised about the reliability of his book as a historical source.

[11] *Ibid.*, p. 41. In his perceptive study of Hitler's policies toward Czechoslovakia, J. K. Hoensch interprets its destruction as one of the consistent objectives of the Nazis from the beginning of the Führer's political career. "Revize a expanze" [Revision and Expansion], *Odboj a revoluce*, VI (1968), No. 3, pp. 49–82.

[12] The relations between Czechoslovakia and Weimar Germany had been cool but "correct." In 1928 and 1931 the Wilhelmstrasse tried to attach Czechoslovakia to Germany by proposing a central European economic union which would also include Austria. Faced with Prague's reluctance and with suspicion on the part of the Western powers, however, Berlin did not press the project. Bruegel, *Tschechen und Deutsche*, pp. 214–16, 222–23.

isolation, the Nazis went so far as to suggest secretly to the Prague government that it conclude a non-aggression treaty with them. Too obviously aimed at weakening Czechoslovakia's ties with France, these overtures met in Prague with a skeptical, though not entirely negative response.[13]

Allied with France since 1926 and with the Soviet Union since 1935, Czechoslovakia seemed to be firmly anchored in the anti-German alliance system. The Nazis were well advised to proceed against it with caution. Only after the reoccupation of the Rhineland in March 1936 had bolstered his self-confidence did Hitler take a bolder course.

In that year, the Nazis dropped the last of their secret feelers with the Prague government, marking a turning point in Germany's policy toward Czechoslovakia. Official Nazi propaganda voiced a growing displeasure with the protection which the Czechs extended to anti-Hitler refugees.[14] Most important, Berlin endorsed the Sudeten Germans' demand for self-determination.

With financial support from Berlin, Czechoslovakia's Germans built a powerful political organization in the early thirties, modeled after Hitler's own. In 1935, the Sudeten German Party (SdP) emerged as the largest single party in the Czechoslovak elections. In the SdP, there fused two distinct currents of Sudeten German nationalism, represented respectively by its chairman, Konrad Henlein, and his deputy, Karl Hermann Frank. Henlein, nourished in his youth by the romantic nationalism of the hikers' movement (*Wandervögel*), was never virulently Czechophobe. He admired Othmar Spann, the Viennese philosopher, whose ideas of a corporative state (*Ständestaat*) were later condemned by the Nazis because of their Catholic connotations. A teacher by profession, Henlein surpassed most of his lieutenants in both intellect and

---

[13] German agents contacted the Czechoslovak government several times between 1933 and 1936. To what extent their actions were backed by the Berlin authorities still remains a matter of controversy. Cf. G. L. Weinberg, "Secret Hitler-Beneš Negotiations in 1936–37," *Journal of Central European Affairs*, XIX (1960), pp. 366–74. R. Kvaček, "Československo-německá jednání v roce 1936" [Czechoslovak-German Negotiations in 1936], *Historie a vojenství* (1965), pp. 721–54. R. Kvaček and V. Vinš, "K německo-českým sondážim ve třicátých letech" [German-Czech Feelers in the Thirties], *Československý časopis historický*, XIV (1966), pp. 880–96. The best general study of the aims and style of Hitler's foreign policy before 1938 is H.-A. Jacobsen, *Nationalsozialistische Aussenpolitik*.

[14] Many anti-Nazi exiles found asylum in Czechoslovakia—paradoxically the only country where free German political life survived. Cf. B. Černý, *Most k novému životu* [The Bridge to a New Life].

civilized manners. He was the ideal man to win the hearts of British sympathizers for the alleged sufferings of his people in 1937–1938.[15]

In contrast to Henlein, Frank, destined to play a prominent role during the Nazi occupation of Bohemia and Moravia, represented Sudeten German nationalism at its worst. He was born into a Carlsbad family of fanatical Schönerer followers. Having studied for one year at the law school of the German university in Prague, he began his career after World War I as a poorly paid clerk, at first working for a steel-producing company, later for the state railroad corporation. A none too successful, semi-educated member of the German middle class, he became a convert to the Nazi faith in the nineteen-twenties. Frank set up a bookstore at Loket, near his native Carlsbad, which specialized in the dissemination of Nazi propaganda. Having joined the SdP at the outset, he was later elected a deputy in the Prague parliament. He was known less for political acumen than for noisy conduct and reckless ambition. As the second-in-command of the Sudeten German Party, Frank was Henlein's perennial rival.[16]

Until 1937, Berlin's support of Czechoslovakia's Germans was not openly subversive. It still served the apparently legitimate purpose of strengthening the emotional ties between Germany and the compatriots abroad (*Auslandsdeutschtum*). From 1937, however, the promotion of Sudeten German nationalism coincided with preparations for the disruption of Czechoslovakia. In June 1937, Germany's military preliminaries took shape in a secret plan called "Operation Green."[17] On the political level, Henlein and Hitler agreed on a common strategy which the Sudeten German leader confidentially summarized by saying that "we must always demand so much that we can never be satisfied."[18]

Hitler's planning, however, went little beyond the anticipated disruption of Czechoslovakia. He did not reveal any specific plans concerning the future of the Czechs. Speculation on this

[15] About Henlein's background, see R. Luža, *The Transfer of the Sudeten Germans*, pp. 63–67, which also gives further references.

[16] Frank file, Berlin Document Center [BDC]. Cf. *Zpověď K. H. Franka* [The Confession of K. H. Frank], pp. 7–8.

[17] Blomberg's directive, June 24, 1937, *Nazi Conspiracy and Aggression*, VI, pp. 1007–11. Cf. E. M. Robertson, *Hitler's Pre-War Policy and Military Plans*, pp. 89–90; and B. Celovsky, *Das Münchener Abkommen*, p. 91.

[18] Note on conversation between Henlein and Hitler, March 28, 1938, *Documents on German Foreign Policy* [*DGFP*], D, II, p. 198.

subject emanated from the Sudetenland, rather than Berlin. In a memorandum for the Führer dated November 19, 1937, it was Henlein who first suggested that the whole of Bohemia and Moravia should become part of the Reich. He stated: "[The SdP] at heart . . . desires nothing more ardently than the incorporation of Sudeten German territory, nay of the whole Bohemian, Moravian, and Silesian area, within the Reich . . ."[19] Later, presumably in the summer of 1938, the leadership of the SdP prepared another memorandum which is the first known comprehensive Nazi statement favoring the incorporation of Bohemia and Moravia. Frank seems to have had a decisive share in its wording. The document, entitled "Grundplanung O.A.," foresaw a preliminary military occupation.[20] After approximately five years of army rule, the "Leader of the Sudeten Germans" was to take over the government. Suppression of all independent Czech political and cultural institutions would follow, the Czech population would be gradually assimilated, and the entire territory would become German in character. After the war this memorandum was found in Henlein's former headquarters at Aš in western Sudetenland. We do not know whether it ever reached Berlin. If it did, it was not officially endorsed.

The directives for "Operation Green" also envisaged "a quick seizure of Bohemia and Moravia"—not of Slovakia—to be followed by the establishment of a military government in the occupied territory.[21] But this measure was considered merely routine and temporary. Although in his secret conferences Hitler justified the destruction of Czechoslovakia by the need for enlarging "the German racial community" and extending its *Lebensraum*, his words did not necessarily imply formal annexation of any territory beyond the predominantly German Sudetenland.[22] His notorious exclamation, "We do not want any Czechs," may have indeed reflected his genuine reluctance to include an ethnically alien population of eight million Slavs in a supposedly homogenous

---

[19] Henlein to Hitler, November 19, 1937, *ibid.*, p. 57.

[20] "Grundplanung O.A.," in V. Král (ed.), *Die Vergangenheit warnt*, pp. 27–38. Although the memorandum is unsigned, its style suggests Frank's authorship.

[21] Keitel's directive, December 21, 1937, *DGFP*, D, VII, p. 636. Instructions about the tasks of the army in the occupied territory, September 7, 1938, Records of Headquarters, German Armed Forces High Command [OKW], T-77, 487, 1651612–13, and T-77, 170, 904328–51, National Archives [NA]. See also OKW, T-77, 168, 901370–578, NA.

[22] Hossbach's notes on the conference of November 5, 1937, *DGFP*, D, I, pp. 29–30.

Reich of the German race.[23] A study prepared by the Armed Forces High Command in June 1938 examined the "geopolitical importance of *an* incorporation" of Bohemia and Moravia, implying that *the form* of incorporation still remained undecided.[24] Although the available evidence leaves no doubts about Hitler's desire to control Bohemia and Moravia, he let the course of events decide the form of his domination.

The international situation in the late thirties bore little promise for the Czechs in their impending showdown with Hitler. Having yielded to the aggressors in the Rhineland, in Ethiopia, in Spain, and in Austria, the Western powers could be suspected of lacking faith in the system of collective security they themselves had tried to create. Small nations seemed helpless against blackmail by their powerful neighbors. Because of the persisting mistrust between the Western democracies and the Soviet Union, each side considered a deal with Germany as a desirable alternative to a common anti-Hitler front.

Thus Czechoslovakia's alliances, though impressive on paper, were less so in reality. Since, according to the terms of the 1935 treaty, Soviet help was contingent upon France's acting first, the key to Czechoslovakia's security lay in Paris. Yet the French, though fearing German expansionism, recalled with anxiety their own enormous sacrifices during World War I and sought British assurances before committing themselves to a policy which might again involve them in war. If France's willingness to help the Czechs was small, Britain's was even smaller. In contrast to the French, who had traditionally sympathized with Czech nationalism, the British attitude was at best ambivalent. At the worst, influential British conservatives tended to side with the Germans. The opinion that Germany suffered unjustly at the hands of the victors at Versailles found more advocates in Britain than in any other Western country. British policy-makers, too ignorant about Nazism to understand its dynamism, took Hitler's word that his ambitions were strictly limited to areas inhabited by Germans. Prime Minister Neville Chamberlain hoped that—as in Bismarck's times—a satisfied Germany would turn into a safeguard of European security. He envisaged Germany as a stabilizing force, a role

[23] *The Speeches of Adolf Hitler*, ed. by N. H. Baynes, II, p. 1526.
[24] "Geopolitische Bedeutung einer Eingliederung Böhmens und Mährens/Schlesiens in das Reich," June 14, 1938, OKW, T-77, 487, 1651679–96, NA.

which France's eastern European allies, products—like Czechoslo-vakia—of the controversial Versailles settlement, were so ob-viously unsuited to play. Although reluctantly, the French adopted the British view, that the best way of dealing with the Czechoslovak crisis was to press Prague into concessions to Berlin.[25]

Quite apart from considerations of international morality, the principal folly of the appeasement policy consisted in the willing-ness to sacrifice Czechoslovakia without receiving in return any tangible security guarantees. Such a policy could only encourage Hitler's ambitions and invite him to take risks which would even-tually make war inevitable. In September 1938, these ambitions did not necessarily include the seizure of Bohemia and Moravia, except as a possible alternative. Although he wished to assert German domination in the area and appeared ready to use force in order to achieve it, Hitler did not aim at any particular political settlement. Not he, but the British and the French decided in September 1938 the form of German control over Czechoslovakia.

The settlement to which Hitler and Mussolini agreed was embodied in the joint statement adopted by the four powers at the Munich conference on September 30, 1938. It provided for the immediate cession of the Sudetenland to Germany. For Czechoslo-vakia this implied new frontiers which would make the rest of the country indefensible. The signatories of the Munich agreement promised to guarantee its integrity in the future. However, by acceding to this settlement, the Western governments acknowledged that Czechoslovakia would be both politically and economically within the German sphere of influence.[26]

Having entrusted her fate to foreign powers who had failed to provide help at the crucial moment, Czechoslovakia now faced the unattractive alternatives of accepting the Munich terms or resisting Germany alone. The Czechs had good reasons to blame the West-ern governments for this state of affairs. The responsibility for the choice, however, was entirely their own.[27] It was an agonizing situation but not a unique one in history. Serbia had faced a choice between surrender and probable defeat in 1914; Finland was to face it in 1939.

[25] Of the extensive literature on appeasement, two especially useful studies are M. Gilbert and R. Gott, *The Appeasers*, and K. Robbins, *Munich 1938*.

[26] The standard work on Munich is Celovsky, *Das Münchener Abkommen*.

[27] Cf. D. Vital, "Czechoslovakia and the Powers, September 1938," *Journal of Contemporary History*, I (1966), No. 4, pp. 37–67.

Before making a decision, the Czechoslovak statesmen had to take into account the attitude of the Soviet Union which—much to the dismay of the Moscow policy-makers—had not been invited to Munich. During the September crisis, the Russians had repeatedly indicated their willingness to stand by Czechoslovakia even if France defaulted. They confirmed this position as late as September 30. By accepting Soviet help, the Czechs would have put Moscow into an embarrassing position. The Red Army would have had to cross either Poland, or Rumania—a violation of sovereignty which neither of these countries was willing to tolerate. Moreover, the Soviet armed forces were hardly ready to act effectively, as their poor performance in the war with Finland in 1939–1940 and their initial response to the German invasion in 1941 were amply to demonstrate. Czechoslovakia's President Beneš later gave the following reasons for not having tested the sincerity of the Soviet offer:

Neither the West nor Russia was ready. I knew that. If Germany had succeeded in provoking war and Russia had somehow come to our help, my fears would have materialized: Daladier and Chamberlain would have left Hitler a free hand to settle his account with the Bolsheviks. [A German] war with the West would have never come; Hitler would have controlled Russia, and we would never have come out from under the yoke.[28]

Although made *post factum*, this seems a plausible explanation. Beneš undoubtedly also feared the increase of Communist influence which the Soviet offer entailed. Saved from an embarrassing situation, the Soviet Union, unlike Britain and France, emerged from the crisis with an undamaged reputation. While the Czechs' traditional sympathy for the West was under strain, their equally traditional pro-Russian feelings remained intact.

The choice between fighting and surrender, however, did not depend solely upon the acceptance or refusal of Soviet help. There was a chance that defiance of the Munich terms, even without foreign support, would either dissuade Hitler from a full-scale attack or persuade other countries to take a firmer stand against him. This possibility would have been worth testing, especially

[28] Smutný's note on conversation with Beneš, July 5, 1941, L. Otáhalová and M. Červinková (eds.), *Dokumenty z historie československé politiky* [Documents on the History of Czechoslovak Politics; *DHCSP*], I, p. 238. J. A. Lukacs' 1953 discussion of the Soviet role during the Munich crisis is still topical, despite subsequent publication of new documents (*The Great Powers and Eastern Europe*, pp. 172–89).

since there would always have been time to surrender after armed resistance had proved hopeless. German military experts later estimated that the Czechoslovak army alone could have resisted for fifteen to twenty days.[29] The morale of the troops, as demonstrated by their mobilization on September 23, was good. In a dramatic conversation on September 29, several Czechoslovak generals urged Beneš to reject the Munich ultimatum and to order the army to fight.[30] Yet the President preferred acceptance. He later explained his reasoning in a conversation with his personal secretary: "Fighting Germany alone means suicide, a sacrifice of countless lives and the odium that peace has been broken because of our apparent desire to hold a territory inhabited by Germans . . . . I have a plan of my own. Although I submit, I know that social forces will push Europe into war. Then Czechoslovakia will be resurrected and will receive satisfaction."[31] For the rest of his life Beneš was torn with doubts about the wisdom of his decision. He tried to persuade himself and others that his action had been a brilliant piece of statesmanship. Yet regardless of later rationalizations, mere reliance upon "social forces" implied, in 1938, relinquishment of any policy, and indeed the demise of Beneš as a statesman.

The striking feature of the surrender was its apparently unanimous acceptance by the nation. The people overwhelmingly respected the President's judgment. The National Assembly did not inquire into his reasons. The generals did not press him. Some of them may have plotted to seize power but their plans remained in the preparatory stage.[32] In compliance with orders, the soldiers laid down their arms, vacating the Sudetenland without incidents or even gestures of defiance. Almost overnight, their fighting spirit

[29] "Erfahrungen über das Verhalten der Armeen Osteuropas in der Spannungszeit 1938," December 1, 1938, Records of Headquarters, German Army High Command [OKH], T-78, 301, 6252033, NA.

[30] E. Beneš, *Mnichovské dny* [The Munich Days], pp. 340–42. Smutný's note on conversations with Beneš, July 5, 1943, *DHCSP*, I, p. 348.

[31] Smutný's note, June 23, 1941, *DHCSP*, I, p. 235. From the Czechoslovak side, information about Munich is brought up to date in M. Lvová, *Mnichov a Edvard Beneš* [Munich and Edvard Beneš], and in the collection of official documents by V. Král (ed.), *Das Abkommen von München 1938.*

[32] Jan Křen, *Do emigrace* [Into Exile], pp. 78–81. The former Czechoslovak Chief of Staff recently denied that such plans had even existed. L. Krejčí, "Obranyschopnost ČSR 1938" [Czechoslovakia's Defense Readiness in 1938], *Odboj a revoluce*, VI (1968), No. 2, pp. 30–33.

gave way to indifference to the further course of events. Emanuel Moravec, who was a colonel in the General Staff in 1938 and who later became the leading Czech collaborator with the Germans, pinpointed some of the causes of the army's behavior: "Politically our generals were lambs; there was among them not a single lion to act as a truly daring and tough soldier . . . . Our soldiers, having been brought up in too much modesty and obedience, limited themselves to curses and tears." [33]

The Czechs' response testified to their uncertainty about the use of power, an uncertainty typical of a small nation. A middle-class people par excellence, they owed their greatest achievements to industrious and peaceful work rather than to the use of arms. In 1938, their statehood was of relatively recent vintage; most Czechs had spent a good portion of their lives under foreign domination, none too oppressive in its Austrian form. Presidential paternalism, the *dictature du respect* [34] characteristic of Czechoslovak democracy between the wars, did not encourage popular initiative when great political decisions were at stake. Munich further weakened the nation's self-confidence. The crucial problem for the future was whether in the hard times ahead the people would recover faith in their own actions or continue to rely upon "social forces."

Born of surrender and despair, the post-Munich "Second Republic" came into existence under the least favorable conditions possible. Demoralization prevailed in political life. George F. Kennan, the recently appointed Secretary of the American Legation in Prague, observed in December 1938 that "every feature of liberalism and democracy . . . was hopelessly and irretrievably discredited." [35]

On October 6, Edvard Beneš, the architect of Czechoslovakia's ill-fated alliances, resigned from the Presidency. The right-wing press singled him out as the scapegoat for the national disaster. Otherwise there was conspicuously little serious soul-searching. Both Beneš's critics and his followers soon agreed that pragmatic accommodation to the new situation was the most urgent demand of the day. An article by Jan Stránský published in Prague's

[33] E. Moravec, *V úloze mouřenina* [In the Moor's Role], pp. 311, 343.

[34] The phrase is M. Baumont's; *La faillite de la paix*, I, p. 438. An excellent short analysis of Masaryk's political theory is the article by R. Szporluk, "Masaryk's Idea of Democracy," *Slavonic and East European Review*, XLI (1962), pp. 31–49.

[35] Letter of December 8, 1938, G. F. Kennan, *From Prague after Munich*, p. 7.

leading liberal daily best expressed the prevailing state of mind: "If we cannot sing with the angels we shall howl with the wolves.... If the world is to be governed by force rather than by law, let our place be where there is greater force and greater determination. Let us seek—we have no other choice—accommodation with Germany."[36]

Beneš's successor as the director of foreign policy was František Chvalkovský, formerly Czechoslovak Minister to Rome, known for his sympathies for authoritarian regimes. His apparent realism stemmed from a lack of principles: Chvalkovský later remarked that "everything could be arranged if only one would yield a point of honor."[37] His country's main hope lay in the guarantees promised by the Munich signatories, which, however, were not forthcoming. For a while, the government gave some thought to courting Mussolini as a counterweight against Hitler and it considered a *rapprochement* with Poland. In November 1938, a delegation of the Polish Foreign Office secretly visited Prague and discussed possible military cooperation.[38] Yet without seriously exploring these alternatives, Chvalkovský tried above all to secure German confidence. In a conversation with Hitler on October 14, he indicated readiness to comply with Berlin's wishes in every respect. To Ribbentrop, Chvalkovský reportedly stated: "And in foreign policy we shall lean on you, *Herr Reichsminister*, if you allow us."[39]

In domestic policy, accommodation was promoted by Rudolf Beran, the boss of the powerful right-wing Republican (Agrarian) Party. A shrewd, though narrow-minded political manipulator, Beran had been among Beneš's foremost opponents before Munich. Along with other Agrarian politicians he had sought a *modus vivendi* with the SdP by maintaining friendly relations with several of its leaders. He was impressed by the efficiency of the totalitarian regimes and by their ability to bolster national morale. Dissatisfied as they were with the multiplicity of political parties before Munich, most Czechs welcomed the introduction of a two-party system, sponsored by the Agrarians. The politicians of the center and the right formed the National Unity Party. The Social Democrats

[36] *Lidové noviny*, October 4, 1938.

[37] *The Von Hassell Diaries*, p. 126.

[38] H. Batowski, *Kryzys dyplomatyczny w Ewropie* [The Diplomatic Crisis in Europe], pp. 168–69. Křen, *Do emigrace*, pp. 143–44.

[39] Conversations with Hitler and Ribbentrop, October 13–14, 1938, *DGFP*, D, IV, pp. 60–63, 69–72. P. Schmidt, *Statist auf diplomatischer Bühne*, p. 428.

created the National Labor Party as a "loyal opposition." Beran became Prime Minister.

The new regime encouraged a transition from democracy to authoritarianism.[40] In December 1938, pre-publication censorship of the press was introduced. The labor unions merged into a single organization dominated by the right-wing Social Democrats of the National Labor Party. The Communist party was abolished. In January 1939, the National Assembly voted an Enabling Act authorizing the executive to legislate by decree in case of emergency. This transformation of the political structure, carried out by the Czechs themselves, was not the result of German interference. On the contrary, the Czech politicians hoped to prevent such interference by adapting their regime extensively, though not completely, to that of Germany. They welcomed totalitarian methods as a means of promoting national recovery but detested excesses, particularly those of anti-Semitism. In practice, however, the balance was precarious.[41] Many Jews, though not suffering any serious persecution, encountered discrimination in public employment and professions.[42] More ominous was the government's unprotesting extradition—into the hands of the Gestapo—of exiles from Germany.[43]

On November 30, the National Assembly elected a new President. It chose Emil Hácha, a sixty-six-year-old retired Chief

[40] The best study on the Second Republic is the unpublished Yale dissertation by I. K. Feierabend, "The Pattern of a Satellite State." Good summaries are A. Fichelle, "La crise interne de la Tchécoslovaquie," *Revue d'histoire de la deuxième guerre mondiale*, LII (1963), pp. 21–38, and H. Bodensieck, "Die Politik der Zweiten Tschecho-Slowakischen Republik," *Zeitschrift für Ostforschung*, VI (1957), pp. 54–71. M. Hájek, *Od Mnichova k 15. březnu* [From Munich to March 15], is an orthodox Marxist account.

[41] The ambiguity of this policy was reflected in the press which—responding to a self-imposed rather than an officially exercised censorship—backed the government with only minor reservations. About the difficulties in interpreting the newspapers of that period see O. Böss, "Die Zweite Tschecho-Slowakische Republik im Spiegel zeitgenössischer tschechischer Pressestimmen," in *Bohemia*, III, pp. 402–25, and H. Bodensieck, "Zur 'Spiegelung' der nach-Münchener tschechoslowakischen Politik in der zeitgenössischen tschechischen Publizistik," in *Zeitschrift für Ostforschung*, XVI (1964), pp. 79–101.

[42] Dispatch of February 17, 1939, Kennan, *From Prague after Munich*, pp. 42–57. H. Bodensieck points out that the moderate anti-Semitism of the Czechoslovak authorities, by encouraging the Jews to emigrate, saved them from later extermination. "Das Dritte Reich und die Lage der Juden in der Tschecho-Slowakei nach München," *Vierteljahrshefte für Zeitgeschichte*, IX (1961), pp. 249–61.

[43] Bruegel, *Tschechen und Deutsche*, p. 517.

Justice of the Supreme Administrative Court. A former Austro-Hungarian civil servant and a profoundly faithful Catholic, Hácha was a nationalist of conservative leanings. His bureaucratic inclinations and experience led him to conceive of his office as one of service rather than leadership. He was as painfully aware of his nation's difficult situation as of the limits of his political talent, and accepted the high office only with great reluctance. Having recognized the inevitability of German predominance, he set for himself the formidable task of promoting Czech-German reconciliation. After his election, Hácha told the cabinet that "the Czechoslovak statesmen should take the national saint, Duke Wenceslas, as their model: Duke Wenceslas fought for German-Czech understanding, although initially he did not find understanding with his own people."[44]

Whatever opposition there was to the new regime, its critics did not question the merit of the government's policies but merely the pace at which they were instituted. On the political left, Beneš's followers—particularly army officers, civil servants, and teachers—blamed Beran for pushing the authoritarian transformation too far. They hoped that Hitler's aggressive ambitions would soon be checked by the European powers and that the former President would return to Prague in triumph. Unable to offer any program beyond this belief, however, the opposition was neither organized nor very active. The same applied to the Communists who only slowly began to build an underground network.

In contrast, right-wing critics of the government, advocating extreme nationalism of a Fascist variety, were very vocal. They formed three major groups which, not being legally recognized as political parties, were frequently targets of police intervention. The National Fascist Community, led by General Rudolf Gajda, regarded as its model Italian Fascism. The Vlajka (The Banner) movement drew inspiration from German National Socialism. ANO (*Akce národní obrody*, Action for National Restoration) emphasized anti-Semitism without offering a specific program. The agitation of these groups attracted public attention, though not any sizable following. Viewed with mistrust by an

[44] Hencke to Foreign Office, December 2, 1938, Records of the German Foreign Office [AA], T-120, 12, 18121, NA. Hácha to Beneš, December 10, 1938, *Memoirs of Eduard Beneš*, p. 97. Cf. F. Lukeš, "K volbě Emila Háchy presidentem tzv. druhé republiky" [The Election of Emil Hácha as President of the So-Called Second Republic], *Časopis Národního musea*, Social Science series, CXXXI (1962), pp. 114–20

overwhelming majority of the Czechs, who were deeply averse to any form of political extremism, the Fascists attached their hopes to German support. In November 1938, ANO intimated to the German Legation a plan for a *coup d'état*. The Nazis, however, proved unresponsive. They harbored justified misgivings about the actual strength of the right-wing opposition and about the Fascists' buoyant nationalism, which had until recently had an anti-German cast. Moreover, the Nazi diplomats had little confidence in the personal qualities of the Czech Fascist leaders. In the estimation of the Germans, Miroslav Hlávka, the author of the proposed *coup d'état*, was "a hard drinker and woman chaser," whereas General Gajda was a "morally inferior" adventurer.[45]

The Second Republic achieved significant progress in the settlement of the nationality question, the principal problem which had plagued the pre-Munich state. Following an agreement between Czech and Slovak politicians, reached at Žilina on October 7, 1938, the Republic became a federal state. Slovakia received internal autonomy, safeguarded by a separate government and a diet. A similar arrangement applied to the Carpathian Ukraine, Czechoslovakia's most eastern territory, with a predominantly Ukrainian population. Although about 230,000 Germans still remained in the diminished territory of Bohemia and Moravia, they were a small minority compared with the more than 6 million Czechs there. Paradoxically, this rump territory was more Czech in population than the Sudetenland was German, since the Czech minority in the Sudetenland numbered over 600,000 as against a German population of 3.5 million.[46] So that Berlin would not have any reason for complaints, the Prague government accorded important privileges to the Germans within its jurisdiction. These included the organization of a Nazi party and an elaborate system of German education from the elementary to the university level.

Although no longer on a democratic basis, post-Munich Czechoslovakia achieved a new stability. By early 1939, its leaders viewed the future with cautious confidence. The chairman of the National Labor Party welcomed the New Year by writing in a contemporary daily: "Although one cannot deny that in the people's subconsciousness a complete adjustment has here and there not taken place,

[45] Hencke to Foreign Office, November 11 and 28, 1938, Documents Assembled for the Nuremberg Trials [Nur], NG-3530, Institut für Zeitgeschichte [IfZ]. Altenburg's notes, February 10 and 20, 1939, AA, T-120, 916, 387199, 387220, NA.
[46] Luža, *The Transfer of the Sudeten Germans*, pp. 158, 163.

one can nevertheless hardly help admitting that the state, particularly its Czech parts, enjoys domestic peace, which, barring extraordinary events, can exert beneficial influence contributing to the full restoration of the national spirit."[47] The viability of the Second Republic, however, did not depend upon the attitude of the Czechs and the Slovaks alone. Berlin's toleration of the new state of affairs was essential for its survival.

Several eminent historians have suggested that Munich, outwardly Germany's diplomatic triumph, actually disappointed Hitler by frustrating his plan to march on Prague.[48] At the Nuremberg trial, Hjalmar Schacht testified that the Führer had blamed "that fellow" Chamberlain for spoiling his entry into the Czech capital.[49] On November 23, 1939, Hitler himself boasted in a speech to his generals: "From the very first moment it was clear to me that I could not be contented with the Sudeten German area. It was only a partial solution. The decision to invade Bohemia was made."[50] After Munich, the plans for Operation Green remained in force. On October 21, 1938, Hitler amended them by the following directive: "It must be possible to smash at any time the remainder of the Czech state should it pursue an anti-German policy."[51]

None of these sources, however, presents conclusive evidence about Hitler's design for the annexation of additional parts of Czechoslovakia immediately after Munich. It seems more likely that in October and November 1938 such a course of action was still an open question for the Nazis.[52] Their policy in regard to the country's nationality problem indicated this uncertainty.

After Munich, the Sudeten German politicians prepared several proposals for settling the matter of Czechoslovakia's relationship

[47] *Národní práce*, January 1, 1939, quoted according to an unsigned article in the periodical *Tvorba*, 1959, p. 234.

[48] J. W. Wheeler-Bennett, *Munich*, p. 331. A. Bullock, *Hitler*, pp. 471–72.

[49] *Trial of the Major War Criminals* [*Trial*], XII, p. 531.

[50] Hitler's address to German officers, November 23, 1939, *ibid.*, XXVI, p. 329.

[51] *DGFP*, D, IV, p. 99.

[52] Although the Nazis obviously tried to strengthen their influence in east central Europe, the exact direction of Germany's expansion after Munich was not immediately clear. As late as November 1938, the journalist Georg Dertinger—who had access to Nazi ruling circles—commented that Hitler was not following any "fixed menu" (*festliegende Speisekarte*) but rather awaiting opportunities as they arose. M. Broszat, "Die Reaktion der Mächte auf den 15. März 1939," *Bohemia*, VIII, p. 262.

to the Reich. One originated in Henlein's immediate entourage, another with his close collaborator Hans Neuwirth, and a third with Ernst Kundt, the leader of the German minority in rump Czechoslovakia. All envisaged strong subordination to the Reich but none of them—in contrast to Sudeten German plans prior to Munich—included outright annexation.[53]

The officials in the Wilhelmstrasse and in the Armed Forces High Command also considered the preservation of Czechoslovakia in its post-Munich form desirable. In October 1938, they weighed the alternatives concerning the future position of Slovakia: independence, autonomy within Czechoslovakia, autonomy within Hungary, autonomy within Poland. They welcomed the second alternative as the best guarantee against Polish and Hungarian designs to establish a common frontier. "It is in our *military interest* that Slovakia should not be separated from the Czechoslovak union but should remain with Czechoslovakia under strong German influence."[54]

Those Slovak politicians who resented the union with the Czechs, realizing that without German support their country would be an easy prey for Hungary and Poland, sought to enlist such support for their independence plans. On October 12 and 19 the Slovak nationalist leaders Jozef Tiso and Ferdinand Ďurčanský pleaded for German backing in secret talks with Göring and Ribbentrop.[55] Although they were graciously received, Berlin offered them little satisfaction. The Nazis, in fact, helped to satisfy Hungary's territorial demands at the Slovaks' expense. The Vienna Award, arranged on November 2 under auspices of the German and Italian foreign ministers, assigned to Hungary extensive portions of southern and eastern Slovakia.

The Vienna Award followed a month after the transfer of the industrial Teschen area to Poland, to which Prague had consented

[53] "Zur Lösung der tschechischen Frage," Král, *Vergangenheit*, pp. 40–43. Neuwirth to Foreign Office, October 15, 1938, in V. Král (ed.), *Die Deutschen in der Tschechoslowakei*, pp. 349–53. Kundt to Foreign Office, October 1938, *ibid.*, pp. 357–62.

[54] Woermann's memoranda, October 5 and 7, 1938, Nur. NG-3056, International Law Library, Columbia University [CU], and *DGFP*, D, IV, pp. 46–47. Keitel to Foreign Office, October 6, 1938, *ibid.*, p. 40.

[55] Note on Göring-Ďurčanský conversation, October 12, 1938, *ibid.*, pp. 82–83. Its date corrected according to Ďurčanský, "Mit Tiso bei Hitler," *Politische Studien*, VII, No. 80 (December 1956), p. 9. Minutes of Ribbentrop-Tiso conversation, October 19, 1938, *DGFP*, D, IV, pp. 86–92.

immediately after Munich under Warsaw's military threats. These concessions to its greedy neighbors ended the partitions of Czechoslovakia in 1938. Germany assumed the role of arbiter in east central Europe but did not endorse any further claims of the neighboring states against the rump republic. In particular, Berlin did not view favorably Hungary's ambition to annex the Carpathian Ukraine.[56]

There is ample evidence suggesting that the Germans wished to stabilize Czechoslovakia's position rather than encourage its further disintegration. As a guideline for the forthcoming talks with Chvalkovský, Woermann, the Assistant State Secretary in the Wilhelmstrasse, noted on October 12: "If it is the intention to establish really close relations with Czechoslovakia, we must not impose a Versailles on the country."[57] It was assumed, however, "that in the future the 'Czech and Slovak' rump state will of necessity depend to a considerable extent upon Germany."[58] Hitler made it clear to Chvalkovský that Czechoslovakia must submit to German leadership in foreign policy, reduce its army, introduce anti-Jewish legislation, further limit freedom of the press, and adjust its economy to the needs of the Reich. "[Czechoslovakia] must realize that she is in the German sphere and it is in her own interest to adapt herself to the conditions of that sphere."[59]

For at least two months after Munich, the Nazi leaders evidently preferred to any other alternative Czechoslovakia's continued existence as a formally independent German satellite. They tried to cement its new status by bilateral treaties. The agreement of November 19, 1938 provided for the construction of a super-highway between Breslau and Vienna, giving Germany extraterritorial rights in the section across Czechoslovakia. Another

---

[56] Hewel to Kordt, October 8, 1938, AA, T-120, 1004, 391064–065, NA. In late 1938, Hitler for a while considered the idea of bringing into existence an "independent" Ukrainian state as his satellite, a plan designed to intimidate both Poland and the Soviet Union. If realized, the project would have implied the amputation of the Carpathian Ukraine from Czechoslovakia. Since, however, that province was both economically and militarily a liability for Prague, its loss would have strengthened rather than weakened Czechoslovakia's cohesiveness. Kennan, *From Prague after Munich*, pp. 58–74. Hitler's Ukrainian plans are analyzed in detail in R. Ilnytzkyj, *Deutschland und die Ukraine*, I, pp. 164–213.

[57] Woermann's memorandum, October 12, 1938, *DGFP*, D, IV, p. 58.

[58] Keitel to Foreign Office, October 6, 1938, *ibid.*, p. 40.

[59] Minutes of Hitler-Chvalkovský conversation, October 14, 1938, *ibid.*, p. 70.

treaty, signed on the same day, envisaged the construction of an Oder-Danube canal.[60]

In November, the German Foreign Office drafted a "friendship treaty" which would have embodied the guarantees of Czechoslovakia's territorial integrity foreseen by the Munich agreement. The draft stipulated that the country must coordinate its foreign policy with Berlin's. It was to withdraw from the League of Nations, accede to the Anti-Comintern Pact, reduce its army and give right of passage to German troops. International trade negotiations concerning Czechoslovakia were to be conducted by Berlin and the two countries were to form a monetary and customs union. The draft was to be presented to Chvalkovský during his visit to Berlin in late December.[61]

Until early December 1938, we have no convincing evidence of Hitler's aggressive designs against the new Czechoslovakia. On the contrary, the "Czech question," as the Nazis understood it, seemed to be settled. The Western powers agreed to regard Czechoslovakia as being within Germany's sphere of power. The Czechs had adjusted themselves to this fact. The Nazis showed no dissatisfaction with the Munich arrangement which enabled them to exercise control over a satellite, though formally independent Czechoslovakia, and they seemed to be working toward making this a permanent situation.

[60] *Ibid.*, pp. 153–154. AA, T-120, 1094, 450629–30, and 1004, 391220–27, NA.
[61] Woermann's memoranda, November 23 and 25, 1938, Nur. NG-3613 and NG-2993, CU. The text of the proposed treaty in H. Bodensieck, "Der Plan eines 'Freundschaftsvertrages' zwischen dem Reich und der Tschecho-Slowakei im Jahre 1938," *Zeitschrift für Ostforschung*, X (1961), pp. 464–73. The *terminus a quo* of the currency and customs union was to be April 1, 1939; AA, T-120, 1159, 468040, NA.

2 *HITLER'S DESIGN*
AND IMPROVISATION

D URING the last four weeks of 1938, the Nazis started revising their policy toward Prague. Between December 1 and 5 of that year, Hitler traveled through the Sudetenland, receiving ovations from the populace, and inspecting the former Czechoslovak fortifications.[1] After the war, General Walter Warlimont, who had been head of the Home Defense Department in the Armed Forces High Command, told the American military interrogators about the following incident:

During lunch at the inn of a small Sudeten town, on the first day of the trip, Hitler dominated the table conversation and startled his audience by declaring that he remained firm in his original plan for the incorporation of Bohemia and Moravia within the Reich. He was confident that he would accomplish this by political means. The Wehrmacht needed therefore to concern itself solely with the problem of the most rapid possible occupation of Bohemia and Moravia . . . .[2]

On December 17, General Wilhelm Keitel, the chief of the Armed Forces High Command, issued an order according to Hitler's instruction. The army was to begin preparations for marching into Bohemia and Moravia: "The case is to be prepared on the assumption that no appreciable resistance is to be expected. Outwardly it must be quite clear that it is only a peaceful action and not a war-like undertaking."[3]

Doubts were later raised as to whether Keitel's instruction was valid evidence of Hitler's intention to take over the rest of Czechoslovakia.[4] But previously unknown documents from the German military archives prove such an intention beyond reasonable doubt.

[1] Hitler's daily activities, p. 34, MA 3(1), IfZ.
[2] Interrogation of Warlimont, pp. 3–4, in De Witt C. Poole Collection, RG-59, NA.
[3] Directive by Keitel, December 17, 1938, *DGFP*, D, IV, p. 186.
[4] A. J. P. Taylor, *The Origins of the Second World War*, p. 193.

From January 12, 1939, onward, select military units received directives concerning their "operational preparedness" for the anticipated occupation.[5] Although no exact timetable was set, the documents used the terms "Y-Day" for the date of the invasion and "Y minus" days for the days immediately preceding it. Initially, a few high officers were informed about the objective of the impending operation. Then at the end of February, lower officers were also told at confidential conferences that the targets were Bohemia and Moravia. They had to sign pledges of secrecy.[6]

Why did Hitler decide to replace his indirect control of satellite Czechoslovakia with outright occupation? His interpreter, Paul Schmidt, later noted that in early 1939 "the Czechs were again the red cloth for Hitler."[7] Yet their actual behavior hardly justified his fury. Other reasons must have accounted for the Führer's change of mind.

After a few months of hesitation, following the takeover of the Sudetenland, Hitler finally decided upon the next target of expansion. He hoped to apply to Poland the methods which had worked so well with the Czechs, and transform that country into another German satellite. By demanding the retrocession of Danzig and an extraterritorial highway across the Polish corridor, he tested the pliability of the Warsaw government. Yet the Poles, fearful that after making these concessions they might easily slip into subjection to Berlin, seemed unresponsive. Such was the impression they made in the conversation between Foreign Minister Józef Beck and Hitler, held on January 5, 1939, and even more during Ribbentrop's visit to the Polish capital on January 26.[8]

The German army instructions for "operational preparedness" against Czechoslovakia were first issued in the period between those two fruitless conversations. Such a coincidence supports the

[5] 72nd Infantry Regiment, "Einsatzbereitschaft für Einsatz Böhmen." Instructions about operational preparedness referred to a basic document received from the headquarters of the 46th Army Division, dated January 12, 1939, H 20-72/1, Bundesarchiv [BA], Militärarchiv [MA].

[6] Order for the 10th Army Division, February 15, 1939, Records of the German Army Areas, T-79, 174, 664–67, and 671–74, NA. Diary of Ulrich Schröder, aide-de-camp of the commander of the 66th Armored Company, 2nd Army Division, pp. 2–3, H 08-20/1 BA, MA.

[7] Schmidt, *Statist auf diplomatischer Bühne*, p. 428.

[8] Minutes of Hitler-Beck conversation, January 5, 1939, *DGFP*, D, V, p. 158. Ribbentrop's note about conversation with Beck, January 26, dated February 1, 1939, *ibid.*, pp. 167–68.

contention that by moving troops into Czechoslovakia Berlin hoped to put additional pressure upon the Poles, who would then be facing a German army along their southern frontier. Then too, the Nazis may have known about the secret feelers between Prague and Warsaw in November 1938, and this may have precipitated their action.[9]

These political and strategic considerations were probably complemented by economic motives. Germany's accelerated rearmament had caused an acute shortage of gold and foreign exchange in late 1939.[10] The pressure on the Reich treasury was likely to be eased if Germany assumed direct control over a still prosperous Czechoslovakia. Moreover, substantial quantities of weapons had been stockpiled in Czechoslovakia since the time of the Munich crisis. These would be a welcome addition to the Nazi arsenal, and directives for their seizure, and for the immediate exploitation of the Czech armament industry, figured prominently in the invasion plans.[11] Hence Göring, as head of the German rearmament program, had viewed even Czechoslovakia's formal independence with displeasure. As early as October 1938 he had favored its further dismemberment, supporting the Slovak separatist demands, and only reluctantly submitting to the official German concept of Czechoslovak integrity.[12]

With the issuance of the first invasion directives, Berlin's attitude towards its satellite stiffened. The Wilhelmstrasse shelved the proposed draft treaty of friendship, indicating that the Nazis were no longer interested in formalizing the country's status. On January 21, Hitler assailed Chvalkovský with complaints about the alleged anti-German course of the Prague government.[13] Since the behavior of the Czechs was in fact beyond reproach—as the German *chargé d'affaires*, Andor Hencke, did not fail to note in his

[9] See Chapter 1, note 38. M. Broszat ("Die Reaktion der Mächte," p. 264) maintains that Hitler was less interested in the physical possession of Bohemia and Moravia than in demonstrating to the world his freedom of action in east central Europe. Other hypotheses about the reasons for the change of Berlin's policy toward Czechoslovakia in winter 1938–1939 are presented by F. Lukeš in "Německá politika po Mnichovu a okupace Československa" [German policy after Munich and the Occupation of Czechoslovakia], *Odboj a revoluce*, IV (1966), No. 2, pp. 10–11.

[10] G. Thomas, *Geschichte der deutschen Wehr- und Rüstungswirtschaft*, p. 131.

[11] Cf. OKW, T-77, 170, 904448–63, NA. See Chapter 4, below.

[12] Note on Göring-Ďurčanský conversation, October 12, 1938, *DGFP*, D, IV, p. 83. Cf. minutes of Göring's conference, October 14, 1938, *Trial*, XXVII, p. 162. Memorandum by Brücklmeier, November 17, 1938, *DGFP*, D, IV, p. 151.

[13] Minutes of Hitler-Chvalkovský conversation, January 21, 1939, *DGFP*, D, IV, pp. 190–95.

reports to Berlin—the Führer's outburst could only be interpreted as an attempt to build up tension. In a public speech delivered nine days later, he hinted ominously at the necessity of "re-establishing order in Czechoslovakia."[14] His remark suggested the strategy the Nazis would use to create an appropriate setting for military intervention. As before Munich, they hoped again to promote internal disruption. But this time the Slovaks were to play the role previously assigned to the Sudeten Germans.

By early February, Berlin's non-committal attitude toward the Slovak separatists had changed decisively.[15] On February 12, Hitler told their emissary, Vojtech Tuka, that he regretted his own earlier misunderstanding of their aspirations: "Had he known then [by the time of the Vienna Award] how things really stood in Slovakia, he would have had the Slovak leaders come and would have guaranteed them the integrity of their country—and this still held good today."[16] In the interview with Tuka, the Führer also hinted that he had devised a "far-reaching solution" to be used against the Czechs. He pointed out that their enmity had not disappeared and that their hostile mentality was probably not going to change. If involved with the Czechs, the Slovaks would be guilty by association and suffer accordingly: "*mitgefangen, mitgehangen.*" Hitler made it clear to his visitor that he wanted the Slovaks to separate themselves in the near future. While he "could not guarantee Czechoslovakia today . . . , he could guarantee an independent Slovakia at any time, even today." Ribbentrop and Göring subsequently extended similar offers to other Slovak leaders, who were now frequent guests in the Reich capital.[17]

---

[14] *The Speeches of Adolf Hitler*, ed. by Baynes, II, p. 1578.

[15] The course of German policy toward Slovakia is the subject of the excellent study by J. K. Hoensch, *Die Slowakei und Hitlers Ostpolitik*.

[16] Minutes of Hitler-Tuka conversation, February 12, 1939, *DGFP*, D, IV, pp. 211–12.

[17] Ribbentrop supposedly told Ďurčanský that "in case of the proclamation of independence the Reich government would be ready to guarantee Slovakia's frontiers against external aggression, provided this step would be taken in a favorable moment." Ďurčanský, "Mit Tiso bei Hitler," p. 5. Cf. excerpts from Keppler's file dated August 9, 1939, Nur. NG-3956, CU. On February 27 or 28, Ernst Kundt, the leader of the German "ethnic group" in Bohemia and Moravia, sent a memorandum to Hitler in which he implicitly pleaded for the country's incorporation into the Reich. He was especially concerned about the rapid weakening of the group by exodus to Germany. Kundt's reasoning may have reinforced Hitler's determination to seek the end of satellite Czechoslovakia by military occupation. See H. Bodensieck, "Zur Vorgeschichte des 'Protektorats Böhmen und Mähren'," *Geschichte in Wissenschaft und Unterricht*, XIX (1968), pp. 713–32.

The Prague government became understandably alarmed about the new German-Slovak intimacy. Hoping to bolster its international position, it addressed to the signatories of the Munich agreement a demand for the promised guarantees. None of them complied, but, while the British and French were embarrassed, the Nazis pretended indignation. Seeking assurances anywhere outside of Germany was for them sure evidence of bad faith on the part of the Czechs.

Trying to soothe the German ire, Hubert Masařík, Chvalkovský's *chef de cabinet*, went to Berlin in early March. He tried to impress the Nazis with promises of most generous concessions. These included the appointment of a German cabinet minister to guarantee that the government's policies would always conform with Reich interests. Masařík indicated that any further suggestions "would be gratefully received." Yet he got no farther than to the head of the Czechoslovak desk in the Foreign Office, Günther Altenburg. His proposals were never considered.[18]

The failure of the Masařík mission indicated that the Nazis did not want to limit their freedom of action by any commitment to the Czechs. They instead awaited the early success of their assiduous efforts to build up a domestic crisis in Czechoslovakia. Yet as late as March 9 they still had no definite timetable. Keeping the date of the invasion open, they expected their future victims to act first.

The Prague government was under pressure from the Czech politicians who urged strong action against the Slovak nationalists. They realized that unless the central government reasserted its authority in the country, the Germans might intervene themselves.[19] Following another trip by prominent Slovak politicians to Berlin, Foreign Minister Chvalkovský called upon Hencke, the German *chargé d'affaires*, on March 9. The minister asked openly whether Germany favored an independent Slovakia but received only an

[18] Altenburg's memorandum, March 1, 1939, *DGFP*, D, IV, pp. 221–24. Memoranda by Altenburg and Wiehl, March 2, 1939, AA, T-120, 283, 213550–57, NA. About another unsuccessful approach, made by a journalist who was close to Prime Minister Beran, see F. Lukeš, "Dvě tajné cesty Vladimíra Krychtálka do Německa" [Vladimír Krychtálek's Two Secret Trips to Germany], *Dějiny a současnost*, IV (1962), No, 2, p. 29.

[19] Cf. L. K. Feierabend, *Ve vládách druhé republiky* [In the Cabinets of the Second Republic], pp. 137–41. Hoensch, *Die Slowakei*, pp. 249–50.

evasive answer. This was an ominous sign, indicating that time, for the Czechs, was running short.[20]

During the night of March 9, President Hácha dismissed the Slovak autonomous government. He sent troops to Slovakia and ordered martial law there. But nothing was done beyond this demonstration of force, and the Czech authorities did not even interfere with the paramilitary units of the separatists. The Prague government, apparently having no specific plan of action, paused to see what would happen next.

For the Nazis, Hácha's move was the signal they had been impatiently awaiting. They hoped that it would precipitate a further crisis, thus facilitating the planned military intervention. Within a few hours, the German timetable started operating.

The hour-by-hour movement of the troops was recorded in a "War Diary," preserved in the files of the Army High Command.[21] At about 2:30 P.M. on March 10, Major Adolf Heusinger of Section I of the General Staff dispatched a directive to prepare marching orders for the SS Body Guard "Adolf Hitler." This SS unit was to be set in motion first, because its task was to occupy the industrial Ostrava region several hours before the bulk of the troops entered the rest of the country. This maneuver was intended to prevent the possible seizure of Ostrava by Poland.[22] Other armed forces units stationed in the Sudetenland, Silesia, Saxony, Upper Palatinate, Bavaria, and Austria received marching orders at 4:57 P.M. On "A-Day," March 12, they were to start moving toward the borders from the north, west, and south. "Y-Day," the date for crossing the frontiers, was set for March 15.

Political developments, however, did not proceed with the precision of the German military timetable. The intervention of the central government in Slovakia, hesitant though it was, impressed the separatist party sufficiently to discourage its actions. To the Nazis' great dismay, the Slovaks neither challenged the established authority themselves, nor asked for outside help. The German Consul in Bratislava, Druffel, grasped the reason for their reluc-

---

[20] Hencke to Foreign Office, March 9, 1939, *DGFP*, D, IV, pp. 230–31. Cf. Hoensch, *Die Slowakei*, pp. 252–57.

[21] "Kriegstagebuch, 5. Abt. (Ic) GenStdH, anlässlich der Besetzung Böhmens/Mährens," OKH, T-78, 301, 6252043–217, NA. Cf. Hencke to Foreign Office, March 8, 1939, AA, T-120, 12, 17645, NA.

[22] Cf. OKW directive, March 11, 1939, OKW, T-77, 820, 5555365–67, NA.

tance in his telegram to Berlin: "In Tiso's circle apprehension that Germans, once they intervene, will never go away."[23]

On March 11, Wilhelm Keppler, the State Secretary for Special Tasks in the Foreign Office, was dispatched to Vienna. In the meantime, Joseph Bürckel, the Nazi party boss in the Austrian capital, had been unsuccessfully trying to arrange common action with the Slovaks. From Vienna, Keppler reported to Berlin that the situation was "a mess" and that the Slovaks had apparently fooled the Germans. In particular, the declaration of independence supposedly promised by Ďurčanský seemed to be a hoax.[24]

From the German point of view, the situation was embarrassing. The army machinery was already in motion and it looked as if the invasion would take place before the separation of Slovakia provided the desired pretext for it. In a document dated March 13 and prepared for publication, the Nazis could refer only to the dismissal of the Slovak ministers as the event which supposedly necessitated intervention.[25] Since such an explanation was hardly convincing, they fabricated supplementary evidence of presumed internal chaos in Czechoslovakia. Their press and radio poured out reports about the alleged oppression of Germans and Slovaks. The Wilhelmstrasse drafted a telegram for dispatch to Prague. It mentioned the "cries for help by Germans, terrorized and persecuted in an inhuman manner," which had caused the Reich government "to take necessary measures immediately."[26] Ribbentrop planned to ask Prague to send a plenipotentiary negotiator.

The Foreign Office withheld the telegram, pending the occurrence of real disturbances to make its assertions more credible. Encouraged by Nazi agents, the German populace of Prague, Brno, Jihlava, Olomouc, and other cities rioted on March 12, the anniversary of the clashes with the Czech troops in 1919.[27] But the

[23] Druffel to Foreign Office, March 10, 1939, AA, T-120, 154, 76353 and 76372, NA.

[24] Altenburg's memorandum, March 12, 1939, Nur. NG-3045, CU. Ďurčanský's draft telegram, whose text has been preserved in the Federal Archives at Koblenz, was apparently not the document the Germans had desired. Cf. Hoensch, *Die Slowakei*, pp. 270–84. M. S. Durica, *La Slovacchia e le sue relazioni politiche con la Germania*, I, p. 78. J. Novák, *Im Zeichen zweier Kreuze*, pp. 32–35.

[25] "An Alle," March 13, 1939, OKW, T-77, 820, 5555376–77, NA.

[26] Draft telegram, probably March 13, 1939, in Král (ed.), *Die Deutschen in der Tschechoslowakei*, p. 380.

[27] About the incidents, see A. Šimka, *Od Mnichova k 15. březnu* [From Munich to March 15], and J. Janák, "Die deutsche Bevölkerung der 'Iglauer Sprachinsel' zwischen München und dem 15. März 1939," *Sborník prací filosofické fakulty Brněnské university*, C 12 (1965), pp. 123–62.

Czechs did not get excited easily. In his report to Berlin, Hencke admitted: "The general situation is quiet. The behavior of the authorities and of the population towards Germans is distinctly patient. They evade provocations as much as possible."[28]

There was still a chance that the Slovaks would agree to proclaiming independence under German auspices without further delay. The Nazi agents did their best to intimidate them by smuggling special commandos into Bratislava and provoking disturbances. Tiso was reminded that Berlin might interpret his passivity as a sign of hostility, and then "everything would be lost for the Slovaks."[29] On March 13, Keppler finally phoned the Foreign Office from Vienna saying that "there is a possibility of Tiso's coming to Berlin."[30] In a private latter, he later described the situation on that day as follows: "Thanks to particularly good luck, it was possible to bring Prime Minister Tiso in time for a conference with the Führer in Berlin."[31]

At 6:40 P.M. on March 13, Hitler received Tiso and Ďurčanský in the presence of the highest Nazi dignitaries. He informed his Slovak guests about the impending occupation of Bohemia and Moravia, and pressed them to proclaim independence immediately. If they "hesitated or refused to be separated from Prague, he would leave the fate of Slovakia to events for which he would no longer be responsible."[32] The statement needed no further elaboration. Slovakia would be left at the mercy of Hungary.

On the following day, the provincial Diet at Bratislava voted the creation of a Slovak state. To conform to this new development, the Wilhelmstrasse significantly reworded the draft of its dispatch destined for Prague.[33] The separation of Slovakia was now cited to justify the military intervention, while the stories about rampant

[28] Hencke to Foreign Office, March 13, 1939, AA, T-120, 12, 170609, NA. Cf. Toussaint and Hencke to Foreign Office, March 11, 1939, *ibid.*, 17626.

[29] Novák, *Im Zeichen zweier Kreuze*, p. 37. In a significant reversal of his earlier policy, Hitler informed the Hungarian Minister on March 12 that Germany no longer objected to the seizure of the Carpathian Ukraine by Hungary. Budapest promptly prepared troops to march into that territory on March 16. J. K. Hoensch, *Der ungarische Revisionismus und die Zerschlagung der Tschechoslowakei*, p. 259.

[30] Heinburg's memorandum, March 13, 1939, *ibid.*, p. 239. Interrogation of Veesenmayer, September 1945, p. 6, De Witt C. Poole Collection, RG-59, NA. Cf. Hoensch, *Die Slowakei*, pp. 284–89.

[31] Keppler to Himmler, July 11, 1939, Nur. NG-2936, CU.

[32] Minutes of Hitler-Tiso conversation, March 13, 1939, *DGFP*, D, IV, p. 245.

[33] "Mitteilung an die Regierung in Prag," March 14, 1939, AA, T-120, 1077, 435188–90, NA.

Czech terror were toned down. Since less than twenty-four hours remained before German troops would cross the frontier as scheduled, the drafters dropped the paragraph asking Prague to send a negotiator.

While the Foreign Office was preparing the telegram for dispatch, the German officials were assessing the possible Czech response. Hencke reported from Prague: "Will to resistance can be discerned neither in military units, nor among the population, and least of all among workers . . . . Population resigned, expects German invasion."[34] Such a state of mind confirmed the Nazis' previous estimates. It was not likely that the Czech resistance would result in fierce fighting. Anticipating general passivity, the German commanders were under orders to avoid bloodshed as much as possible. In comparison with the swift brutality of later Nazi military operations, the behavior prescribed in the directives for the occupation of Bohemia and Moravia sounds decorous indeed, more appropriate to medieval than to modern warfare:

At the beginning of the invasion, each unit will send forward a negotiator —an officer with a white flag equal in rank to the respective local Czech commander—accompanied by a signal trumpeter, an interpreter and sufficient armed protection. He will establish contact with the local Czech commander and inform him about the invasion . . . as a pacification measure against which any resistance is useless . . . .[35]

Only in the unlikely event that a besieged garrison refused to surrender was it to be subdued by force of arms.

By March 14, the Germans had completed both their military and political preparations. They merely had to notify the Prague government of the impending invasion and ask it formally to abstain from armed resistance, a demand which was not likely to be rejected. Still, such a course of action would have appeared to the world as what it was, namely public blackmail. But an unexpected initiative from Hácha saved the Nazis even this last embarrassment. Knowing that the key to his country's troubles lay in Berlin, Jiří Havelka, Hácha's closest adviser, had suggested that the President seek personal contact with Hitler.[36] And, with Hácha in Berlin for this purpose, the dispatch of an ultimatum to Prague was no longer necessary.

[34] Hencke to Foreign Office, March 13, 1939, AA, T-120, 12, 17609, NA. Cf. Hencke to Foreign Office, March 15, 1939, *ibid*, 1094, 447231–32, NA.

[35] Order for the Third Army Group, March 13, 1939, H 20-72/2, BA, MA.

[36] Hácha to Chvalkovský, November 15, 1941, *DHCSP*, II, p. 638. Cf. *ibid*., p. 687.

Did the Hácha government receive advance warning about the impending invasion? The Czechoslovak military intelligence had apparently known about the German troop movements by the first week of March and about the exact timetable of the invasion by March 11. They received the information from their French colleagues and especially from Paul Thümmel, a master double agent who worked with the German Counter-Intelligence, the *Abwehr*, in Dresden.[37] Czech officers testified after the war that they had immediately reported the alarming news to the cabinet, but that Foreign Minister Chvalkovský had forbidden its dissemination. The cabinet ministers—questioned while under indictment, in 1947, for collaboration—resolutely denied any advance knowledge of the German military preparations.[38] And Chvalkovský's behavior in those days hardly indicated a mind weighed down by awareness of an impending disaster. He found both the time and the composure to attend parties at foreign legations in Prague, as "genial and unperturbed" as ever.[39]

Whether or not the Czechoslovak leaders had been forewarned, they would apparently have been unwilling, in any case, to believe the shocking news. But they must have sensed that a showdown with the Germans was approaching. The cabinet endorsed Hácha's projected visit to Hitler, which apparently was aimed at shedding light on the Führer's intentions, rather than advancing any specific Czechoslovak proposals.[40]

In the night of March 13, a few hours after Tiso's visit to Berlin, Chvalkovský invited Hencke to a meeting with Hácha at 9 P.M.[41] Since the President was likely to inquire about German intentions

---

[37] E. Strankmüller, "Československé ofenzívní zpravodajství v letech 1937 do 15. března 1939" [The Czechoslovak Intelligence Service from 1937 to March 15, 1939], *Odboj a revoluce*, VI (1968), No. 2, pp. 64–67. The author was a high officer of the Czechoslovak intelligence in 1939. The French assistant military attaché in Berlin confirms in his memoirs that the *Deuxième Bureau* knew about the German troop movements against Czechoslovakia in advance. P. Stehlin, *Témoignage pour l'histoire*, p. 136.

[38] Testimony of Generals Fiala and Moravec at the Beran trial, February 1947, reported in the daily *Právo lidu*, February 19, 1947. F. Lukeš, "Příspěvek k objasnění politiky české a německé buržoazie v předvečer 15. března" [The Policy of the Czech and German Bourgeoisie on the Eve of March 15], *Časopis Národního musea*, Social science series, CXXX (1961), pp. 65–68. Beran's defense speech, in R. Beran, *Die Tschecho-Slowakei zwischen "München" und Besetzung*, pp. 98–101.

[39] Notes on March 21, 1939, Kennan, *From Prague after Munich*, pp. 80, 84.

[40] Cf. Beran, *Die Tschecho-Slowakei*, pp. 36–37.

[41] Hencke to Foreign Office, March 13, 1939, *DGFP*, D, IV, p. 248.

and since the Nazis had not yet succeeded in making the Slovaks proclaim independence, Hencke had every reason for avoiding the interview. Following Ribbentrop's earlier instruction, he declined the invitation, stating that any communication must be sent to the Legation in writing. On March 14, at 11 : 25 A.M., Chvalkovský transmitted a letter to Hencke asking Hitler to grant an interview to Hácha.[42] By that time Slovak independence was a certainty, and the request was granted. Hácha, along with Chvalkovský, left for Berlin on the night of March 14.

By 5 : 30 P.M. on March 14, the SS Body Guard "Adolf Hitler" had already started to occupy the Ostrava region. The progress of this operation proved that the Nazis had been correct in expecting no significant resistance. Local officials at Ostrava were merely concerned about preserving order. Apparently in anticipation of events, they stationed unarmed policemen along the streets where the German columns were to march. Only at Místek, south of Ostrava, did the garrison fight the invaders for over three hours before it surrendered upon higher orders.[43] Government officials throughout the country were so resigned that they did not even attempt to destroy their confidential files. Significant exceptions in this general helplessness were several officers of the military intelligence. On March 14, eleven of them took off for London on their own initiative, carrying along the most important secrets of their department.[44]

In a public statement before his departure from Prague, Hácha observed that historically as well as geographically, the Czech state belonged to the sphere of German power.[45] By the time he and Chvalkovský arrived in Berlin, they learned that the German troops had already occupied Ostrava. We do not know what conclusions the President drew for his impending conference with Hitler. Yet

[42] Chvalkovský to Hencke, March 14, 1939, AA, T-120, 1077, 435232, NA.

[43] Report of the Armed Forces High Command, Foreign Department, March 14, 1939, Nur. NG-3088, IfZ. German Consulate Ostrava (Dopffel) to German Legation Prague, March 20, 1939, AA, T-120, 1307, D 495442–45, NA. Cf. F. Crkovský "Ostravsko a 15. březen 1939" [The Ostrava Country and March 15, 1939], *Slezský sborník*, LIX (1961); pp. 475–90. E. Vavrovský, "Obrana Čajánkových kasáren ve Frýdku-Místku" [The Defense of the Čajánek Barracks at Frýdek-Místek], *Těšínsko*, 1959, No. 9, p. 1.

[44] OKW, T-77, 977, 4465720, NA. Strankmüller, "Československé ofenzívní zpravodajství," pp. 68–73.

[45] K. Megerle, "Deutschland und das Ende der Tschecho-Slowakei," *Monatshefte für auswärtige Politik*, VI (1939), p. 770.

it is hard to avoid the impression that he was already prepared to negotiate an incorporation of his country into the Reich.[46]

On the night of March 14, Hitler was in no hurry to receive the Czechoslovak President. Watching a movie with his entourage, he let his visitor wait for about two hours.[47] From the military point of view their conversation could make no difference. Since the seizure of the Ostrava area had proceeded smoothly, there was every reason to expect that the advance into the rest of the country would be equally easy. Still, the political effect of the occupation depended on Hácha's response.

The midnight conference between the two statesmen, attended by a retinue of high Nazi officials, has usually been interpreted as a show staged by the Germans.[48] Yet it was the Czech visitor, not Hitler, who spoke first. He criticized the politics of pre-Munich Czechoslovakia and expressed doubts about whether independence had been at all fortunate for his people. Having concluded that their fate was now in the Führer's hands, he did not advance any specific proposals.[49]

Hitler had never met Hácha before. As Göring told Mussolini one month later, "the Reich Chancellor was completely surprised" by the President's submissiveness.[50] Quickly taking advantage of the obvious weakness of his visitor, Hitler announced that within six hours the German forces would enter Czechoslovakia from three sides and warned that any resistance would be crushed

---

[46] Interrogation of Paul Schmidt, October 1945, p. 27, De Witt C. Poole Collection, RG-59, NA. Hácha's note on conversation with Hitler, March 20, 1939, *DHCSP*, II, p. 420.

[47] *The Memoirs of Field-Marshal Keitel*, p. 79.

[48] Many historians have taken at face value the dramatic description of the interview by Robert Coulondre, the French Ambassador to Berlin. Coulondre's report, however, based on fourth-hand knowledge, abounds in inaccuracies and statements which are not supported by other evidence. *The French Yellow Book*, pp. 96–97. About Coulondre's informers, see the memoirs by V. Szathmáryová-Vlčková, *Putování za svobodou* [Pilgrimage for Freedom], p. 23.

[49] Hewel's minutes of Hitler-Hácha conversation, March 15, 1939, *DGFP*, D, IV, pp. 263–64. Hácha's note on conversation with Hitler, March 20, 1939, *DHCSP*, II, p. 421. Hitler's table talk, May 20, 1942, in H. Picker (ed.), *Hitlers Tischgespräche*, p. 91.

[50] Note about conversation between Göring and Mussolini, April 15, 1939, Nur. PS-1874, IfZ. Cf. examination of Keppler, pp. 18–19, De Witt C. Poole Collection, RG-59, NA. *United States v. Weizsäcker, Proceedings* (in English), p. 12916, CU. Examination of Meissner, *ibid.*, pp. 4541–42. Meissner, *Staatssekretär unter Ebert, Hindenburg und Hitler*, pp. 476–79.

ruthlessly. Under the impact of this information, Hácha panicked. Unlike his Nazi partners, he anticipated terrible bloodshed. Since he was about to collapse, the Führer's physician gave him an injection.[51] Göring continued to play Hitler's game and told Hácha that the German Air Force could reduce Prague to rubble if resistance were attempted. He was bluffing. Not only had all German military plans envisaged a minimum of compulsion, but physical conditions would have made this threat difficult to carry out. Three years later, Hitler recalled in a private conversation: "I would have irremediably lost face if I'd had to put this threat into execution, for at the hour mentioned fog was so thick over our airfields that none of our aircraft could have made its sortie."[52]

Hácha telephoned Prague and ordered that there be no resistance to the invading troops. Although peaceful occupation was a foregone conclusion, the President, haunted by the vision of a wholesale slaughter, anxiously tried to reassure the Germans that he was doing everything in his power to prevent violence. He consented to sign the following declaration supplied by the Germans:

The Czechoslovak President declared that, in order . . . to achieve ultimate pacification, he confidently placed the fate of the Czech people and country in the hands of the Führer of the German Reich. The Führer accepted this declaration and expressed his intention of taking the Czech people under the protection of the German Reich and of guaranteeing them an autonomous development of their ethnic life as suited to their character.[53]

Having himself emphasized, in his first words to Hitler, the close dependence of his country upon Germany, Hácha was hardly in a position to question the substance of this statement. But except for insignificant details, he also left unquestioned its devious wording, which was a masterpiece of deceptive understatement.

Soon, however, Hácha was to have reason to doubt the wisdom of his compliance. He correctly anticipated that he would be judged severely by future historians. Taylor, for example, writes that "he signed as required; and harbored so little resentment that he served as a faithful German subordinate until the end of the war."[54]

[51] Hewel's minutes, *DGFP*, D, IV, pp. 265–67. Hácha's note, *DHCSP*, II, p. 421. Schmidt, *Statist auf diplomatischer Bühne*, p. 430.

[52] *Hitler's Table Talk*, p. 204. Hácha's note, *DHCSP*, II, p. 422. Cf. Henderson to Halifax, May 28, 1939, *Trial*, XXXI, p. 246.

[53] *DGFP*, D, IV, p. 270.

[54] Taylor, *Origins of the Second World War*, p. 202.

Shirer describes him as a person who "shed all human dignity by groveling before the swaggering German Führer" and points out that Hácha's words "nauseate the reader even so long afterward as today."[55] Such opinions do little justice to the difficult human situation of an aged and frail man, insufficiently familiar with politics, let alone with political gangsterism. Hácha believed that the Czechs could only survive if they retained, at any price, the good will of the Germans. He hoped to solicit it by humility and submissiveness. In him the Nazis had found the person they needed; a man respected by many Czechs for his unquestionable devotion to his people, yet one who was pliable and easily open to intimidation. Thus, despite the honesty of his motives, Hácha's means were pathetically inadequate.

Hitler, although he did rely in the last resort upon military force, proved most effective in his use of political resources against Czechoslovakia. Uninhibited by moral scruples, he skillfully fomented the discontent of the Sudeten Germans and later the Slovaks. In the ensuing crises he acted with caution, keeping alternatives open, waiting for his adversaries to make mistakes, and learning their weaknesses. Like the Western powers in September 1938, the Czech leaders in March 1939 were taking pains to appease him. Taking full advantage of this, and using the crises he had created in Czechoslovakia to destroy that country's independence and extend German power, Hitler was able to attain his maximum goals with a minimum of effort.

But, in their single-minded pursuit of power, the Nazis underestimated the liabilities their ruthless actions had incurred. Other nations, witnessing a confirmation of the dictum *l'appétit vient en mangeant*, realized that Hitler's appetite had increased by what it fed on at Munich. They began to prepare a firmer stand against further German aggression. In Bohemia and Moravia, the Nazis created for themselves the new problem of governing a non-German people, subdued and demoralized but distinctly unfriendly. This presented an unfamiliar challenge to Nazi statecraft.[56]

[55] W. Shirer, *The Rise and Fall of the Third Reich*, p. 444.
[56] Cf. V. Mastny, "Design or Improvisation," in *Columbia Essays in International Affairs*, ed. by Andrew W. Cordier, pp. 127–53.

PART II

THE OCCUPATION—PRESENCES AND POWERS

3 THE ORIGINAL CREATION
OF NAZI STATECRAFT

THANKS to their agreement with Hácha, the Nazis were spared even the necessity of being the first to announce the occupation. The first word of it came from Radio Prague on March 15, at 4:30 A.M. Its broadcasts repeatedly warned the population to abstain from any resistance to the German army, which would start advancing at 6 A.M.[1]

At 5 A.M., Goebbels read over the Berlin radio Hitler's "Proclamation to the German People." It referred to alleged excesses committed by the Czechs against their ethnic minorities and to the breakdown of the Republic because of the Slovak secession. As a further justification of Germany's military intervention, the document stated that "for over a thousand years [Bohemia and Moravia had] in fact belonged to the Reich."[2] Hácha's consent to the occupation was not mentioned. The omission may have been deliberate, intended to impress the German people with still another triumph of the Führer's will. Yet it is more likely that Hácha was not mentioned because the proclamation had been drafted before his meeting with Hitler. Only at 6:10 A.M., ten minutes after the beginning of the invasion, did the Berlin radio broadcast the text of their agreement.

On that day, the weather was the Nazis' only serious opponent. An unusually severe blizzard hindered the advancing army. In its struggle against the elements, Hitler's military machine did not perform very well. There were embarrassing breakdowns of tanks and other vehicles. Yet, except for the delays caused by weather, the operation proceeded according to schedule. The troops entered Prague about 9 A.M., and by afternoon they were in possession of the whole country.[3]

[1] *Keesing's Contemporary Archives*, 1939, p. 3485.
[2] *The Speeches of Adolf Hitler*, ed. by Baynes, II, p. 1585.
[3] Diary of Ulrich Schröder, pp. 11–12, H 08–20/1. BA, MA. *Tagesziel: Prag* and *Marschbefehl: Mähren* are official army publications about the operation.

Although many people had expected the occupation, they were nevertheless shocked once it came. Still asleep when it began, they awakened to the sudden sight of foreign soldiers. When the German mechanized columns reached Prague, the streets were crowded with people, who, obeying the appeals of the government, were on their way to work. Several anti-Nazi Western observers present on the scene reported that the invaders had been received with whistles, boos, tears, and clenched fists. Contemporary photographs, frequently reproduced ever since, also showed such displays of emotion. On the other hand, the German soldiers were often surprised at the helpfulness of the local population. The Czechs willingly gave them directions and even manifested curious, though cautious, interest in the military equipment on the scene. Some of the soldiers believed that their reception was quite friendly.[4] George Kennan, the unprejudiced and perceptive American eye-witness noticed "embittered but curious Czechs [who] looked on in silence" at an armored car in the streets of the city. On the German side, he saw "hundreds and hundreds of vehicles plastered with snow, the faces of their occupants red with what some thought was shame but what I fear was in most cases merely the cold."[5]

The Czechs were depressed and fearful about the intentions of their new rulers. Yet their apprehensions were not fully justified by the few decisions the Nazis had taken so far. The only German blueprint was to be found in routine directives of the army concerning the temporary administration of a foreign territory. These had been included with little change in the successive plans for "Operation Green," having also been applied to the Sudetenland in the first three weeks after its incorporation into the Reich in 1938.[6] In Bohemia and Moravia, the German army authorities used posters and radio announcements to proclaim their assumption of power immediately after the invasion. But they did not take into account the Hácha-Hitler declaration, according to

[4] Newton to British Foreign Office, March 31, 1939, *Documents on British Foreign Policy*, 3rd series, IV, p. 563. V. Sabeau, "Le 15 mars vu de Prague," *L'Europe nouvelle*, April 29, 1939, p. 466. J. Doležal and J. Křen (eds.), *Czechoslovakia's Fight*, illustration No. 2. Schröder diary, p. 9, H 08–20/1, BA, MA.

[5] Notes of March 21, 1939, Kennan, *From Prague after Munich*, p. 87.

[6] OKW, T-77, 168, 901370–578; and *ibid.*, 733, 1959726–42, NA. Administrative chart for Bohemia, March 10, 1939, Wi/IF, 3.188, BA, MA. J. Vrbata, "Přehled vývoje veřejné správy v odtržených českých oblastech v letech 1938–1945" [The Development of the Public Administration in the Separated Czech Territories in 1938–1945], *Sborník archivních prací*, XII (1962), No. 2, p. 49.

which the occupation was at least technically a result of bilateral Czech-German agreement. If they did not want to waste this propaganda asset, the Nazis had to decide the future position of the country quickly.

The Wilhelmstrasse, sensitive to the international implications of the intervention, urged a clarification of the political status of Bohemia and Moravia. A few hours after Hitler's conference with Hácha, Friedrich Gaus, the head of the Legal Section of the Foreign Office, prepared a memorandum about this matter. He proposed that Hitler proclaim the establishment of two "protectorates," one in Bohemia, the other in Moravia.[7] Such an action "would forestall any attempt to make the settlement an object of an international conference." He emphasized that it was desirable to preserve "the fiction that the new regime is based upon an agreement with the existing Czechoslovak central government and not upon the arbitrary decision of the occupation power." The protectorates were to elect their own governments, approved by a German "General Resident," and receive a constitution which would guarantee their autonomous development. The form of their dependence upon the Reich in foreign policy, military, and economic matters was to be defined later.

Gaus's reasoning indicated that Hácha's visit to Berlin had influenced the decisions made by the Nazis. Although the intervention of the Czechoslovak President did not change anything about the invasion itself, it helped to shape German thinking on the form of the occupation regime. Hitler spoke the truth when he told Hácha during their nighttime conference that "Germany's attitude will be decided tomorrow and the day after tomorrow."[8] To implement this statement, he left Berlin in the early morning of March 15, accompanied by a retinue of administrative experts and some of the highest dignitaries of the Party, government, and armed forces.

Rarely did Hitler appear so ill at ease as during his hastily improvised trip of March 15, 1939. Heinrich Lammers, who participated as chief of the Reich Chancellery, later testified that the Führer's decision to travel to the conquered country had been made on the spur of the moment.[9] Although Prague was already

---

[7] Foreign Office memorandum, March 15, 1939, AA, T-120, 1094, 447271–73, NA.

[8] *DGFP*, D, IV, p. 266.

[9] Hitler's daily activities, p. 38, MA 3(1), IfZ. Examination of Lammers, *United States v. Weizsäcker, Proceedings* (in English), p. 20829, CU.

safely in German hands, Hitler did not venture to go there directly. Even before reaching the Bohemian frontier, he had his train diverted from the main Berlin-Prague line, heading instead for Česká Lípa, a railroad junction which was still in the Sudetenland. After a two-hour break, he surprised his entourage by expressing a desire to go to Prague. Frank, Henlein's notorious deputy, directed the Führer's motorcade on icy roads congested by the advancing troops.[10] It was already dark by the time they reached the outskirts of the capital. In the meantime, the German army, having taken possession of Prague Castle, prepared it hurriedly for the reception of the Führer's party. After a drive through the streets, deserted because of the approaching curfew, Hitler slipped into the Castle about 8 P.M. So inconspicuous was his presence that later that night, after Hácha's return from Berlin, the Czech cabinet met in one part of the Castle without knowing of the unexpected guests who had taken residence in the other. Once settled, Hitler finally staged a modest celebration. Breaking his strict principles as a vegetarian and teetotaler, he had Prague ham and Pilsner beer as an evening snack.[11]

Hitler's pointed restraint during his entrance into Prague contrasted with the ebullience of his behavior on other similar occasions. In March 1938 he had paraded through Vienna amidst cheering crowds and eighteen months later he entered Danzig as a triumphant conqueror. During the Polish campaign, as Germany's warlord, he was frequently with his troops along the front line. None of these postures, however, was suitable for Prague in 1939. On the one hand, an ovation by local Nazis, whose number in the allegedly German country was embarrassingly small, would only have accentuated the less-than-enthusiastic reception by the Czechs. On the other hand, any stance suggesting conquest would have detracted from the credibility of the agreement with Hácha.

Apart from these practical considerations, Hitler behaved as if he could not believe his easy success to be really true. He may have had doubts whether the submission of the Czechs was complete enough to preclude unpleasant incidents. He regarded them as perfidious people filled with hatred. So often had he described them as bloodthirsty oppressors of the poor Sudeten Germans that he

---

[10] *Völkischer Beobachter*, March 16, 1939. *Zpověd K. H. Franka* [The Confession of K. H. Frank], p. 50.

[11] Hácha's note on conversation with Hitler, March 20, 1939, *DHCSP*, II, p. 422. *The Memoirs of Field-Marshal Keitel*, p. 81.

seems to have finally believed the inventions of his own propaganda. After his arrival in Prague, Hitler supposedly wished to visit the numerous hospitalized victims of Czech terror claimed by the German press, and he was surprised to learn that his wish could not possibly be fulfilled.[12]

Hitler's fears about possible incidents were not justified. The population universally obeyed orders and abstained from resistance. While the President was still on his way back from Berlin, other officials already cooperated with the occupation authorities to preserve order and assure a smooth transfer of power. The mayor of Prague sought out the German commanding general on the morning of March 15. Later that day, Havelka, Hácha's *chef de cabinet*, conferred with Ribbentrop and Henlein, who had arrived in the capital along with the Führer.[13]

Reassured by the calm aspect of the country, the Nazi chieftains, assembled at Prague Castle, settled down to business in the night of March 15–16. Some of them later testified that the debate on the future of Bohemia and Moravia had taken place amidst great confusion. Göring and Ribbentrop competed in trying to influence the decision. Hitler finally appointed Wilhelm Stuckart, State Secretary in the Ministry of the Interior, to draft the basic document.[14]

Stuckart was a lawyer who had distinguished himself as an attorney for the Nazi party in its early days. After Hitler's seizure of power, he came to the Interior Ministry as Himmler's confidant. As the author of many new bills, he had a prominent share in the Nazification of German law. Besides anti-Jewish legislation, his specialty was legal incorporation of new territories, such as Austria and the Sudetenland.[15] Gaus probably assisted Stuckart in preparing the new "constitution" for Bohemia and Moravia. Having earlier drafted the proposed German-Czechoslovak "friendship" treaty in November 1938, Gaus was also the author of the memorandum about the two "protectorates."

[12] N. Henderson, *Failure of a Mission*, p. 215. Cf. Newton to British Foreign Office, March 1939, *Documents on British Foreign Policy*, 3rd series, IV, p. 405.

[13] *Völkischer Beobachter*, March 16, 1939. *České slovo*, March 17, 1939.

[14] Examination of Stuckart, *United States* v. *Weizsäcker*, *Proceedings* (in English), pp. 24542–45, CU. Examination of Lammers, *ibid.*, pp. 20831–32, 22379. Affidavit by Gaus, Nur. NG-1635, CU. *Zpověď K. H. Franka*, p. 106. Cf. M. Schubert's memoir, "Konec druhé republiky" [The End of the Second Republic], *Naše hlasy* (Toronto), March 14, 1964.

[15] Stuckart file, BDC.

While Gaus's suggestion for dividing the occupied territory into two separate units was not heeded, his idea of a "protectorate" appeared in the final text of the "Führer Decree Concerning the Establishment of the Protectorate of Bohemia and Moravia." This form of dependence was unusual in Europe. Some authors have speculated that the Nazis had adapted for Bohemia and Moravia the 1881 protectorate treaty between France and Tunisia.[16] Comparison of the two documents, however, reveals only a superficial resemblance. The Protectorate of Bohemia and Moravia was indeed, as Stuckart liked to point out with pride, an original creation of Nazi statecraft. The term was a common German euphemism for a satellite country in an especially close form of dependence.[17]

The preamble to the Decree repeated the same themes as Hitler's "Proclamation to the German People" broadcast in the early morning of March 15. In the text proper, Bohemia and Moravia were together declared an autonomous part of the Reich. The Germans living in the country became Reich citizens (*Reichsbürger*); the Czech inhabitants were referred to as Protectorate nationals (*Protektoratsangehörige*). Germany assumed control over foreign affairs and defense but preserved native administration in internal matters. Although incorporation into the Reich implied the abolition of state sovereignty, the Nazis—in an apparent tribute to Hácha—conceded to him the formal vestiges of a head of state, including the title of "State President." He was responsible to a Reich Protector, appointed to safeguard Germany's interests in the country. The cabinet ministers, though chosen by the President, required the Protector's confirmation.[18]

Although the Decree was hailed in Nazi propaganda as a historic document, its provisions actually settled very little. The thirteen short articles were no constitution but rather a statement of intentions calculated for public consumption. The crucial provisions were vague. Thus article three stated ambiguously that "[the Protectorate] exercises sovereign rights conceded to it within the framework of the Protectorate, in conformity with the political,

[16] E. V. Erdely, *Germany's First European Protectorate*, pp. 34–37. E. Sobota, *Co to byl protektorát* [What the Protectorate Was], pp. 30–31. Cf. E. Rouard de Card, ed., *Les traités de protectorat conclus par la France, 1870–1895*, pp. 159–61.

[17] W. Stuckart, *Neues Staatsrecht*, p. 186. *Idem*, "Das Protektorat im Grossdeutschen Reich," Nur. NG-2496, CU.

[18] Decree of March 16, 1939, *DGFP*, D, IV, pp. 283–86.

military and economic requirements of the Reich." Equally
nebulous was the delimitation of the Protector's powers over the
autonomous authorities. He could "protest against measures calculated to harm the Reich, and if there is danger in delay he can
order measures necessary in the common interest." Besides these
equivocations, which were apparently deliberate, a number of
others resulted from hurried preparation. Thus, for example, the
territory of the Protectorate was defined as "the areas of the former
Czechoslovak Republic occupied by German troops in March
1939." Taken literally, this would have included the western parts
of newly independent Slovakia, where the German army had
temporarily entered on March 15.[19]

Hácha often argued that internal autonomy was the main asset
of his agreement with Hitler. He found consolation in the belief
that his submission had prevented the Nazis from enforcing a
harsher regime.[20] Indeed, we have no evidence of their intention to
grant self-government before the President's visit to Berlin. Yet
the actual value of this concession should not be overestimated.
The Germans made it of their own free will and in their own
interest. They retained the right, as well as the power, to determine
the extent of autonomy. Hermann Raschhofer, a leading Nazi expert in constitutional law, put it bluntly in a manuscript written in
1940: "It is clear that the implementation of the Führer's promise
. . . is entirely up to him . . . . By Hácha's act, the authority to
supply a framework for the political organization of the Czech
people was completely transferred to the Führer."[21] Rather than
upon the letter of Hitler's decree, Czech freedom of action depended exclusively upon the Nazis' willingness to abstain from
interference in the future.

Hitler's program for March 16 was devised to show his benevolent attitude toward the vanquished. That morning, Ribbentrop
read the Protectorate Decree over the Prague radio. Shortly after
noon, the Führer successively received the mayor of the city, Hácha,
and General Jan Syrový, the Czechoslovak Minister of Defense.

[19] Weizsäcker to Druffel, March 15, 1939, Nur. NG-5304, CU.

[20] Cf. Sobota, *Co to byl protektorát*, p. 27.

[21] H. Raschhofer, "Rechtliche Betrachtungen zum Reichsprotektorat Böhmen und
Mähren," quoted in K. Fremund, "Z činnosti poradců nacistické okupační moci"
[The Activities of the Advisers to the Nazi Occupation Regime], *Sborník archivních
prací*, XVI (1966), No. 1, p. 4.

The handclasp between Hitler and the General, who in the mobilization of September 1938 had been considered the foremost champion of national defense, symbolized the extent of the conquerors' triumph and of the victims' capitulation.[22]

Hitler gave only small satisfaction to the local Germans who burst into a frenzy of enthusiasm as soon as they had learned of his presence. He briefly appeared in the window to greet the cheering crowd. Later, he reviewed in the courtyard of the Castle a group of bandaged Nazi students who claimed to have been wounded in clashes with Czech terrorists. Yet by that afternoon the Führer had left Prague as inconspicuously as he entered it, to spend the night in the Sudeten section of Silesia. Only on the following day did he return to the Protectorate to visit Olomouc and Brno, the Moravian cities with sizable German minorities. At Brno, he gave his blessing to a group of Nazi fanatics, led by Oskar Judex, who had seized the city hall shortly before the arrival of German troops. From Brno, Hitler left by train for Vienna, where he arrived about 5 P.M. on March 17.[23] This had been his first and last visit to Bohemia and Moravia. The memory of his uneasy triumph, along with his limitless contempt for the Czechs, may explain why he left that part of Europe out of his future itineraries.

On March 18, Hitler summoned Konstantin von Neurath to the Imperial Hotel in Vienna to appoint him Protector of Bohemia and Moravia. Neurath had served during the Weimar Republic as the German envoy to Rome and to London. From his diplomatic career he enjoyed the reputation of a moderate and easygoing, though not particularly bright man. He had been Foreign Minister under Papen, Schleicher and Hitler, a record attesting to his considerable adaptability to different governments. Although as a conservative south German aristocrat Neurath disliked the lawlessness of the Nazi upstarts, he was enough of a nationalist to welcome their regime. He initially hoped that, given responsibility for the conduct of government, they would become civilized, but did not draw any conclusion after this hope had proved to be an illusion. The well-informed and observant Rauschning noted about Neurath that "in Hitler's presence, the big, corpulent man became painfully like a smart young subordinate on pins to make himself

[22] *Völkischer Beobachter*, March 17, 1939. *České slovo*, March 17, 1939. V. Král, *Pravda o okupaci* [The Truth about the Occupation], following p. 208.

[23] Deutsches Nachrichten-Büro [DNB] dispatch, March 17, 1939, No. 413, R 43 II/1327, BA. *Völkischer Beobachter*, March 18, 1939.

useful."[24] Having outlived his usefulness as a respectable façade for Hitler, he was replaced in the Foreign Office by the ardent Nazi Ribbentrop in February 1938. Sixty-six years old at that time, Neurath received the honorific and meaningless titles of "Minister without Portfolio" and "President of the Secret Cabinet Council." (The Council, supposedly the Führer's advisory body in foreign policy matters, never even met.) Neurath's apparent assets—respectability, circumspection, and moderation—tended to degenerate into deficiencies—indolence, lack of character, and servility; but these were precisely the qualities which made him, for Hitler, a likely candidate for the new office. A bureaucrat rather than a politician, he would be an appropriate counterpart to Hácha at Prague Castle.

Hitler appointed Frank as Neurath's deputy with the title of State Secretary. Frank was to assure strict adherence to the Nazi line and provide the Protector with knowledge of the Czech milieu. Although his appointment was a token concession to the Sudeten Germans, who regarded the Protectorate as their own domain, it did not imply recognition of their decisive influence in the country. Frank had attempted to pack the occupation government with his former colleagues from the Sudeten German Party. But his efforts miscarried after meeting with firm opposition in Berlin. Stuckart, who was in charge of selecting the personnel for the new administration, ruled that "experts from the Reich and from the Sudetenland should be employed in a fixed ratio."[25] Although the Sudeten Germans were employed generously in the lower echelons, officials from other parts of the Reich filled the most important positions, generating resentment among the local office-seekers.

After the war, Neurath told the Nuremberg tribunal that Hitler had originally entrusted him with the mission of conciliating the Czechs, an assertion which the court did not take very seriously.[26] Devoid as he was of both magnanimity and tact, the Führer was hardly ever interested in genuine reconciliation, which would have required some sacrifice of German interests. Yet we have no reason

[24] H. Rauschning, *Makers of Destruction*, p. 109, Cf. P. Seabury, *The Wilhelmstrasse*, pp. 26–41. *Ambassador Dodd's Diary*, pp. 139, 424. L. Schwerin von Krosigk's memoir, *Es geschah in Deutschland*, p. 311. J. C. Fest, *Das Gesicht des Dritten Reiches*, pp. 209–19. H.-A. Jacobsen, *Nationalsozialistische Aussenpolitik*, pp. 28–33.

[25] Correspondence between Frank and the Ministry of the Interior, March–April 1939, Rk 8817B, R 43 II/1329, BA.

[26] *Trial*, XVI, p. 655. Cf. *Zpověď K. H. Franka*, p. 51.

to doubt his desire to create a regime which would be palatable to the Czechs and acceptable abroad. Voicing the directives he had just received from Hitler, Stuckart told a March 25 confidential meeting of the State Secretaries from all Reich Ministries that "according to the Führer's will, the Czechs should be treated in a conciliatory manner, though with the greatest strictness and relentless consistency . . . . The treatment according to strict principles should obviously be fair . . . . The autonomy of the Protectorate should be restricted only if absolutely necessary. . . ."[27] In a private conversation, Stuckart later explained that, also according to the Führer's will, the regime in Bohemia and Moravia . . . "as the first embodiment of the German concept of the protectorate must avoid everything that would be likely to deter other nations, which perhaps might later express the same desire of being added to the German Reich as protectorates."[28]

Stuckart's key role in the shaping of the German Protectorate policy is significant. Hitler entrusted the implementation of his guidelines to a bureaucrat, an indication that he considered the problems of the country administrative rather than political. Reassured by the Czechs' submission, he did not anticipate any serious difficulties in governing them. From April 1939, he devoted most of his energy to diplomatic maneuvers in relation to the impending confrontation with Poland, letting his subordinates worry about the situation in Bohemia and Moravia.

The military authorities ruled the country from March 15 until April 16, the date the Protector officially assumed control over the government. The commanding general in Bohemia was Johannes Blaskowitz; in Moravia, Sigmund List. Both later became known for their brutality on the battlefield, the former in Poland, the latter in Russia. Yet they were more moderate behind the front lines, and Blaskowitz opposed the excesses of the SS against civilians in defeated Poland. (Arrested in 1945 for alleged complicity in war crimes, he committed suicide, a gesture indicating that he was not indifferent to the notion of military honor.) In the occupied

[27] Notes on conference with Stuckart, March 25, 1939, AA, T-120, 257, 195988, and T-120, 1505, D 632806–07, NA.

[28] Pancke's note on conversation with Stuckart on April 25, 1939, NS 2/55, BA. In his report to the State Department, dated May 4, 1939, G. F. Kennan assessed the German intentions in almost identical fashion; Kennan, *From Prague after Munich*, p. 147.

Bohemia of 1939, Blaskowitz handled the subdued adversary with tact. He ordered his soldiers to treat Czechoslovak officers with respect and to give a military salute when passing by the Tomb of the Unknown Soldier in Prague. In his first interview with the Beran cabinet, Blaskowitz assured the ministers of his sympathy for their national feelings. At a German military parade held in downtown Prague on March 19, Czech government representatives received places of honor and their national flag was flown side by side with the swastika. Throughout the country, the German soldiers maintained good discipline and avoided provocations.[29]

A technical rather than a political measure, the military administration was that of any occupation army. Courts-martial were set up to try offenses against the military establishment. The population had to surrender firearms and radio transmitters.[30] The Beran government remained in office pending further decisions but was obliged to secure for all its measures prior approval by the "chiefs of civil administration." These were the *Gauleiter* Henlein and Bürckel, assigned as advisers to the commanding generals in Bohemia and Moravia respectively. But even the two notorious party bosses used their powers with restraint. Only when the Beran government took the initiative in regard to the substantial Jewish property in the country did they intervene decisively. They blocked the ordinance about "forced managers" which would have enabled the government to appoint Czech trustees in Jewish enterprises, and thus forestall possible confiscation by the Germans.[31]

Behind the reasonable and reassuring façade of the military administration, however, arbitrary persecution was not altogether absent. The very presence of the German troops inspired horror in many people, especially in those—like the refugees from Hitler's Germany—with first-hand knowledge of Nazi methods. Foreign diplomatic missions were besieged by desperate persons seeking in vain for asylum.[32]

[29] Blaskowitz's address to the cabinet, March 16, 1939, Wi/IF 3, 173, BA, MA. Newton to British Foreign Office, March 31, 1939, *Documents on British Foreign Policy*, 3rd series, IV, p. 561. *České slovo*, March 21 and 28, 1939.

[30] *Verordnungsblatt für Böhmen und Mähren*, 1939, pp. 2–4.

[31] Ordinance of March 21, 1939, *Sammlung der Gesetze und Verordnungen des Protektorates Böhmen und Mähren* [*SGV*], 1939, pp. 331–33. Ordinances of March 20 and 31, 1939, *České slovo*, March 21 and April 1, 1939.

[32] Kennan, *From Prague after Munich*, pp. 85–86. J. W. Bruegel, "Zur Erinnerung an die Besetzung Prags 1939," *Deutsche Rundschau*, LXXXV (1959), pp. 220–25.

On the very morning of March 15, a high German officer requested the Provincial Government of Bohemia to arrest all suspected Communists. The Nazis dubbed this operation, which also took place in Moravia, *Aktion Gitter* (Operation Bars). Neither the Gestapo nor the army participated in its initial stages, leaving its implementation to the Czechs. The provincial government, having sent instructions to the districts, later added that the roundup should also include refugees from Germany. Since no names were available, the local authorities were often at a loss about who was to be arrested. The gendarmes usually decided the matter in consultation with mayors and other notables. Although their zeal understandably varied from place to place, several thousand persons were taken into custody throughout the country. After a few days, when prisons began to overflow, the Germans intervened to stop the operation. Only at this stage did the Gestapo move in, interrogating the detainees and deciding their fate. Most of them were released after signing a promise to abstain from subversive activities. But the German refugees were immediately deported to concentration camps.[33]

The fact that *Aktion Gitter* was not a typical example of Gestapo methods indicates the improvised nature of German rule in Bohemia and Moravia at this early stage. The success of the roundup depended in the last analysis upon the Czech authorities. Their shocking cooperation can be partly explained by the agreement of January 23, 1939, which provided for mutual assistance by the Czechoslovak and German police in the suppression of Communist activities.[34] Still the persecution was much less extensive than in Austria after the *Anschluss*,[35] let alone Poland in September 1939. Most notably, there was no organized violence against the Jews, except for sporadic outbursts by the Czech Fascists.[36]

[33] M. Görtler, "Akce Gitter ve středních Čechách" ["Operation Bars" in Central Bohemia], in *Středočeské kapitoly z dějin okupace*, pp. 7–38.

[34] Agreement of January 26, 1939, in *Mnichov v dokumentech* [Munich in Documents], II, pp. 351–52.

[35] Over 70,000 persons were arrested after the Nazi takeover of Austria. F. Engel-Janosi, "Remarks on the Austrian Resistance," *Journal of Central European Affairs*, XIII (1953), p. 108. Cf. G. E. R. Gedye, *Betrayal in Central Europe*, pp. 289–302.

[36] By March 20, 2000 persons had been arrested, of whom 1500 were kept under detention. Among them were 150 German refugees; the rest were Czech Communists. Hencke to Foreign Office, March 20, 1939, AA, T-120, 12, 17562, NA. Other German sources give the number of arrests from March 15 till May 23 as 4639. Between March 15 and April 4, 927 Communists were reportedly arrested. V. Král, *Otázky hospodářského a sociálního vývoje v českých zemích, 1938–1945* [Economic and Social Development in Bohemia and Moravia in 1938–1945], I, pp. 24–25.

But, although the Germans were under instructions to act with restraint, there were frequent incidents of arbitrary interference on the lower administrative level. In several cases, the Nazi supervisors ordered local Czech authorities to submit all business correspondence for their approval or even insisted on the use of German for the conduct of business in local Czech agencies. In a few towns with German minorities, they closed down Czech schools and replaced mayors with appointed commissioners. In a Moravian town with a ninety-nine per cent Czech population, street signs had to be put into German, the Czech form only in small letters in parentheses. Lacking a pattern, such pinpricks were usually the "revenge" of the Sudeten German "experts" who assisted the military.[37]

On the balance, despite these occurrences, the German occupation was at this initial stage less oppressive than many Czechs had expected. Formal independence disappeared but the daily life of the people changed hardly at all, a significant difference from the countries which were occupied later in the war. As the first non-German nation to be subjugated by the Nazis, the Czechs were in a unique situation. They had not suffered a military defeat. They were of course the subjects and the Germans the masters, but this relationship was not a result of the occupation. The people's spirit had already been broken at the time of the Munich Pact, and March 15 only confirmed their subjugation. Since the invasion brought so few significant changes there seemed to be no compelling reasons to revise the attitude toward the Germans which, though certainly not friendly, at least encouraged accommodation to the new conditions. The country's official representatives followed initially in the steps of the President and confined themselves to facilitating the formal transfer of power.

The first to draw political conclusions from the recent events were the Czech Fascists. On the morning of March 15, they penetrated into the parliament building and proclaimed the creation of a Czech National Committee with General Gajda as chairman. It included mostly members of the three major right-wing groups—Gajda's own National Fascist Community, the pro-Nazi Vlajka (Banner) group, and ANO, the anti-Semitic Action for National

---

[37] Hácha's notes for conversation with Neurath, April 1939, *DHCSP*, II, pp. 425–28. Cf. reports by the *Oberlandräte* after the conclusion of the military administration, 320/2894, Geheimes Staatsarchiv [GSA].

Restoration. But several moderate politicians, unwilling to leave the field to the Fascists, also joined. In a special proclamation, the committee welcomed incorporation into the Reich and urged the population to abandon its "totally unjustified mistrust of Germany." On the following day, General Gablenz, the new German commander of Prague, received the self-appointed Czech representatives and recognized their claim to speak in the name of the entire people.[38]

The very existence of the Czech National Committee obviously challenged the authority of President Hácha and his government. But the President, still under the spell of the excruciating experience he had undergone the previous night in Berlin, was too resigned to act decisively. In the evening of March 16, he addressed his people by radio, urging them to become reconciled with incorporation into Germany:

When twenty years ago all Czech hearts were filled with joy [at the proclamation of national independence], I stood apart from those historic events. My joy about our unbelievable success was overshadowed by anxiety about the external and internal guarantees which would assure the permanence of our success. Now, after twenty years, I can see with grief that my anxieties were not without foundation. What we held for a solution to last for ages proved to be merely a short episode in our national history . . . . By our union with [Germany] the former unity of the Reich has been restored.[39]

Hácha's speech had not been dictated by the Germans. It expressed the view of a former Austrian civil servant for whom subordination to foreign rule was normal rather than unusual. He may have shared the hope of many Czechs of his generation that German rule would not be significantly harsher than that of the Austrian regime before 1918. Even limited autonomy had some advantage over precarious independence. And would the subjects' loyalty not be rewarded by the masters' generosity?[40]

The President's political brains were Prime Minister Beran and

---

[38] Nečas to Beneš, December 17, 1940, *DHCSP*, I, pp. 153–56. Sobota, *Co to byl protektorát*, p. 53. *České slovo*, March 18, 1939. Cf. T. Pasák, "K činnosti Českého národního výboru na počátku okupace" [The Czech National Committee at the Beginning of the Occupation], in *Z českých dějin*, ed. by Z. Fiala and R. Nový, pp. 289–315.

[39] U. Thürauf (ed.), *Schulthess*, LXXX, p. 62.

[40] Cf. contemporary criticism of these illusions by O. Odložilík, "Stará nebo nová situace?" [An Old or a New Situation?], *Brázda*, II (1939), pp. 238–40.

Jiří Havelka, once Hácha's junior colleague at the Supreme Administrative Court. Although not a professional politician, Havelka devised the strategy the government should follow in dealing with the Germans. In order to avoid clashes, it should anticipate their wishes and itself initiate inevitable measures, painlessly and in a watered-down form. Some Czechs resented such strategy as opportunistic and nicknamed him "the climber."[41]

Havelka and Beran guided the President's steps against the Fascists, contending that the existing government enjoyed the full confidence of the Führer and that Gajda's Committee was therefore superfluous. The Germans rescinded their earlier support of it and the military authorities were reprimanded by Berlin for their precipitate action. Henlein stated in a confidential directive that "the settlement of party affairs in the Protectorate should be left to the autonomous authorities." The Committee saw the only way out of the confusion in disbanding itself.[42]

The next measures of the administration bore the unmistakable imprint of Havelka's strategy. The President abolished the National Assembly and dissolved the two remaining political parties. He appointed instead a fifty-member Committee of National Solidarity, which was to become the nucleus of a mass political movement. Its program repudiated parliamentary democracy and socialism, condemned Jewish influence and demanded state direction of the economy. Individual members of the new organization referred to the President as the "Leader" and professed a desire to establish close ties with the Nazi party.[43]

In a situation where the Germans exercised final authority, the totalitarian terminology used by the Czech leaders could no longer be taken seriously. It was little more than window dressing, intended to impress the Nazis and to deny the domestic Fascists a cause for which to fight. The National Solidarity Movement (NSM) officially received a monopoly of political organization, a measure which implicitly, though not formally, abolished the Fascist parties. ANO joined the NSM and Vlajka, too, reluctantly

---

[41] *DHCSP*, II, p. 815, lists the nickname.

[42] Dispatch of the Deutsches Nachrichten-Büro, No. 417, March 18, 1939, R 43, II/1327, BA. "Tagesbefehl No. 9," March 28, 1939, Wi/IF 3.173, BA, MA. Cf. note on Hitler's conversation with Keitel on March 31, Wi/IF, 3.166, BA, MA.

[43] Hácha's statement, quoted in Popelka to Chvalkovský, December 1, 1941, *DHCSP*, II, p. 643. *České slovo*, March 22–25, 1939. Cf. Sobota, *Co to byl protektorát*, pp. 44, 54–57. H. Ripka, *Munich*, p. 388.

announced its adherence. Gajda assured Hácha of his loyalty, although he took no practical steps to disband his followers.[44]

With the imminent Fascist danger averted, the government consolidated its power. Having secured Neurath's approval, the President reorganized the cabinet on April 27. Its composition changed little and the shifts that were made indicated that the Germans had not masterminded the change. Most Czechs welcomed the elimination of the unpopular Prime Minister Beran, although the old manipulator continued to exercise influence informally. In recognition of his indispensability, Havelka became Deputy Prime Minister. On the other hand, two men who had compromised themselves by apparently unnecessary servility had disappeared from the scene. Foreign Minister Chvalkovský and Defense Minister Syrový were conveniently eliminated along with their ministries, although Chvalkovský was sent to Berlin to head the Czech "legation" there.

The new Premier, General Alois Eliáš, had served as Minister of Transport in the former cabinet but was not a prominent political personality. An engineer by profession, he started his military career as an Austrian officer, joined the Czechoslovak Legion in Russia during World War I and later became a deputy chief of staff under the Republic. As Beneš's military adviser, he took part in the Geneva disarmament conferences in the early thirties. There he met Neurath, with whom he remained on good terms. Even in their new positions in the Protectorate, the two men, in allusion to their Geneva days, reportedly communicated in French. Thus Eliáš, despite his earlier membership in the "treacherous" Legion and his association with Beneš, did not arouse German apprehensions. Frank initially considered him a moderate and "prudent" man.[45]

The Prime Minister respected Hácha but did not share his fatalism and timidity. He did not expect the German rule to last long and wished above all that the Czechs survive it with a minimum of sacrifices. Neither he nor his ministers had much faith in their ability to resist German pressures. Yet they calculated that the Protectorate's autonomy, limited though it was, still offered

[44]Cf. J. Jelínek, *PÚ-Politické ústředí domácího odboje* [The Political Center of Home Resistance], pp. 42–52. Sobota, *Co to byl protektorát*, p. 65.

[45]*Trials*, XII, p. 895. Cf. Král, *Pravda*, p. 25. T. Pasák has published several thoughtful articles about Eliáš, most recently, "General Eliáš a problémy kolaborace" [General Eliáš and the Problems of Collaboration], *Dějiny a současnost*, X (1968), No. 6, pp. 33–37.

an opportunity to look after the nation's interests. In April 1939, this was a sensible attitude and the first reception of the cabinet by Neurath abounded in mutual expressions of good will.[46]

The two fields where the disappearance of national sovereignty had most obvious repercussions were defense and foreign affairs. Hitler ordered the Czechoslovak army demobilized and the military service of Protectorate nationals abolished. He did not wish again to witness Czech troops defecting en masse, as they had done in World War I. He thought it advisable to order good pensions for the officers who were forced to retire, hoping that this would be the safest way to curb their militancy. The Protectorate was allowed to maintain only a pathetic Government Force. It consisted of 7000 men armed with light weapons and intended for auxiliary police duties.[47]

Even after Berlin had forced the liquidation of the Czech Foreign Service, the Hácha government, always sensitive to legalistic considerations, still hoped to preserve an appearance of international legal entity. Chvalkovský became "Minister" to Berlin where he was to represent Czech interests—an anemic counterpart of the Protector's office in Prague. The Nazis, however, never accorded Chvalkovský the status of a diplomatic representative and treated him with assorted insolence. They issued a special decree to make it clear that, rather than enjoying diplomatic immunity, the envoy was subject to the jurisdiction of German courts to the same extent as any ordinary Czech national.[48]

In another action intended to demonstrate that state sovereignty had not been entirely relinquished to the Reich, the Hácha administration claimed membership in the Universal Postal Union as Czechoslovakia's successor. Neurath, however, checked this effort at the outset. But the Nazis were pragmatic enough to grant Bohemia and Moravia vestiges of sovereignty whenever it suited their own interests. Thus the Protectorate was allowed to negotiate separate commercial treaties with foreign countries in 1939—a

[46]Thürauf, (ed.), *Schulthess*, LXXX, pp. 125–26.

[47]Note on Hitler's directives to Brauchitsch, March 25, 1939, *DGFP*, D, VI, pp. 117–19. Note on conversations between Hitler, Keitel, and Friderici, March 31, 1939, Wi/IF 3.166, BA, MA. *Der Neue Tag*, August 1, 1939. Cf. F. Nesvadba, "Vládní vojsko a jeho odsun do Itálie" [The Government Force and Its Transfer to Italy], *Historie a vojenství*, 1968, pp. 924–61.

[48]Decree of December 26, 1939, *Reichsgesetzblatt* [*RGB*], 1940, I, p. 22.

move calculated to avoid threatened foreign boycotts of German-made goods. Even later, the Hácha government acted as a signatory in international agreements to settle Czechoslovakia's debts.[49] But regardless of these expediencies, there could be little doubt that the occupied country was part of the Reich, albeit with a status *sui generis*.

In internal affairs, German interference was relatively limited until the outbreak of the war. There was little physical contact between the Neurath and Hácha administrations. Adopting Havelka's strategy, the autonomous government tried to forestall Nazi pressures by acting first. Initially many anti-German puns and allegories appeared in the press, but soon Czech censors began to eliminate anything which was likely to arouse Nazi displeasure.[50] In place of the National Assembly, which had been dissolved by the President, the cabinet assumed exclusive legislative power. It issued executive decrees in accordance with the Enabling Act of January 1939.[51] On the lower level, provincial and district assemblies, though never very important before, disappeared altogether. In the municipalities, where local self-government had been most advanced, no elections took place. Appointive officials assumed decisive power everywhere.[52]

Like the French under Pétain in 1940, the Czechs in 1939, haunted by the memory of their imperfect democracy, were prepared to accept the paternalism of the Hácha regime. They welcomed its program of political concentration in the name of national unity. By May 1939, 98.4 per cent of the eligible male citizens had registered with the National Solidarity Movement—an impressive show of confidence in what a contemporary observer termed their *ersatz* leadership.[53] The Nazis did not fail to realize

[49] Cf. Sobota, *Co to byl protektorát*, pp. 34–38.

[50] The situation of the press during the Second Republic and at the beginning of the Protectorate is analyzed in T. Pasák, "Problematika protektorátního tisku a formování tzv. skupiny aktivistických novinářů na počátku okupace" [The Protectorate Press and the Origins of the Group of the So-Called Activist Newsmen], *Příspěvky k dějinám KSČ*, VII (1967), pp. 52–71.

[51] On December 12, 1940, Neurath indefinitely extended its validity, *Verordnungsblatt des Reichsprotektors in Böhmen und Mähren* [*VOB*], 1940, p. 604.

[52] For comparison with the earlier administrative system in Czechoslovakia, see E. Taborsky, "Local Government in Czechoslovakia, 1918–1948," *American Slavic and East European Review*, X (1951), pp. 202–215.

[53] Pešl's message for Beneš, June 6, 1939, *DHCSP*, I, p. 440. *České slovo*, May 4, 1939. Cf. Sobota, *Co to byl protektorát*, pp. 57–58.

the significance of this gesture and Frank became alarmed that "the Czechs were closely uniting and concentrating."[54]

The success of the NSM strengthened the government on the eve of the decisive showdown with the Fascists. Between May 19 and 28, the Vlajka and the "Fascist Action Committee," a radical faction impatient with Gajda's hesitant leadership, rioted in Brno and to a smaller extent in Prague also. Several hundred of them roamed through the streets molesting pedestrians who wore NSM badges. In familiar Nazi fashion, they dragged Jews out of cafes and beat them up. Gajda and the leading Vlajkaists met with the President and demanded key political positions. They proposed the adoption of the Nuremberg laws and the creation of a new secret police to be appropriately called the "Czestapo." Among the Fascists in Brno, there was also some talk about separating Moravia from Bohemia.[55]

The attitude of the Germans remained ambiguous. On the one hand, they secretly financed anti-Semitic propaganda by the Czech Fascists.[56] But when the Hácha government used the police to put down the disturbances, the Nazis did not interfere. Prime Minister Eliáš supposedly bribed Gajda, who was hard-pressed by his creditors, to exact from him a promise to withdraw from politics.[57] While his followers grudgingly joined the NSM, the erratic general kept his word and vanished from the scene. The crisis clarified the situation: the opposition had exposed its weakness and the Vlajka remained henceforth the only extreme right-wing organization of any importance.

The consolidation of the nation was no mean accomplishment of the Hácha administration. After a series of disasters, the government acquired an appreciable measure of popularity. It helped to awaken the people from their political apathy. Their opposition

[54] Quoted in Stuckart to Lammers, May 2, 1939, *Trials of War Criminals*, XII, p. 896. Cf. E. V. Erdely, *Germany's First European Protectorate*, p. 195. On the significance of the NSM campaign, see Kennan's report to the State Department, May 11, 1939, Kennan, *From Prague after Munich*, pp. 157–58.

[55] Sobota, *Co to byl protektorát*, pp. 61–62. Pešl's message for Beneš, May 21–28, 1939, *DHCSP*, II, pp. 433–35. The most recent study of Moravian Fascism is T. Pasák, "Problematika moravského extrémně-pravicového hnutí v roce 1939" [The Extreme Right-Wing Movements in Moravia in 1939], *Slezský sborník*, LXVI (1968), pp. 16–27.

[56] Main Office of the Security Service, Jelínek folder, June–July 1939, CCXXXIV-3, Centre de documentation juive contemporaine [CDJC].

[57] J. Havelka, "Vzpomínka na generála Eliáše" [A Reminiscence of General Eliáš], *Dějiny a současnost*, VII, (1965), No. 3, p. 41.

against the oppressor was taking shape. In June, a Czech observer noted that "rarely was the nation in as good a moral condition as today."[58] As in other occupied countries later on, the people reaffirmed their nationality in symbolic demonstrations. Theater and concert audiences rose spontaneously to sing the national anthem. Passers-by laid flowers at the Tomb of the Unknown Soldier. The transfer of the remains of a nineteenth-century Czech poet from the Sudetenland to Prague served as an occasion for patriotic festivities. Pilgrimages, attended that year by unusually large crowds, reinforced both the religious and the national faith.[59]

The Czechs recovered confidence in the future. A high Nazi official reported to Berlin that "people only wait until Germany will be forced to give up the Protectorate through some international entanglements and they look forward to a sanguinary revenge."[60] In the tense weeks of August 1939, especially before the signing of the Nazi-Sovet nonaggression pact, the majority of the population awaited the outbreak of the war with serenity. They confidently believed that Germany would be promptly defeated and they would regain their freedom.

Although united and in good spirits, the Czechs were not free from important weaknesses which would inevitably be aggravated during a prolonged occupation. Their government was likely to sink into an ever-greater dependence upon German good will as it clung to its residual autonomy. The ministers often contemplated resignation in protest against its violation, but they lacked the determination to act decisively. The majority of the people, given to an exaggerated optimism about an early liberation, tended to underestimate the demoralizing impact of their temporary acquiescence to the German-imposed reality. Thus, despite their inner opposition, they were capable of behavior which amounted, for all practical purposes, to collaboration with the enemy. This disposition could be turned to great advantage by the Germans, if they could only find appropriate policies by which to encourage it.

[58] Pešl's message for Beneš, June 6, 1939, *DHCSP*, II, p. 439.

[59] PVVZ message for Beneš, May 8–9, 1939, *ibid.*, p. 432. Kennan to State Department, May 11, 1939, Kennan, *From Prague after Munich*, pp. 158–59. Cf. F. Janáček, *Dva smery v začiatkoch národného odboja* [Two Trends at the Beginning of the National Resistance Movement], pp. 175–76. On the general pattern of resistance at the early stage of the occupation in various European countries, see L. de Jong, "Zwischen Kollaboration und *Résistance*," in *Das Dritte Reich*, p. 142.

[60] Reinhard to Dellbrügge, April 21, 1939, 320/2894, GSA. Leaflets and official reports about acts of defiance from March to November 1939 are quoted in J. Radimský, "Z prvního roku okupace" [From the First Year of the Occupation], in *Brno v minulosti a dnes*, VII, pp. 183–92.

4 *THE ECONOMIC PARTNERSHIP*

I N T H E Nazi drive for European hegemony, the seizure of Bohemia and Moravia was an operation of secondary importance; thus, once it was accomplished, the Germans largely improvised the political settlement in the country. In contrast, the economic aspects of the undertaking were handled with a precision comparable to that brought to bear on the military strategy. At least three months before the invasion, the Army High Command had drawn up detailed plans for the seizure of arms and for the control of defense industries. These plans were meticulously executed as soon as the occupation had started.[1]

General Georg Thomas, the head of the War Economy and Armaments Board, dispatched his agents to secure the entire stock of Czechoslovak weapons and ammunition. They speedily shipped the loot to Germany, giving the stupefied Czechs little chance to hide away any sizable quantities of arms.[2] With similar efficiency, the Technical Emergency squads secured installations of military importance, such as power stations and gas works, taking precautions against possible sabotage. During the subsequent few weeks Thomas's men inspected all defense plants in the country, collecting data on their current output and productive capacity. The managers were obliged to furnish the pertinent data in detailed questionnaires. At the same time, the Germans captured over two-hundred thousand technical designs and patents, many of them of considerable value.[3]

Such activities suggest that the Nazis assigned high priority to exploiting Bohemia and Moravia for Germany's rearmament.

[1] See Chapter 2, note 11, above.
[2] "Erfahrungsbericht," March 13–31, 1939, OKW, T-77, 733, 1959752–63, NA.
[3] "Geschichte der Rüstungs-Inspektion Prag," p. 49, WO 8-122/21, BA, MA. Cf. OKW, T-77, 732, 1958404–27, and 733, 1959752–63, NA; Wi/IF 3.23, 3.207, 3.208, BA, MA.

From the time of the Munich crisis, there was an important stock of arms available in the country. Just how much, however, the Czechoslovak equipment strengthened the military potential of the Third Reich is difficult to estimate. As Table 1 shows, the figures given in Hitler's speech of April 28, 1939 differ considerably from those compiled after the war by Czechoslovak historians:

TABLE 1. *Arms and Ammunition Seized by the Germans in Czechoslovakia in 1939*[4]

	According to Hitler's speech of April 28, 1939	According to Czechoslovak sources
Airplanes	1,582	1,231 (plus material ready in factories for 240)
Field artillery	2,175	2,253 (plus 1,966 anti-tank guns)
Anti-aircraft guns	501	..
Tanks	469	810
Rifles	1,090,000	603,000
Machine guns	43,000	57,000
Revolvers	114,000	..
Infantry cartridges	1 billion	..
Artillery cartridges	3 million	..

In 1938, the Reich's total defense expenditures amounted to 15,850 million marks.[5] The Germans later assessed the total value of the seized armaments, expressed in terms of the 1939 purchasing power of the mark, at only 77 million marks.[6] Although a defense budget does not consist only of items relating to the manufacture of arms, the vast discrepancy between the two figures indicates that the contribution represented by the Czechoslovak equipment should not be overrated.

Moreover, the Nazis used only some of the seized arms for their own troops. In the Polish campaign the Czechoslovak equipment reportedly supplied ten divisions, while the police and SS utilized small firearms of Czech origin.[7] On the other hand, however, the Germans sold a considerable portion of the booty

[4] Hitler's Reichstag speech of April 28, 1939, in *Speeches of Adolf Hitler*, ed. by Baynes, II, pp. 1610–23. Hájek, *Od Mnichova*, p. 153.

[5] S. Andic and J. Veverka, "The Growth of Government Expenditure in Germany since the Unification," *Finanzarchiv*, XXIII (1964), p. 258.

[6] Official German army estimate, October 10, 1944, Nur. EC-86, IfZ.

[7] F. Halder, *Kriegstagebuch*, I, pp. 17–18. G. Stein, *The Waffen SS*, p. 55.

abroad, in particular to the Balkan countries and to Turkey, Iran, and China. They did not immediately block the orders these countries had previously placed with the armament plants in Bohemia and Moravia. Surprisingly enough, they even contemplated the sale of Czechoslovak airplanes and tanks to France and Britain, evidence of how lightly they took into account a possible war with these two countries.[8] Germany was arming for short local campaigns rather than for a major war which would inevitably involve France and Britain as its adversaries. Rather than stockpiling the Czech weapons for its armed forces, Berlin hoped to exchange them for sorely needed foreign currency.

The economies imposed in the Protectorate soon after the invasion testified to the Nazis' overwhelming need for hard cash. A special Reich Bank supervisory board in Prague decided the allocation of foreign exchange quotas for imports—especially of raw materials—giving preference to firms working on German orders.[9] Berlin also showed immediate concern about the Czechoslovak gold reserve. The Reich Bank dispatched to Prague a special representative who arrived on March 15 along with the advance columns of the army. Backed by the military authorities, he forced the governors of the Czechoslovak National Bank to order the disposal of the gold reserve stored in the vaults of the Bank of England. This operation, conducted through the Bank for International Settlements at Basel, was eventually successful—a pathetic by-product of the follies of appeasement. Despite formal British embargo on Czechoslovak assets and despite indignation in the House of Commons, the London officials allowed 809,984 ounces of gold to be shipped to Germany in June.[10]

[8] Keitel's circular, March 29, 1939, Wi/IF 3.166, BA, MA. Wiehl's memorandum, April 1, 1939, AA, T-120, 1094, 447366, NA. Cf. *DGFP*, D, VI, pp. 960–61. *Trial*, XXXVIII, pp. 369–70. Papal Nuncio Valeri reported from Paris in July 1939 that the Germans were negotiating the sale of 1400 airplanes, which they had seized in Czechoslovakia, to France. P. Blet (ed.), *Actes et documents du Saint-Siège*, I, p. 200.

[9] L. Chmela, *Hospodářská okupace Československa* [The Economic Aspect of the Occupation of Czechoslovakia], pp. 43 and 49.

[10] The Germans failed to capture additional Czechoslovak gold deposited on different accounts in both Basel and London. After the June incident and especially after the outbreak of the war, the British enforced the embargo vigorously. Cf. note by A. Drucker, January 5, 1943, *DHCSP*, I, pp. 300–302. *Parliamentary Debates*, *House of Commons*, 1939, vol. 345, pp. 1481–88, 1713, and vol. 348, pp. 35, 882, 1524, 2006. Chmela, *Hospodářská okupace Československa*, pp. 41–42. Erdely, *Germany's First European Protectorate*, pp. 121–23.

For German business firms, the seizure of Bohemia and Moravia opened up prospects for profitable investment. Encouraged by the Berlin government, particularly by Göring, German capital had already made substantial inroads on Czechoslovak industry between Munich and March 15. After that date the economic penetration further increased. Czech-owned companies were either forced to sell part of their stock at prices dictated by German buyers, or were required to increase their capital to an amount which would guarantee a German majority among the stockholders. Through these operations, the Hermann Göring Works, the semi-governmental armament concern, acquired capital control over Škoda and Brünner Waffen, the leading producers of arms in the Protectorate, as well as over Poldi and Vítkovice, the largest steel works. Interlocking directorates and executives who sat on the managing boards served as the instruments of German control. On the first day of the occupation, for example, representatives of the Dresdner Bank and the Deutsche Bank, which had close connections with the Nazi party and government, forcibly removed the Jewish members of the board of directors in the two largest German-owned banks in Prague. The two institutions became subsidiaries of the Dresdner and Deutsche banks. Business enterprises which the Gestapo had confiscated from Jews and exiles were entrusted to German firms or to individual Nazi managers.[11] The nominal value of German-owned stock in Bohemia and Moravia increased tenfold during the occupation.[12] Although allowance must be made for the gradual depreciation of the mark, this figure indicates a substantial expansion of German business interests in the country.

It would nevertheless be preposterous to view these figures as evidence of reckless exploitation—as the Nuremberg tribunal did after the war—unequivocally harmful to the Czechs. Implementing Berlin's blueprint for the economic incorporation of Bohemia and Moravia, the German firms kept their activities within strict limits. They were supervised by Hans Kehrl, a high official of the Reich Ministry of Economics. On March 15 he arrived in Prague as a special plenipotentiary of Walter Funk, the Minister of Economics, and of Göring, who was the head of the Four Year Plan authority, Germany's supreme planning board. Kehrl arbi-

[11] Examination of Körner, *United States v. Weizsäcker*, *Proceedings* (in English), pp. 14204–205, CU. Král, *Otázky*, II, pp. 27–91, 150–58, 174–212.

[12] V. Vilinskij, "České koncerny za války" [The Czech Concerns during the War], *Statistický obzor*, 1946, p. 59.

trated between competing firms, such as the two rival banks, Dresdner and Deutsche, and decided their spheres of influence. In conformity with Göring's instruction that Czech business interests must not be disregarded, Kehrl tried to prevent excesses which would cause disruptions.[13]

Although most Czechs believed that their country was being mercilessly plundered, the Nazis in fact shipped away little except the arms. At the beginning of the occupation, Berlin decreed a temporary freeze upon all new purchases and prohibited German firms from placing new orders in the country without special authorization. In a decree dated March 28, the Ministry of Economics explicitly banned the shipment to Germany of raw materials, semi-finished goods, and other enumerated articles.[14]

The Nazis handled prudently the issue of a customs union between Germany and the Protectorate, which Göring had originally pressed as the necessary first step towards economic incorporation. This plan caused alarm among Czech businessmen and economic experts. In his April 1939 memorandum for Berlin, the governor of the Prague National Bank, Ladislav František Dvořák, warned that the project would undermine the country's ability to earn foreign exchange, which the Nazis considered highly desirable. He argued that, because of the overvaluation of the mark in relation to the Czech crown, the abolition of the tariff barrier would suddenly force prices up to adjust to the higher German level. The cost of production would increase so much as to seriously impair the competitive power of Protectorate industry abroad. In view of the ensuing marketing difficulties, production would have to be curtailed, causing, in turn, widespread unemployment and social unrest. Dvořák concluded that the customs union would harm German interests no less than Czech ones.[15]

Kehrl was favorably disposed to such reasoning. He, too, held that the Protectorate must maintain its high level of exports. In the decisive discussions with Funk, which took place in Berlin on May 12, Dvořák scored a significant success. The Nazi Minister

13Kehrl to Himmler, September 30, 1939, Nur. NID-14621, IfZ. Göring's instruction, March 16, 1939, OKW, T-77, 733, 1960561–62, NA. Minutes of the conference between the representatives of the Economics Ministry and German banks, March 21, 1939, Nur. NID-13394, IfZ.

14Ordinance of March 28, 1939, *RGB*, 1939, I, pp. 654–55. Directive of March 31, 1939, OKW, T-77, 732, 1958301, NA.

15"Voraussetzungen der wirtschaftlichen Entwicklung des Protektorates Böhmen und Mähren," R 2/5835, BA. Cf. *DGFP*, D, IV, p. 82.

of Economics agreed to postpone the customs union, although preparations were to be made for its realization in the near future.[16]

Before the war started, the Nazis had proceeded ruthlessly to satisfy their immediate needs in the Protectorate. They seized the arms and tried to put gold and foreign exchange at their command. As a long-term economic policy, however, they avoided measures which would drive the Czechs to desperation. The system left the Czechs enough room for their own economic activity.

The Nazis had excellent experience with German big business. The industrialists, regardless of their reservations about Hitler, eagerly seized the opportunities his regime offered. In return for guaranteed profits, they readily submitted to regimentation. They welcomed the boom sustained by rearmament.[17]

The Protectorate was the first occupied country where the Nazis tested whether nationalism or interest in profit would determine the attitude of native businessmen. They had few doubts about the outcome of this experiment. On March 30, 1939, General Thomas assured his Prague staff that the Czech industrialists would be cooperative as long as their profits were safeguarded.[18] General Udet, Göring's aide in charge of aircraft production, urged that political differences should not obstruct businesslike relations. In a letter to Keitel he noted: "The past should be forgotten; cooperation should be based upon mutual confidence."[19] On March 20, 1939, Göring met with the leading representatives of Czech industry. He emphasized that their compliance would be rewarded with ample contracts. As promised, the German army, navy, and air force soon flooded Protectorate factories with orders.[20]

While strengthening commercial ties between the occupied country and Germany, the Nazis did not wish to harm existing Czech foreign-trade connections. The Reich market was to supplement rather than substitute for the traditional Western markets. As Table 2 indicates, despite Czechoslovakia's growing political dependence upon Germany after Munich, its commercial links with the West had remained strong. In 1938, Britain had been its second-

---

[16] Král, *Otázky*, I, pp. 128–32.
[17] Cf. A. Schweitzer, *Big Business in the Third Reich*.
[18] "Geschichte der Rüstungs-Inspektion Prag," pp. 7–10, W 08-122/21, BA, MA.
[19] Udet to Keitel, December 1939, S 391/FD, 5590/45, Imperial War Museum, [IWM].
[20] *Ibid.*

largest, the Netherlands its fifth-largest, and the United States its
sixth-largest customer. American imports to Czechoslovakia had
been outmatched only by the German ones.

TABLE 2. *Czechoslovakia's Foreign Trade
in the Fourth Quarter of 1938*[21]

(*in million crowns*)

Export		Import	
Germany	450,000	Germany	465,500
Great Britain	160,783	United States	132,538
Rumania	109,750	Rumania	83,810
Yugoslavia	72,787	Great Britain	74,597
Netherlands	69,415	Yugoslavia	71,543
United States	61,508	France	60,257

The restriction of foreign trade which occurred after March 15
was not enforced by the Germans. Western firms were the first to
sever their contacts in protest against the occupation of Bohemia
and Moravia. On March 23, President Roosevelt annulled the
existing trade agreements with Czechoslovakia. In the United
States, goods from the Protectorate suffered from the boycott of
German products. Although the boycott was far from complete,
it nevertheless caused the American agents of the Prague Export
Institute to worry about growing marketing difficulties by the
summer of 1939.[22] With encouragement from Berlin, the Czechs
tried to remedy the situation. Jan Baťa, the leading shoe and rubber
manufacturer, received Göring's blessing to travel to the United
States in search of new customers and new sources of raw materials.
Although Baťa later stayed abroad and even established relations
with anti-German exiles, the Allies nevertheless considered it
advisable to keep the overseas affiliates of his company on their
black list as enemy firms.[23]

Despite initial difficulties, Protectorate industry adjusted itself
with remarkable ease to the new market orientation. The Czech
economic journals praised the benefits of association with a big
state, while the exporters took full advantage of the German demand.[24] They found additional outlets in the Balkan countries.

21 Král, *Otázky*, I, p. 110.
22 Cf. *SGV*, 1939, p. 375. Král, *Otázky*, I, pp. 139–40.
23 *Ibid.*, II, p. 457.
24 Quoted *ibid.*, I, pp. 125–26, 165. Cf. Křen, *Do emigrace*, p. 162.

Not only did the occupation cause no economic difficulties but Czech industry in 1939 enjoyed its greatest boom since the Depression. After the Molotov-Ribbentrop pact of August 1939, the new friendship between Berlin and Moscow seems to have further bolstered its prosperity. According to the German-Soviet agreements of October 23, 1939, and February 11, 1940, the Protectorate shared in the expanded trade between the Reich and the Soviet Union.[25]

The Czech business community warmly welcomed the link with Russia. On November 3, President Václav Hromádko of the Škoda Corporation presented to the Germans a plan in which he outlined how Soviet wishes could be best met. Nine of the largest firms formed a syndicate to distribute the Soviet contracts among its subsidiaries. Several delegations of industrialists visited Moscow in late 1939 and early 1940, causing the Nazis to wonder about the possible pan-Slavistic connotations of such contacts. Yet the Soviets, faithful to their Berlin alliance, limited themselves strictly to business. In their dealings with the Czechs, they avoided anything which might arouse German displeasure.[26]

For a definite answer concerning the volume of the Protectorate's trade with Russia we must await the declassification of the papers of the Soviet Purchasing Commission in Prague, currently held by the Department of the Army in Washington. The exchange of goods between the Reich and the Soviet Union, motivated on the German side by an overwhelming need for raw materials and foodstuffs, grew to considerable proportions in early 1940. In return, the Germans supplied industrial products, including military items. On March 30, 1940, Hitler is said to have stated privately that the "delivery of military *matériel* to Russia should have priority over German army deliveries."[27] His words seem to be confirmed by our data showing that German armaments exports conspicuously increased after the Molotov-Ribbentrop pact. Despite the war,

[25] M. Beloff, *The Foreign Policy of Soviet Russia*, II, pp. 293–94. G. Weinberg, *Germany and the Soviet Union*, pp. 65–75. Schnurre's memorandum, February 26, 1940, *Nazi-Soviet Relations*, p. 132.

[26] Armament Inspection Board Prague, "Kriegstagebuch Nr. 1," fols. 69, 74, W 08-122/1, BA, MA. Armament Inspection Board to Defense Economy Board, November 22, 1939, fol. 40, W 08-122/24, BA, MA. During his 1947 trial, former Prime Minister Beran wanted to describe the commercial relations between the Protectorate and the Soviet Union; the State Prosecutor, fearing damage to Moscow's reputation, forbade him to testify—see Beran, *Die Tschecho-Slowakei*, pp. 135–36.

[27] Thomas, *Geschichte*, p. 229.

these exports remained high in volume in the first six months of 1940. In the second half of 1939, the Reich—including the Protectorate—sold 321,145,770 marks worth of military equipment abroad.[28] Exports from a single Protectorate factory, the Škoda works, accounted for a fourth of this amount. Foreign deliveries by the country's two other major producers, Brünner Waffen and Českomoravská-Kolben-Daněk (ČKD Prague), also increased substantially:

TABLE 3. *Value of Exported Military Equipment* [29]

	(in marks)	
	July–December 1939	*January–June 1940*
Brünner Waffen	2,782,774	37,816,478
ČKD Prague	564,947	12,690,416

Although our sources do not state the destination of the exported products, there is little doubt that the Soviet Union was their principal recipient.

Since by late spring 1940 the heyday of the Nazi-Soviet honeymoon had already passed, the total quantity of arms actually delivered to Russia was probably not large. Yet trade in non-military items, including heavy machinery, continued, though on a diminishing scale, until June 22, 1941—despite Hitler's military preparations against Russia. By that date there were at least four Soviet trade representatives still present in the Protectorate upon whom the Gestapo could lay their hands.[30]

Surprisingly enough, the total volume of industrial production in Bohemia and Moravia decreased in the second war year, 1940–1941.[31] This may have been caused partly by the decline of the Russian trade, although it is more likely that the recession took place primarily in the light industries which were more and more affected by the shortage of raw materials. The output of heavy industry remained the same or even increased. Yet the expansion

[28] Statistics compiled by the War Equipment Export Association, S 361/FD, 5455, ABC/45, IWM.

[29] *Ibid.*

[30] Defense Economy Inspection Board to OKW, September 9, 1939, W 01-8/295, BA, MA. Armament Command Brno, "Kriegstagebuch Nr. 7," fol. 66, W 09-70/6, BA, MA.

[31] V. Průcha and R. Olšovský, "L'occupazione nazista e l'economia cecoslovacca," in *L'occupazione nazista in Europa*, ed. by E. Collotti, p. 328.

in this sector, which produced the bulk of military items, was not sufficient to cause a rise in the total output figure.

Such a situation indicates that until 1941 the Protectorate hardly conformed to the customary image of an occupied country whose economy had been "militarized" and pillaged. Bohemia and Moravia presented the same picture of a very incomplete economic mobilization which—as Western scholars discovered after 1945— was also typical for Germany at that time. The Nazi planners, who were not anticipating a war of attrition, geared the Reich economy to supporting swift *blitzkrieg* campaigns. Requirements for military goods therefore fluctuated with the specific needs of these campaigns.[32]

In the Protectorate, firms were not compelled to accept military contracts until September 1940. But according to reports sent to Berlin by the German Armament Inspection Board in Prague, the contracts were "highly welcome and desired" and were "executed promptly."[33] In July 1940, following the defeat of France, Berlin suddenly cancelled a number of pending military orders, causing considerable anxiety among Czech businessmen. Not until a month later did new orders replace the cancelled ones. Similar fluctuations in the demand for armaments occurred as late as the summer of 1941, when the Nazis still believed that a quick conclusion of the Russian campaign was imminent.[34]

Although the Nazis did not insist upon total economic mobilization during the first two years of the occupation, they nevertheless established a strict system of controls. With all the Protectorate's resources at their command, they were able to get what they wanted. The economic structure of the country greatly facilitated their task. Since the Depression, the role of the government had been steadily increasing, a process which had gained momentum especially after Munich. The National Solidarity Movement, the only legal Czech political party after the invasion, included in its

[32] Cf. B. H. Klein, *Germany's Economic Preparations for War*, and A. S. Milward, *The German Economy at War*.

[33] Ordinance of September 19, 1940, *SGV*, 1940, p. 697. Armament Command Brno, "Kriegstagebuch Nr. 2," fol. 44, entry for March 3, 1940, W 09-70/2, BA, MA. Armament Inspection Board Prague, "Kriegstagebuch Nr. 1," fol. 97, W 08-122/1, BA, MA.

[34] Armament Command Brno, "Kriegstagebuch Nr. 4," fols. 10, 24–25, 45, W 09-70/4, BA, MA. Thomas, *Geschichte*, pp. 233–34, 284–86. Cf. Klein, *Germany's Economic Preparations*, pp. 188–89.

program the demand for a state-directed economy. When the Hácha administration began to put this program into practice in the summer of 1939, it acted with German blessing, though not on German orders.

The government decree of May 10, 1939 established the Supreme Office of Prices, a separate agency at the ministerial level, which was intended to supervise the setting of prices. Another decree, dated July 20, prohibited price increases without official authorization. The state assumed control over foreign trade.[35] The law of June 23, 1939 laid the foundations of an "organic structure" for the economy. It created "Central Associations" to represent the main fields of business activity: industry, commerce, banking, insurance, and others. In conformity with the German model, seven such associations were established during the subsequent two years.[36]

Business in Bohemia and Moravia, as in Germany, had been highly organized even before the advent of totalitarianism. Along territorial lines, businessmen had been joined in chambers of commerce; along functional lines, they were joined in interest associations, such as the Union of Manufacturers. Yet under the Nazi regime the character of these organizations changed. Analogous to the Reich Groups, the Central Associations in the Protectorate embodied three basic principles: compulsory membership, unity of representation, and appointive leadership. All firms had to join. The Associations enjoyed the monopoly of organization in each branch.[37] Rather than being elected by its members, the leading officers of each Association were appointed by the Minister of Industry, Commerce and Trade. He chose most of them from among the representatives of large companies, thus assuring the predominance of big business.

The Protectorate government tried to maintain a strong influence in economic life. The Czechs tailored the new system after the German model in order to forestall Nazi criticism. But they also

[35] Ordinances of May 10, June 23, July 20, 1939, *SGV*, 1939, pp. 385–93, 441–43, 498.

[36] Ordinance of June 23, 1939, *ibid.*, p. 596. Others quoted in M. Durmanová, "Řízené hospodářství a správa Ústředního svazu průmyslu za nacistické okupace" [Guided Economy and the Administration of the Central Association of Industry under the Nazi Occupation], *Sborník archivních prací*, XVI (1966), p. 378.

[37] Cf. A. and V. M. Toynbee (eds.), *Hitler's Europe*, pp. 171–73. Schweitzer, *Big Business*, p. 249.

hoped that, tightly organized, they would be able to remain materially strong and thus withstand pressure more easily. Economic and political concentration were to complement each other. The ultimate goal was a corporative order reminiscent of Fascist Italy. The employers and the employees would join in the same corporations, and national unity would increase as class conflicts presumably receded.[38]

In preparation for the corporative system, the Committee of National Solidarity tried to bring labor unions under its control. They had already been amalgamated into a single organization as of December 1938. The former party-affiliated or independent unions had merged into the National Union of Employees (NOÚZ), organized by industries and dominated by right-wing Social Democrats. The unions feared that subordination to the NSM would limit their freedom of action and further weaken their bargaining powers. The Hácha government had already prohibited strikes after wage disputes in southeast Moravia in June 1939. During decisive negotiations in July 1939, the NOÚZ upheld its separate existence, thus frustrating the corporative projects. Until 1940 the unions enjoyed a margin of freedom which enabled them to negotiate collective contracts.[39]

The Nazis, too, viewed the plans for a full-fledged corporative system with apprehension. They believed that subject peoples should be denied the benefits of such concentration, and even the Italians under the puppet regime of Salò in 1944 would prove to be no exception to this rule.[40] But the regimentation of business and industry as foreseen in the "organic structure" plan was well suited to German purposes. The Nazis transformed the newly created Czech institutions into instruments subject to their own control. They only needed to impose their own appointees in the Central Associations to make use of the sweeping powers provided by the system. The Associations decided on marketing, as well as on the assignment of government contracts, the distribution of raw materials, and the allocation of production quotas. Bernard

[38] Cf. Král, *Otázky*, III, pp. 75–76.

[39] L. Lehár, "Vývoj Národní odborové ústředny zaměstnanecké v prvních letech nacistické okupace" [The Development of the National Union of Employees in the First Years of the Nazi Occupation], *Historie a vojenství*, 1966, pp. 587–95, 601. Security Police to Lammers, July 10, 1939, AA, T-120, 1505, D 632588-89, NA. *Der Neue Tag*, June 14, 1939.

[40] Cf. F. W. Deakin, *The Brutal Friendship*, pp. 665–77.

Adolf, a Sudeten German industrialist from Liberec, assumed the chairmanship of the key Central Association of Industry.

The separation of the NOÚZ from the NSM exposed the unions to German interference. In late 1940, State Secretary Frank appointed Wilhelm Köstler, a high-ranking official of the German Labor Front, to serve as "intermediary" between him and the NOÚZ. Bypassing the Hácha administration, the Nazis dealt with labor directly. They emphasized their special concern for the welfare of the working class. In July 1939, General Erich Friderici, the chief of the German armed forces in the Protectorate, stated at a conference with the Nazi supervisors at the Škoda factory: "Director von Bolschwing and I have taken the responsibility, as far as our means allow, for carrying out social welfare measures in such a way as to make the workers perceive that they are better off in the Protectorate than before."[41] It was Friderici who later sponsored the free-meal program in the armament factories. In May 1940, Neurath, disregarding the general freeze decreed by the Eliáš government, ordered a wholesale increase of wages, which especially benefited the low-income brackets.[42] In his public speeches, Frank seldom missed a chance to court the workers as allies against "irresponsible" intellectuals, whom he presented as the main obstacle to Czech-German understanding.

The Nazis exercised direct economic control through two networks. The first extended over the provinces and districts from the Economics Department in the Office of the Protector and served as a prolonged arm of the Berlin Ministry of Economics. The departmental chief, Walter Bertsch, acted as the Ministry's top regional representative. He was a career bureaucrat with a good, though not outstanding, Party record. Bertsch and his staff supervised the autonomous government to assure the coordination of its economic policies with the needs of the Reich. He and his subordinates regulated the business activities of German firms and selected confidants to serve in the managing boards of Czech firms, Central Associations, and other economic agencies.

The German army created the second network to administer military contracting. From late August 1939 onward, General Thomas's War Economy and Armaments Inspection Board operated

[41] Minutes of the conference of May 17, 1939, Nur. NID-9382, IfZ. Cf. Lehár, "Vývoj," pp. 602–11.
[42] Ordinance of May 20, 1940, *VOB*, 1940, p. 214. Cf. Král, *Otázky*, III, pp. 153, 156.

in the Protectorate through the local Armament Inspection Board, regional commands in Prague and Brno, and armament officers in individual plants.[43] The Central Office for Public Contracts coordinated the military production with other economic programs. The Armament Inspection Board, headed by General Wolfgang Weigand, not only placed the contracts but also supervised their fulfillment on the spot.[44]

In order to prevent sabotage in the factories, Hitler ordered in February 1940 that hostages be selected from among the managers and foremen to guarantee undisturbed production. Since Neurath hesitated, considering such a measure to be unnecessarily harsh, Weigand issued the required order. The hostages had to sign the following statement: "Today I have been notified by the Armament Inspector, Major-General Weigand, that I bear personal responsibility, with all its consequences, for the prevention of any acts of sabotage in my plant. I pledge to keep this notification secret."[45]

A result of Hitler's whim, this drastic measure did not conform to the German pattern up to this time. Until the advent of total mobilization in early 1942, the Nazis were not seriously pressed by the needs of war and therefore preferred more gentle means. Their paramount desire was to unite the Protectorate economically with Germany, rather than to exploit it for the conduct of the war. After careful preparations, the tariff barriers between the two countries finally fell on October 1, 1940, without causing any adverse repercussions. The customs union implied a far-reaching economic equalization. From the Nazis' point of view, Bohemia and Moravia were part of the German homeland, and their resources should therefore be used in the same fashion as those of Germany.[46]

Since from October 1940 onward German statisticians treated Germany and the Protectorate as one entity, the share of the

[43] The Defense Economy Board, founded in Prague on March 30, 1939, was renamed "Armament Inspection Board" effective November 29, 1939. "Geschichte der Rüstungs-Inspektion Prag," fol. 7, W 08-122/21, BA, MA.

[44] Thomas's circular, March 15, 1939, Wi/IF 3.166, BA, MA. Weigand to OKW, September 5, 1939. Göring's circular, October 9, 1939, *ibid.*

[45] Keitel to War Economy and Armaments Board, February 29, 1940, Nur. PS-1154, IfZ. Armament Inspection Board Prague, "Kriegstagebuch Nr. 3," fols. 10, 14, 21, 23, 78, W 08-122/2, BA, MA.

[46] E. von Wedelstädt, "Die wirtschaftliche Eingliederung des Protektorats," *Die deutsche Volkswirtschaft*, IX (1940), pp. 290–93. "Protektoratswirtschaft im Zollanschluss," *Der Neue Tag*, March 15, 1941.

Czech resources in the economy of the Third Reich is impossible to compute. The only reliable figures are those concerning the "matricular contribution" paid every year from the Protectorate government budget to Berlin. (See Table 4.) This sum, though increasing yearly, was relatively modest and did not exceed its equivalents in comparable occupied countries, such as Norway and the Netherlands.

TABLE 4. *The Protectorate's " Matricular Contribution"* [47]

(in million marks)

	Nominal value	1939 purchasing power
1940	300	262
1941	500	412
1942	800	646
1943	1000	795

Bohemia and Moravia had more to gain than to lose from economic association with Germany. In the international division of labor within the Nazi New Order, every nation was supposed to contribute those goods which it was best suited to produce. For most countries, this apparently sensible plan implied their transformation into economic appendages of the Reich. The Balkans were to contribute little but agricultural products and raw materials; France, products of light industry; Poland, slave labor. The manufacture of sophisticated industrial goods—a substantially more profitable specialization—was reserved for the Reich.[48]

Bohemia and Moravia, whose economic structure was similar to that of Germany and therefore could not complement its needs, belonged to this privileged zone. The Germans invested heavily there, following the same pattern as at home. As a special task, the Protectorate—along with Austria—was to participate in the economic conquest of southeast Europe. The Nazi chiefs attended the semi-annual Prague trade fairs and praised the advantages of Balkan trade for the Czechs. The base of the Southeast Europe Company, which served as the German spearhead in that area, was extended from Austria to Bohemia and Moravia.[49]

[47] Official army estimate, October 10, 1944, Nur. EC-86, IfZ.

[48] Cf. A. and V. M. Toynbee (eds.), *Hitler's Europe*, pp. 165–71.

[49] H. Kehrl, "Das Protektorat im grossdeutschen Wirtschaftsraum," *Zeitschrift des Vereins Berliner Kaufleute und Industrieller*, XXII, No. 4 (1941), p. 23. Report of the Armament Inspection Board Prague, October 14, 1941, Acc. No. 4378–162, *World War II Records Division, Alexandria, Va.* [Alex.]. Frank's speech, September 11, 1940, *Der Neue Tag*, September 12, 1940. D. Orlow, *The Nazis in the Balkans*, pp. 62–64.

The promise of partnership, along with immediate profits, prompted the Czech businessmen to eager cooperation with the Germans. In their hearts, they desired liberation and national independence, like the rest of their compatriots. But in their acts, they prepared for the alternative of permanent German rule.

It would be unfair to single out the "capitalists" for their susceptibility to the lure of material gain. The armament boom tempted the working classes as well. The most striking example of this attraction is the story of Czech migrant labor in 1939–1941.

As early as January 20, 1939, the Czechoslovak government, responding to Nazi demands for foreign labor, agreed to permit twenty thousand workers to accept temporary jobs in Germany. In March 1939, recruiting agents of various Reich firms came to Bohemia and Moravia along with the occupation army. So extensive were their activities that the German military authorities soon prohibited the "wild" recruitment in order to protect the stability of the country's labor market. The Protectorate government eventually assumed authority in matters of employment. In July 1939, it created Labor Offices to direct the disposition of manpower.[50]

As a rule, workers were not forced to take jobs in Germany until the Nazis put the Labor Offices under their own control in early 1941. Only exceptionally did the Czech officials apply indirect pressure by withholding substitute jobs when an applicant was reluctant to go to Germany.[51] As the chart below indicates, the voluntary labor migration reached its climax during the first month of the occupation. This may have been the effect of the initial "wild" recruiting. Seasonal decline occurred during the winter months, but in the spring and summer of 1940 the influx of workers again increased, although it no longer approached the level of April 1939. The reported figures did not include the so-called *Grenzgänger*, who were resident in the Protectorate and crossed the border regularly to work in the Sudetenland. The figures also did not take into account the several hundred Czech engineers who took advantage, in 1939, of the great demand for

---

[50] Král, *Otázky*, I, p. 187. Third Army Group, "Besondere Anordnungen Nr. 6," March 20, 1939, Wi/IF 3.173, BA, MA. Ordinance of July 25, 1939, *SGV*, 1939, pp. 623–24.

[51] "Geschichte der Rüstungs-Inspektion Prag," fols. 26–27, W 08-122/21, BA, MA. Cf. Král, *Otázky*, I, p. 89.

technical specialists and the high salaries in Germany. Their competence and diligence earned high praise there.[52]

LABOR MIGRATION FROM THE PROTECTORATE
TO OTHER PARTS OF THE REICH
MARCH 1, 1939—DECEMBER 31, 1941 [53]

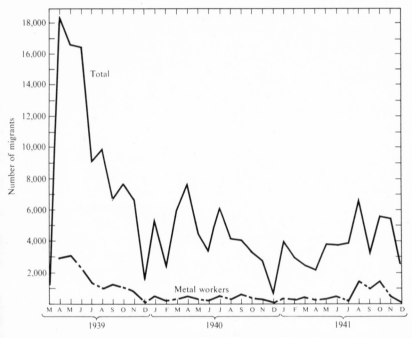

Political factors do not seem to have significantly influenced the trend of the migration. The workers, most of whom found employment as unskilled labor in the construction industries, were attracted above all by high wages. Some of them were disappointed by the living conditions in Germany and may even have returned home before the expiration of their contracts. But the majority evidently thought that the advantages outweighed the disadvantages and remained for the entire period they had signed for, usually one year. In 1939 alone, the migrants sent home remittances

[52] Interrogation of Otto Saur, July 14, 1945, 3049/49, File No, 1, IWM.
[53] W 08-122/22, BA, MA. Cf. also E. M. Kulitscher, *The Displacement of Population in Europe*, p. 133.

amounting to the not insignificant sum of 7.5 million marks.[54] The gradual decline of the movement of workers to Germany in 1940 and 1941 resulted primarily from the expansion of employment opportunities at home. By 1940, jobs were plentiful for the first time since the Depression.[55]

The cost of living rose rapidly from March 1939 onward. As predicted by Czech financial experts, association with Germany forced the prices in the Protectorate to adjust to the higher German level. The postponement of the customs union only slowed down but did not arrest the general rise of prices. The government tried to avert inflation by holding wages down. Hoping to regulate the disproportion between living expenses and incomes, from time to time it authorized upward wage adjustments by industries.[56] Only in March 1940 did the Protector arbitrarily decree an overall increase in order to gratify the workers. In the period before mid-

TABLE 5. *Changes in the Indices of Wages and Living Expenses*[57]

	Index of nominal weekly wages (all workers in all industry)	*Index of living expenses (working class family, average compiled for 27 cities)*
1939:		
March	100.0	100.0
July	103.0	103.9
September	104.0	105.0
1940:		
January	119.0	117.0
April	123.4	123.6
July	130.4	133.4
October	144.0	137.2
1941:		
January	146.2	143.3
April	154.0	151.0

[54] Armament Inspection Board Prague to War Economy and Armaments Board, April 10, 1940, W 08-122/24, BA, MA.

[55] From 1939 to 1941, the Protectorate's labor force increased by 10.5 per cent; Průcha and Olšovský, "L'occupazione," p. 328.

[56] Ordinance of December 21, 1939, *SGV*, 1939, pp. 943–44. Cf. Král, *Otázky*, III, pp. 148–51.

[57] Computed from *Ergebnisse der vierteljährlichen Lohnerhebungen für die Monate März, Juni und September 1943*, p. 1; and *Statistisches Jahrbuch für das Protektorat Böhmen und Mähren*, II, p. 123. Cf. H. Wirth, "Löhne, Preise und Kaufkraft im Protektorat," *Böhmen und Mähren*, August 1940.

1941, the real wages developed as indicated in Table 5. Comparison of the two columns shows a remarkably constant ratio between wages and prices, a tribute to their competent management by the Czech government. Although the growth of wages did not apply equally to different industries, most workers probably improved their real earnings during this period. Since, in addition, more women took advantage of the new employment opportunities, the actual incomes of many working-class families must have significantly increased.

In the regimented economy of the Protectorate, however, not even the index of real wages was a reliable indication of the material condition of the population. The growing scarcity of consumer goods set a definite limit to the amount available for purchase. Moreover, the rationing of certain essential products immediately resulted in dual prices, those fixed by the government and the higher black market prices. We have no reliable way of determining the level of the latter for this period.

In Bohemia and Moravia, the Nazis ordered rationing only in October 1939, several weeks after they had introduced it in Germany itself. Although the Czechs administered the system, the Germans determined the size of the rations. In 1939, rationing was still more generous in the Protectorate than in Germany, a feature which the Nazis—fearing resentment at home—forbade the Czech Minister of Agriculture to mention in a public speech.[58] The rations in 1940 can be seen from Table 6, adapted from a 1946 League of Nations publication. Those of flour products, the staple diet of the Czechs, remained relatively high. Sugar rations, also significantly larger than in Germany, were intended to satisfy the traditional preferences of the consumers. The allocation of meat was approximately the same in both countries. On the other hand, fats, always a deficit item in Bohemia and Moravia, were available in a much smaller quantity for the Czechs than for the Germans. The supply of fats would have had to be subsidized by imports, for which the Nazis were reluctant to appropriate their scarce reserves of foreign exchange. Although rations kept steadily diminishing, they were at least honored. The system, though burdensome, did not discriminate against the Czechs.[59]

[58] *Der Neue Tag*, October 1, 1939. Government ordinances of September 18 and 29, 1939, *SGV*, 1939, pp. 653–55, 672–75. Feierabend, *Ve vládě Protektorátu*, p. 104.

[59] Cf. K. Brandt, *Germany's Agricultural and Food Policies in World War II*, II, p. 286. Ziemke to Foreign Office, November 15, 1940, AA, T-120, 1279, 484599–600, NA. *Zpověď K. H. Franka*, p. 182.

TABLE 6. Food Rations in the Protectorate and in Germany[60]

(in grams per week, P = Protectorate, G = Germany)

| | Bread and Flour | | | | | | Sugar | | Meat | | | | | | Fats | | | | | |
| | normal consumers | | heavy workers | | very heavy workers | | | | normal consumers | | heavy workers | | very heavy workers | | normal consumers | | heavy workers | | very heavy workers | |
	P	G	P	G	P	G	P	G	P	G	P	G	P	G	P	G	P	G	P	G
1940:																				
I	2900	2400	3800	3800	4800	4800	350	250	500	500	1000	1000	1200	1200	155	270	185	395	340	740
II	2650	2400	3800	3800	4800	4800	300	225	500	500	1000	1000	1200	1200	155	270	275	395	620	740
III	2650	2250	3800	3650	4800	4650	300	225	575	500	1075	1000	1275	1200	155	270	275	395	620	740
IV	2250	2250	3400	3650	4800	4650	300	225	500	500	1000	1000	1200	1200	155	270	260	395	565	740
1941:																				
I	2250	2250	3650	3650	4650	4650	300	225	500	500	1000	1000	1200	1200	155	270	275	395	620	740
II	2250	2250	3650	3650	4650	4650	300	225	500	500	1000	1000	1200	1200	155	270	285	395	630	740

[60] Adapted from Food, Famine and Relief, pp. 128–29, 136–37.

Contemporary descriptions of the people's material conditions are often contradictory and tainted with the political biases of the commentators, so that a definite conclusion is difficult to reach. There was undoubtedly a tendency toward the equalization of economic status. The workers were able to get a greater share of the available consumer goods than before. The farmers were not worse off because of the occupation. Until the outbreak of the war, the Protectorate government, in which agrarian influences remained strong, continued its former policies of supporting high farm prices. During the war, the farmers had to deliver most of their produce to the state at dictated rates, but were still able to sell the surplus at premium prices in the black market.[61] Men with fixed incomes, in particular civil servants and other public employees, and professional people were hit hardest, but since their incomes had usually been higher than those of the rest of the population, they were generally in a better position to withstand the hardship. As in Germany, the standard of living in the Protectorate did not seriously deteriorate in 1939–1941.

From the Nazi point of view the German economic management of Bohemia and Moravia was quite successful. It supplied enough guns for the soldiers while leaving enough butter for the civilians. Yet even a reasonably fair economic policy did not inspire among the Czechs genuine sympathies for the regime. Although the Germans did not go so far as they could have in using the Protectorate's resources to support their military machine, most Czechs were unhappy about their using them at all. Similarly, although the Nazis did not require from their subjects significantly greater material sacrifices than from their own people, the Czechs deeply resented any sacrifice for an alien cause. They hated the occupation regime on political rather than economic grounds, and it was on the political level that the Nazis had to seek a solution to the problem of integrating these hostile people into their domain.

[61] Cf. Report of the Reich Attorney-General of the People's Court, April–June 1940, Nur. NG-682, IfZ.

5 STRUGGLES BEHIND THE SCENES

THE LACK of authoritative guidance from Berlin was hardly conducive to the development of a coherent German policy for Bohemia and Moravia in the summer of 1939. As far as Hitler was concerned, his sketchy initial instructions to Stuckart—which explained tactics rather than long-term objectives—indicated limited interest in the Protectorate.[1] The Führer did not elaborate any ideological goals to be pursued in the country. While international concerns absorbed his attention, diplomatic and military considerations still held priority over ideology.

Influential elements within Germany's hierarchy, however, were dissatisfied with this set of priorities. The Party and the SS—institutions which could only justify their existence on ideological grounds—pressed for a rapid realization of the radical tenets of the Nazi ideology. In these organizations, upstarts who owed their careers exclusively to adherence to the Hitler movement sought ruthlessly for personal advancement. They challenged the role of the bureaucracy and the army which—as traditional institutions antedating the Third Reich—were usually inclined to exercise a moderating influence. The rivalry of the radicals and the moderates made a deep imprint upon the politics of Nazi Germany. Paradoxically, it often shaped the policies of Hitler's "Führerstaat" more decisively than did directives from the center of authority.

Hitler sanctioned the role of the Nazi party in Bohemia and Moravia on March 21, 1939.[2] Its organizational structure disregarded the frontiers of the Protectorate; the whole territory was partitioned into four sections and these were added to the adjacent districts (*Gaue*): the Sudetenland, Bavarian Ostmark, Upper Danube, and Lower Danube. Such an arrangement gave the

[1] See Chapter 3, notes 27 and 28, above.
[2] Directive No. 59/39, March 21, 1939, Db 15.02, IfZ.

provincial Party bosses a vested interest in Czech affairs. Time and again they made their ideas about the treatment of the Czechs known in Nazi circles. Some authors of these proposals, notably those from the Sudetenland, wished them to be treated harshly: the Protectorate should be abolished and the city of Prague purged of its Slavic inhabitants.[3] Others favored a more benevolent course and would have preferred to have the Czechs Nazified rather than eliminated. Many of the leading Party officials in Germany subscribed to this view. *Der Stürmer*, the notorious anti-Semitic newspaper published by Julius Streicher, suggested that the Germans and the Czechs should join in a partnership to crack down upon the Jews.[4]

The higher Nazi authorities soon intervened to keep these self-styled policy makers in line. In May 1939 the Party headquarters in Munich ordered its locals in the Protectorate to abstain from both fraternizing with the native Fascists and molesting the Jews.[5] The Propaganda Ministry reprimanded *Der Stürmer* and ruled that it should henceforth cease writing about the Czechs "in either a positive or a negative sense." At that time, Hitler still wished the "Jewish question" to be handled by the Czechs themselves. The Party was required to solicit the Protector's approval for any meetings in Bohemia and Moravia at which political speeches would be made.[6]

No such restrictions, however, applied to the activities of the Nazi elite corps, the SS. This organization of hard-core fanatics, established along military lines under the leadership of Heinrich Himmler, had by 1939 achieved a considerable degree of independence. In May, the constitution of the SS "Sector No. 39" in the Protectorate formalized their presence in the country, a presence which in fact dated from the very beginning of the German occupation.[7]

[3] A typical document is printed in F. Štěpán (ed.), "Nové dokumenty o protičeskoslovenských plánech dnešních revanšistů z let 1938–1939," [New Documents concerning Anti-Czechoslovak Plans of Today's Revanchists in 1938–1939], *Příspěvky k dějinám KSČ*, I (1961), pp. 735–39.

[4] Cf. "Judas Glück und Ende an der Moldau," *Der Stürmer*, 1939, No. 18; similar articles in the April and May issues.

[5] Frank to Central Office (Stuckart), June 20, 1939, R 43 II/1324, BA. Circulars of May 4, 1939, R 43 II/1329, BA.

[6] Propaganda Ministry to *Der Stürmer*, May 20, 1939, G-41, Institute for Jewish Research [Yivo]. Cf. Stuckart's note, March 21, 1939, 320/376, GSA. Ordinance No. 160/39, August 13, 1939, Db 15.02, IfZ.

[7] Himmler's circular, May 30, 1939, Schumacher collection, folder 308, BA.

Although the SS regarded themselves as the vanguard of Nazism, they developed interests of their own, distinct from those of the state and the Party. The SS played a prominent role in *Aktion Gitter* and—in apparent disagreement with Hitler's intentions— they tackled the Jewish "problem" immediately. They pioneered a simple method of handling confiscations: "Non-Aryans entrust their property to German banks and receive in exchange a permit to emigrate."[8]

Soon the Nazis began using the Czech ordinance about "forced management" for the very Germanization of Jewish property the Beran government had unsuccessfully hoped to avert. The value of the confiscations which the Gestapo carried out during the three months following March 29 amounted to 44 million marks. The new managers were partly "deserving" SS and Party members, partly holding companies controlled by Himmler. Industrial plants, ranging from sugar refineries and breweries to brick factories and quarries, constituted the nucleus of the SS economic empire in the country.[9]

The ambitions of the SS in the Protectorate extended still further. On April 18 they dispatched to Prague a contingent of "experts" from the Race and Settlement Head Office (RuSHA). This group immediately seized the Land Office, the government agency which had been in charge of Czechoslovak agrarian reform; shortly afterward they established control over the state-owned lands and forests. A number of officials in the Ministry of Agriculture were conveniently arrested because of alleged mismanagement. *SS-Oberführer* Curt von Gottberg assumed the direction of the Land Office as "Commissioner-in-Charge."[10]

The declared purpose of Gottberg's mission was to redress injustices which Germans had supposedly suffered as a result of the agrarian reform. Its real objective was to amass land which would be settled later by German farmers. Günther Pancke, the head of the RuSHA, emphasized in a confidential letter that this was a task par excellence for the SS, because the bureaucracy supposedly

[8] Herbeck to Basche, March 23, 1939, Nur. NID-13365, IfZ.

[9] SD Prague to RSHA, June 28, 1939, R 58/954a, BA. Schmidt-Klevenow to Gross and Pancke, March 6, 1940, Nur. NG-872, IfZ. Cf. E. Georg, *Die wirtschaftlichen Unternehmungen der SS*, pp. 80–83. The papers concerning the enterprises are in the collection "Deutsche Wirtschaftsbetriebe" (DWB), Alex.

[10] Henschel to Gottberg, April 18 and 26, 1939, NS 2/141, BA. Gottberg to Heydrich, May 24, 1939, NS 2/141, BA. Cf. AA, T-120, 1505, 632581-87, NA.

lacked the "necessary political understanding." In May, Gottberg and Friedrich Hildebrandt, the head of the SS in the Rhineland, founded a German Association for Welfare and Settlement Assistance. Originally intended to accelerate the sequestration of church property in Germany, the Association extended its activities to the Protectorate.[11]

Gottberg had installed himself in the Land Office with Frank's support and over Neurath's opposition. Neurath objected to the arrogant commissioner-in-charge and his rowdy staff, and he took exception to the aims of Gottberg's mission. He complained to Berlin that they "greatly prejudiced the policy which I am supposed to carry out in this country."[12] Walther Darré, the Reich Minister of Agriculture, took Neurath's side. Although Darré had been the original founder of the RuSHA, he had later broken with Himmler and opposed colonization projects outside of Germany. Stuckart tried to mediate the controversy, pressing for the subordination of Gottberg to Neurath and for a slowdown of the confiscations.[13]

The conflict was approaching a climax toward the end of May 1939 when the riots of the Czech Fascists broke out. We may suspect that the SS welcomed the disturbances as embarrassment for Neurath. In any case, both topics were undoubtedly on the agenda of the urgent meeting with Hitler, on May 31, which the Protector had evidently requested in order to marshal support from Berlin.[14] The political constellation, however, was not propitious for Neurath. Hitler was exuberant about two recent triumphs of his diplomacy: the Pact of Steel with Italy on May 22 and the state visit of Prince Regent Paul of Yugoslavia on the very day of the

[11] Pancke to Heydrich, March 31, 1939, Nur. NO-3162. Cf. examination of Günther Pancke, *United States v. Greifelt, Proceedings* (in German), p. 655, CU. Hildebrandt to Pohl, October 14, 1940, Records of the German National Socialist Workers Party [NSDAP], T-81, 41, 38308, NA. Note about the investigation of the Association's activities, March 1–5, 1940, Records of the Reich Leader of the SS and Chief of the German Police [RFSS], T-175, 188, 2726178–81, NA. Cf. F. Zipfel, *Kirchenkampf in Deutschland, 1933–1945*, pp. 231–32.

[12] Neurath to Lammers, June 22, 1939, R 43 II/1324a, BA.

[13] Correspondence among Darré, Lammers, Neurath, and Stuckart, May 17–22, 1939, AA, T-120, 1505, 632383–93, NA. Affidavit by Hans Werner von Aufsess, *United States v. Weizsäcker*, defense document book I, A 9, CU. Pfundtner to Neurath, July 20, 1939, 320/376, GSA.

[14] Neurath to Lammers, May 19, 1939, R 43 II/1329, BA. M. Domarus, *Hitler: Reden und Proklamationen*, II, p. 1203.

conference with Neurath. The Protector must have returned empty-handed, as the immediate relapse to a tough line in Bohemia and Moravia indicated.

On June 4, State Secretary Frank delivered a menacing speech at Budweis, in which he warned the Czechs that "the German Reich was no Austria-Hungary and that another 1918 would never be repeated."[15] Four days later, the murder of a German policeman in the mining town of Kladno served as a pretext to demonstrate the difference between Austrian and Nazi methods. Although there was no evidence of Czech complicity, the Gestapo arrested the entire Kladno city council and a number of other persons, some of whom subsequently died as a result of mistreatment. The city was saddled with a fine of half a million crowns as an additional punishment.[16]

There followed a series of stiff laws intended to show the Czechs who was master in the house. The pre-occupation Czechoslovak national defense law was amended, to allow Reich authorities to suspend civil rights in an emergency. The Protector assumed the power to revise or annul laws passed by the autonomous government. A new language ordinance was especially irritating to the Czechs. Not only were all official texts to be bilingual, with the German version coming first, but certain expressions, such as *Reichsprotektor in Böhmen und Mähren* and *Deutsches Reich*, were not to be translated at all. Finally, the Protector arbitrarily dismissed Czech municipal councils in six major cities and replaced them with German commissioners.[17]

Most conspicuous was the radical turn in the treatment of the Jews. Having rejected a draft with numerous escape clauses which the Eliáš government had prepared, the Protector issued a comprehensive decree. It defined the term "Jewish" in accordance with the notorious Nuremberg laws of 1935 and placed Jewish affairs under German jurisdiction. The SS expert Adolf Eichmann came to Prague from Vienna, to apply in the Protectorate the methods he had previously tested in Austria. He tried especially

[15] *Der Neue Tag*, June 5, 1939.

[16] *České slovo*, June 10–11, 1939. A. Pěnička, *Kladensko v boji za svobodu* [The Kladno Country in the Struggle for Freedom], pp. 32–34. Cf. Cardinal Kašpar to Hácha, July 5, 1939, *DHCSP*, II, p. 442.

[17] *VOB*, 1939, p. 44. Neurath to Hácha, June 24, 1939, and circular of the Ministry of the Interior, July 24, 1939, AA, T-120, 1505, 632517-29, NA. Cf. Neurath to Hácha, June 28, 1939, *DHCSP*, II, p. 441.

to force Jews to emigrate, but this method became more and more difficult as foreign governments began closing their doors to Jewish immigrants. Instead, the Nazis in August started preparations for concentrating in the capital all Jews from the provinces, a plan which ominously foreshadowed later deportations.[18]

Not only the Jews were to be resettled on the eve of the war. Following the conclusion of his alliance with Mussolini, Hitler intended to transfer German-speaking South Tyrolians from Italy to the Reich. Himmler proposed Moravia as their future home.[19] They would join other German colonists in breaking up compact Czech settlements. The army was already busy drawing up plans for vast training grounds which would ultimately serve the same purpose. After five years, the troops were scheduled to withdraw and let German farmers move in. The confiscation of ecclesiastical property, whose registration the Land Office concluded by the end of August, was expected to make additional land available. Gottberg drafted the statutes of a Foundation for the Promotion and Support of Settlers in Bohemia and Moravia, devised to finance new homesteads on government land "whose ownership status is currently not clear." In connection with the resettlement project he finally proposed the shipment of fifty thousand persons from the Tábor area in Bohemia and of thirteen thousand peasant families from Moravia to Germany for "labor duty."[20]

While the SS firebrands were plotting to prepare Bohemia and Moravia for the Nazi millennium—as they conceived it—the German bureaucrats were engaged in the more prosaic task of

[18] Ordinance of June 21, 1939, *VOB*, 1939, pp. 45–49. Cf. K. Lagus and J. Polák, *Město za mřížemi* [A City behind Bars], pp. 40–41. Wolf to RSHA, June 14, 1939, R 58/954a, BA. "Wochenbericht der Jüdischen Kultusgemeinde in Prag," August 19 and 25, 1939, Berichte 1939, Yad Vashem [YV].

[19] C. F. Latour, *Südtirol und die Achse Berlin-Rom*, p. 34. Gottberg to Heydrich, July 29, 1939, NS 2/139, BA. The subsequent story of the abortive resettlement of the South Tyrolians into the Sudetenland is summarized in Z. Antoš, "Jihotyrolská otázka za II. světové války a naše země" [The South Tyrolian Question during World War II and the Czech Lands], *Slezský sborník*, LXIV (1966), pp. 390–93.

[20] Gottberg to Himmler, June 8, 1939, NS 2/165, BA. Gottberg's instruction, July 22, 1939, RFSS, T-175, 188, 2726201–202, NA. A. Haas, "Vyvlastňování české půdy na Českobudějovicku za okupace" [The Expropriation of Czech Land in the Budweis Country during the Occupation], *Jihočeský sborník historický*, XXXI (1962), p. 173. "Stiftungsurkunde," August 7, 1939, NS 2/139, BA. Král (ed.), *Die Deutschen*, pp. 391–92. On the resettlement plans in 1939, see also R. L. Koehl, *RKFDV: German Resettlement and Population Policy*, pp. 27–28.

building the institutional foundations of their power in that area. The structure of the occupation government took shape during the spring and summer months of 1939 and was finally formalized by two decrees, issued on September 1.[21] The system—as established at that time—was to last without substantial changes until mid-1942.

Stuckart was the chief architect of the German administrative system in the Protectorate. Under this system, the Nazis did not replace the native bureaucracy but rather added their own in a parallel fashion. The Office of the Protector was first intended as a small supervisory body. But Hitler's decrees of March 22 and June 7, 1939 had already initiated a departure from mere supervision to actual governing.[22] The Protector was made exclusively responsible to the Führer and equipped with unlimited legislative powers. In practice, he either pressed the Czech government to legislate according to his wishes or issued ordinances himself.

Czech autonomy continued to shrink as the Protector gradually assumed direct authority over additional sectors of public life. According to the decree of March 16, 1939, these were to include defense and foreign affairs only. By the summer of 1941 as many as twenty-four more sectors had been added: political police, citizenship, Jewish affairs, labor allocation, foreign trade, broadcasting, the motion picture industry, fuel management, and others.[23] The Office of the Protector grew into a leviathan which hardly fit into the enormous Czernin Palais, the former seat of the Foreign Office in Prague. It was subdivided into departments and sections, analogous to ministries.[24] Despite the officially proclaimed unity of the country, the Protector also maintained a separate regional

[21] Ordinances of September 1, 1939, *VOB*, 1939, p. 126–28. The structure of the German administration is described in S. Šisler, "Příspěvek k vývoji a organizaci okupační správy v českých zemích v letech 1939–1945" [The Development and Organization of the Occupation Administration in Bohemia and Moravia in 1939–1945], *Sborník archivních prací*, XIII (1963), No. 2, pp. 46–95.

[22] *RGB*, 1939, I, pp. 549 and 1039. Cf. folder R 43 II/1329, BA.

[23] Werner Best, "Die deutschen Aufsichtsverwaltungen in Frankreich, Belgien, den Niederlanden, Norwegen, Dänemark, und im Protektorat Böhmen und Mähren," Records of German Field Commands, T-501, 101, 1362–63, NA. Cf. H. Hufnagel, "Organisation der Verwaltung im Protektorat Böhmen und Mähren," *Böhmen und Mähren*, 1940, No. 1.

[24] Ordinance of September 18, 1940, *VOB*, 1940, pp. 425–26.

office in Brno, to serve the *amour-propre* of the Moravian Nazis.[25]

The Czechs asserted that the Protector's confidence in the President and his cabinet sanctioned the performance of their entire administration, thus making any German interference on the lower level unjustified.[26] But the Nazis disagreed with this argument and even created special regional government bodies, presided over by the so-called *Oberlandräte*. These had no Czech counterparts and their fiefdoms, which were smaller than the Czech provinces (*Länder*), always consisted of several districts (*Bezirke*). They handled the affairs of the German citizens, represented the Protector in sectors of his direct jurisdiction, and above all supervised the local Czech agencies. The *Oberlandräte* regarded themselves as "local governors among savages."[27] In addition, several hundred German officials served directly in the autonomous administration, usually as deputies and executive vice-presidents.

Omnipotent in relation to the government, the Protector was closely dependent upon Berlin. Hence, regardless of his impressive formal powers, Neurath was expected to implement the Berlin line rather than to pursue a course of his own. The intermediary between Neurath and Hitler was Heinrich Lammers, the chief of the Reich Chancellery. Although a bureaucrat rather than a politician, Lammers held a key position as the person who facilitated access to the Führer. He decided upon the items to be placed on Hitler's agenda and translated his often erratic statements into practical directives. Both Neurath and Frank kept on good terms with Lammers.

The "Central Office for the Protectorate" in the Ministry of the Interior, headed by Stuckart, was originally intended as a clearinghouse between the Protector and the central agencies of the Reich. All their measures concerning Bohemia and Moravia were first to be cleared by Stuckart who would then secure the Protector's cooperation. (A similar arrangement applied for several other occupied countries, but there, as in the Protectorate, it never worked.) Neurath frequently complained about being bypassed and

[25] It was abolished by the ordinance of November 25, 1942, *VOB*, 1942, pp. 307–308.

[26] Šisler, "Příspěvek," p. 50.

[27] Craushaar to Dellbrügge, April 18, 1939, 320/2894, GSA. The structure of German provincial administration in one Bohemian region is described in J. Letocha, "Okupační veřejná správa 1938–1945 ve Východočeském kraji" [The Occupation Administration in East Bohemia in 1938–1945], in *Východní Čechy 1964*, pp. 20–42.

Stuckart, although he tried hard, could not help him. Except for drafting laws upon outside orders, the Central Office had nothing to do, and it was finally abolished in 1943.[28]

Neurath posed rather pretentiously as the supreme representative of the Reich in Prague, but in reality his position was hardly comparable to that of his counterparts in occupied Norway, the Netherlands, Luxembourg, and other countries. There such old Nazi hands as Terboven, Seyss-Inquart, and Simon firmly held the reins of power, whereas Neurath was handicapped by his low Party status. Moreover, he was notably averse to systematic work and little enjoyed the everyday conduct of government affairs. His principal adviser, Hans Völckers, who had formerly been the German Minister to Havana and Madrid, was a nonentity, poorly suited to make up for the deficiencies of his superior.

The main credit for the performance of the Protector's administration must be given to Kurt von Burgsdorff, the Assistant State Secretary. Burgsdorff, who came from a family with civil service traditions—his father had held the fancy title of *wirklicher Geheimrat* in the kingdom of Saxony—was respected by the Nazis as an administrative wizard. A conservative nationalist and a staunch Protestant, he was despite his Party membership a perfect specimen of the "unpolitical" civil servant.[29] He did not object to the regime as such but was courageous and resourceful enough to fight political patronage for the sake of efficiency. Earlier this led to a clash with *Gauleiter* Martin Mutschmann of Saxony, who had been pushing his incompetent proteges into the civil service. Not surprisingly, Frank was Burgsdorff's principal adversary in the Protectorate.

The Protector's authority further suffered because of the special status held by as many as nine administrative branches. Justice and finances were to a considerable extent run by the respective ministries of the Reich. The Armed Forces High Command controlled

---

[28] Ordinance of March 22, 1939, *RGB*, 1939, I, p. 549. Examination of Stuckart, *United States v. Weizsäcker*, *Proceedings* (in English), p. 24435, CU. For Stuckart's attempt to uphold the Protector's authority, see the following documents: March 20, April 1 and 11, 1939, AA, T-120, 2561, 310933-96, NA; January 3 and February 22, 1940, AA, T-120, 1505, D 632619-24, NA. Cf. A. and V. M. Toynbee (eds.), *Hitler's Europe*, pp. 106–108.

[29] Cf. *Der Neue Tag*, April 16, 1943. Burgsdorff's RSHA dossier, vita dated July 1, 1943, RFSS, T-175, 58, 2573048-050, NA.

the army. Most important, the police force—operating under Frank—was the exclusive domain of the SS.[30]

The Nazis maintained a complex system of courts. The military tribunals created on the very first day of the occupation merely adjudicated offenses against the army establishment and never achieved great importance.[31] Since, however, German criminal law officially applied in the Protectorate, the same civilian courts functioned there as in Germany. These tried all cases even remotely concerning the citizens of the Reich, as well as political cases, defined with considerable flexibility.[32] Czech courts remained, but their agenda was limited to routine matters. Their decisions could be reviewed by the German judiciary, and the Protector held, though seldom exercised, the right of pardon.

Extraordinary courts proliferated in the course of the war. The Special Courts were first used in occupied Poland but later also in the Reich proper—including the Protectorate—to try political offenders only.[33] The verdicts of their three-judge panels were final. The infamous People's Court in Berlin examined the most serious cases. Later, after it had become overloaded, the Superior Courts in Dresden and Leitmeritz helped to handle cases from Bohemia, and their counterpart in Breslau handled those from Moravia. *Ad hoc* summary courts operated temporarily in 1941–1942.[34]

The multiplication of courts poorly concealed the continuous decline of legality. The police were officially authorized to impose "protective custody" arbitrarily, and ship to concentration camps

30 The other separate jurisdictions were the Reich railroads, Reich postal services, German institutions of higher education (University of Prague and Technical Universities in Prague and Brno), Reich Radio Station "Bohemia," and the Representative of the Foreign Office.

31 Decree of May 8, 1939, *RGB*, 1939, I, pp. 903–904. The jurisdiction of military courts over Protectorate nationals ended by the ordinance of January 24, 1942, *RGB*, 1942, I, p. 47. The organization of the judiciary is described in Šisler, "Příspěvek," pp. 88–91, and J. Macek, "Okupační justice v českém pohraničí a její vývoj (1938–1945)" [The Occupation Judiciary in the Czech Borderland and Its Development (1938–1945)], *Sborník archivních prací*, XIII (1963), No. 1, pp. 63–118.

32 Ordinances of April 14, 1939, *RGB*, 1939, I, pp. 752–54, 756–58, of August 26, 1939, *VOB*, 1939, pp. 83–84, and of January 11, 1940, *ibid*, 1940, p. 3.

33 Decree of February 21, 1940, *RGB*, 1940, I, p. 405. *Deutsche Justiz*. 1940, p. 323.

34 See chapters 10 and 11. There was also a special court to try offenses against the SS and police establishments. Ordinance of July 15, 1942, *RGB*, 1942, I, p. 475.

persons who had never been tried, or had been found not guilty by courts, or had served their regular prison sentences.[35]

Frank, the Higher SS and Police Leader in the Protectorate, controlled the police and also presided over the SS. In this capacity he was responsible to Himmler rather than to Neurath. But he was at the same time the State Secretary, a position which enabled him, as a deputy of the Protector, to influence the entire administration. Frank, though formally obliged to act in conjunction with Neurath, ignored him more and more boldly, thus adding to the natural aversion between the pretending grandseigneur and the half-educated politico from the Sudetenland, who was fittingly characterized as the "perfect image of the German *Halbgebilde-ter.*"[36] As early as May 1939, Ulrich von Hassell, the conservative critic of the Nazi regime, noted the obvious "helplessness of Neurath" before Frank.[37] The Führer himself sanctioned the Protector's inferiority shortly afterwards by ordering that German authorities in Bohemia and Moravia should heed the State Secretary in all important matters, in order to "arrive at politically correct decisions."[38]

Hitler's original suggestion to Stuckart, that the police establishment in Bohemia and Moravia be limited, was never seriously followed. All types of German police appeared on the scene. The Regular Police, which used to be the relatively harmless uniformed force, was there to conduct arrests, suppress demonstrations, and— if need be—carry out reprisals against civilians, including mass shootings. If it operated with less brutality in Bohemia and Moravia than later in eastern Europe, it was because of the generally milder treatment given the Czechs, rather than any essential difference in methods. The Czech police and gendarmerie performed routine tasks under administrative supervision by the Protectorate Ministry of the Interior but were actually controlled by the commander of the Regular Police.[39]

[35] Ordinance of September 20, 1940, *VOB*, 1940, p. 484. Cf. Thierack to Gürtner, August 14, 1940, Nur. NG-369, IfZ.

[36] Kennan to the State Department, August 19, 1939, Kennan, *From Prague after Munich*, p. 218.

[37] *The Von Hassell Diaries*, p. 43.

[38] Frick to Neurath, July 14, 1939, AA, T-120, 1505, 632515–16, NA.

[39] The organization and methods of the German police are described in "Nacistický bezpečnostní aparát na Moravě v letech 1939–1945" [The Nazi Security Machinery in Moravia in 1939–1945], *Sborník Matice moravské*, LXXXIV (1965), pp. 232–57.

More important than the uniformed regular force was the other branch of the system, the Security Police. It consisted of the Criminal Police—in charge of crime in general—the Gestapo—which specialized in political offenses—and the Security Service. Although the interrogation methods of the Gestapo in the Protectorate were as notorious as everywhere else, its efficiency stemmed less from brutality than from systematic gathering and filing of information.[40] In this respect the task of the Gestapo was complemented—and often duplicated—by the Security Service, originally the Nazi party's intelligence bureau. Both agencies alternated intimidation with corruption as methods of recruiting an impressive network of native informers, among whom the Vlajkaists figured prominently. Trying to diagnose symptoms of political opposition before it could become active, the Security Service minutely analyzed the state of public opinion and reported its findings to Berlin.[41] In the absence of normal channels of expression, these reports, biased though they were, offer an invaluable insight into the public mind under the occupation.

Next to the courts and the police, the army ranked a poor third among the instruments of repression. In the "Defense Area Bohemia-Moravia," troops were stationed, until late in the war, much as they were in Germany.[42] Since the Protectorate never became a major theater of war, service there was an enviable sinecure, and the interests of the German officers tended to converge on socializing rather than on military and political affairs.

General Erich Friderici, the Armed Forces Plenipotentiary, had in 1939 entertained wild ideas about the expulsion of the Czechs,

---

[40] From the material preserved in former Nazi archives in one Czech region, the system has been reconstructed by J. Kmoníček in "O některých formách práce nacistického okupačního aparátu proti odboji na Královéhradecku" [The Working Patterns of the Nazi Occupation Machinery Used against Resistance in the Hradec Králové Country], *Historie a vojenství*, 1965, pp. 755–72.

[41] The most important information was included in a confidential news bulletin issued by Himmler, *Meldungen aus dem Reich* [*Meld. Reich*]. Cf. the introduction by H. Boberach (ed.) to *Meldungen aus dem Reich*, a work that draws upon these confidential bulletins as source material. The organization of the Security Service in the Protectorate is the subject of the study by Č. Klapal, "Několik poznámek k působení SD v okupovaném Československu" [The Security Service in Occupied Czechoslovakia], *Odboj a revoluce*, V (1967), No. 5, pp. 82–96.

[42] Most of the troops which had participated in the March invasion left the country soon afterwards. Cf. note of April 5, 1939, AA, T-120, 1094, 447369, NA. Hitler to Brauchitsch, March 25, 1939, *Trial*, XXXVIII, p. 275.

but in practice he was a relatively moderate man.[43] He was on close terms with Neurath. Friderici had, however, incurred Frank's hostility by claiming influence in security matters as supervisor of the Government Force, an auxiliary police unit.[44] The State Secretary pulled strings to get rid of him, and in 1941, as a result of Frank's machinations, General Friderici was transferred away from Prague, and ultimately to the eastern front.

The uneasy relationship between the SS and the army was accentuated by their rivalry in fighting subversive activities. The Security Police, particularly its Reich chief, Reinhard Heydrich, nourished deep distrust toward the *Abwehr*—the military intelligence—and their suspicions were amply justified, at least in the Protectorate. Paul Thümmel, the officer who had reportedly warned the Czechs about the impending invasion in March 1939, was installed in the Prague headquarters of the *Abwehr*, and regularly supplied Czech underground organizations with news for the Allies.[45]

In the permanent tension between the moderates and the radicals in the Protectorate, the latter held undeniable advantages. The vague delimitation of competencies favored ruthless individuals who could easily impose their will upon their obedient and conscientious colleagues of more moderate persuasion. Yet despite personal differences and rivalries, an overwhelming majority of the officials were guided by a common, unquestioning loyalty to the regime. Thus the administration of the occupied country was perhaps erratic and top-heavy but not necessarily ineffective. A comparison of the Protectorate with other countries which eventually fell under Hitler's domination reveals the peculiar characteristics which made the system function in Bohemia and Moravia.

Although they later spoke of a "New Order" of integrated Europe, the Nazis did not follow any master plan for the administration of their rapidly growing European domains. The circum-

---

[43] E. Friderici, "Das tschechische Problem," July 12, 1939, in Král (ed.), *Die Vergangenheit warnt*, pp. 44–48.

[44] Daluege to Bonhard, September 30, 1940, R 19/335, BA.

[45] Thümmel's code name, *René*, appears frequently in the secret messages exchanged between Prague and London in 1941, OKW, T-77, 1050, NA. Two books about Thümmel, written by Czech journalists, are spy stories of questionable trustworthiness—although the authors undoubtedly used archival documents: R. Ströbinger, *A-54: Spion mit drei Gesichtern*; Č. Amort and I. M. Jedička, *Tajemství vyzvědače A-54* [The Secret of Agent A-54].

stances of their seizure varied, leaving a permanent imprint upon the character of each occupation regime. Thus the brutal dismemberment of Poland was to a large extent punishment inflicted upon a nation unwilling to follow the Czechs in peacefully submitting to German overlordship. In contrast, the relatively lenient occupation of Denmark was a by-product of the Nazi strategic thrust against the Allies in Scandinavia. The Low Countries also fell under German rule in the course of military operations against France and Britain. In France, the unpredictable collapse of the country decisively influenced its later partition and the double standard followed by the Nazis in running its two portions. Yugoslavia was both punished for its evasive maneuvers to avoid the grip of Germany's alliance system, and needed as a base for military operations to help Mussolini's abortive adventure in Greece. The invasion of the Soviet Union was an undertaking *sui generis* in which both strategic miscalculations and ideological dreams shaped the occupation policies.

Bohemia and Moravia shared with Poland the doubtful privilege of being the first non-German countries added to the Nazi empire. They were also geographically close to Germany and contained substantial German minorities. But here the parallels ended. The extent of actual incorporation differed significantly for each of the two Slavic nations. The Nazis did not wish to transform the Government-General, which was the ethnically most homogeneous remainder of former Poland, into a German country but rather to set it aside as a future preserve of slave labor. There was also too strong a resistance movement in the region to make the prospect of fusion with Germany anything but illusory. In contrast, the Protectorate was stable enough to make possible a large-scale transplantation of the administrative institutions of Germany proper. This applied especially to the judiciary, the provincial administration, and the police. In this respect, Bohemia and Moravia resembled some of the territories already incorporated: Luxembourg, Alsace and Lorraine, the Suwałki and Ciechanów districts in northeastern Poland.[46]

Nowhere was the amalgamation of Bohemia and Moravia with Germany more apparent than in the German civil service establishment. Only at first sight does its size—9632 persons in the fall of 1941—seem small in comparison with almost 400,000 employees

---

[46]Cf. A. and V. M. Toynbee (eds.), *Hitler's Europe*, pp. 91–93.

of the autonomous government.[47] If we consider the ratio of population to officials, rather than the total number of officials, the difference from other occupied countries becomes evident. The German bureaucratic machinery in the Protectorate exceeded that in Norway by four and a half times, that in the Netherlands by seven times, that in the occupied part of France by twenty times, and that in Denmark by fifty-three times. The above figure does not include 4706 German officials who were technically employees of the autonomous government as of May 1940.[48]

The situation was strikingly different with the armed personnel. The strength of the Regular Police in the Protectorate was reported to be, in 1942, only half of that in Norway and was sharply lower than in Poland or Russia.[49] There were proportionally one and a half times as many policemen in Bohemia and Moravia as in the Netherlands, and four times as many as in occupied France. Yet in France and the Netherlands multitudes of soldiers supplemented the police force, whereas, at least until late 1944, the proportion of regular troops in the Protectorate seems to have been no higher than it was in Germany. (There are no exact figures about the armed SS units [*Waffen SS*]. Their number kept increasing but probably no more than everywhere else in the Reich.)

The hope of early incorporation was not the only reason why officials and troops were deployed in the Protectorate in much the same fashion as in Germany. The main reason was undoubtedly that little armed force was needed to keep the local population subdued. In March 1939, the Nazis acted on the assumption that the Czechs, after initial hesitations, would willingly accept the new regime. Although the forecast later proved unrealistic, the people's behavior never justified any substantial increase in armed personnel. The invaders continued to feel reasonably secure, the resentment of their subjects notwithstanding.

[47] Best, "Aufsichtsverwaltungen," p. 1367 (see note 23, above). Cf. Král, *Otázky*, I, 13, quoting the Statistical Annual for the Protectorate for 1943.

[48] Computed from the data given by Best, "Aufsichtsverwaltungen," p. 1367.

[49] Daluege's report of February 1, 1943, Nur. NO-2861, IfZ. This report seems to give a reliable basis for comparison although it tends to underestimate the total strength of the Regular Police, probably by counting only its major subdivision, the Protective Police (*Schutzpolizei*). According to Daluege, the Regular Police in the Protectorate consisted in 1942 of 3764 men. According to Paul Riege, its former commander in Prague, the figure throughout the war was about 6925 men; Riege's letter to the author, January 12, 1967. The German statistics usually included the Security Police among administrative personnel.

The extent to which the Nazis allowed Czech officials to govern —under strict supervision, to be sure—was unparalleled in other countries. In most of them, unlike Bohemia and Moravia, the occupation upset the native administration. In Norway and Holland, for example, the governments fled abroad and were not fully replaced by German appointees. The government of the Dutch state secretaries was rudimentary compared with the complete cabinet in the Protectorate. In eastern Europe the Nazis usually liquidated the upper echelons of the local bureaucracy, keeping lower officials merely to execute orders. Only in Denmark, which the Germans initially treated as a satellite rather than an occupied country, did the administrative institutions remain relatively intact.

The apparent autonomy of Bohemia and Moravia did not impede their effective incorporation into the Reich. Many Czech civil servants found it hard to distinguish between serving their own people and serving the oppressors. As early as April 1939, the former Social Democratic mayor of Brno, who soon afterward fled into exile, observed bitterly that all too many officials did not find subordination to the Nazi masters detestable. The older generation, having already served under Austria, "had experience in serving foreigners."[50] The structure of the civil service and its patterns of work, shaped by the Austrian tradition, had much in common with the German style. Like his German colleague, the Czech bureaucrat regarded as his duty "unpolitical" service to the state, no matter what kind of regime happened to be in power. Devoted to civil service as an institution, he felt above the unsavory business of politics. Although nationalist feelings might cause him to serve with inner reluctance, all the same they would not prevent him from performing reliably. Hence sabotage of orders was an exception; their conscientious execution was the rule.[51]

Contrary to widespread belief, premeditated and open use of force played a subordinate role in the functioning of the occupation regime. Mere threat of force, improvised use of expediences and sometimes just bluffing usually sufficed to make it work. The Czechs' susceptibility to such methods, stemming ultimately from their lack of self-confidence, was a necessary pre-condition for the

---

[50] Ečer to Beneš, April 14, 1939, quoted in Křen, *Do emigrace*, pp. 165–66.
[51] Cf. Neurath to Hitler, August 31, 1940, *Trial*, XXXIII, p. 254.

Nazis' success. Significantly, the regime took roots during the uncertain last months of European peace in 1939, a period in which both sides found it advisable to exercise restraint. Once the war came, their clash of interest became more obvious; yet, despite increasing tension, the already established patterns of behavior made an open confrontation unlikely. The country maintained its stability while the Czech-German conflict continued to boil under the surface.

PART III

THE GROWING CONFLICT
FORCES AND EVENTS

6 CZECH NATIONALISM

RESURGENCE AND REPRESSION

ALTHOUGH most Czechs had anticipated the war, the actual course of events in late August and early September 1939 discouraged them. The Molotov-Ribbentrop pact frustrated their widely cherished hopes for a Western-Soviet alliance. In August, immediately after the pact, the Nazis had observed "a considerably friendlier mood" in the Protectorate.[1] Markedly fewer anti-German leaflets appeared at this time than in the preceding months. The Hácha government, as surprised by the sensational pact as almost everybody, hailed it as a triumph of German diplomacy and expressed hopes for the expansion of trade between the Protectorate and the Soviet Union. Bent on further promoting the good will of the Nazis, the President inaugurated the Union for Cooperation with the Germans and appointed some of the country's leading Germanophiles to head it.[2] The supporters of the Vlajka group, of course, continued to castigate the government's efforts as insufficient and insincere. Heartened by the apparent international triumphs of Nazi Germany, they found this an auspicious time to defy the President by walking out of the official political party, the NSM. On the eve of the war, an organization of Fascist-minded Czech veterans of the Austrian army announced that they would fight on the German side if need arose.[3]

Once the hostilities opened, many Czechs feared that this might not be the kind of war they had been hoping for. Although this time the British and the French had kept their word and had

---

[1] Prague headquarters of the Regular Police to Frank, October 24, 1939, in F. Kropáč and V. Louda, *Persekuce českého studentstva za okupace* [The Persecution of the Czech Students during the Occupation], p. 32.

[2] *Der Neue Tag*, August 24 and 31, 1939. *České slovo*, August 31, 1939.

[3] T. Pasák, "Vývoj Vlajky v období okupace" [Vlajka's Development in the Occupation Period], *Historie a vojenství*, 1966, pp. 850–51. *České slovo*, August 27, 1939.

declared war on Germany, they nevertheless let their Polish ally succumb. This spectacle seemed to justify the opinion that for a small nation submission to a superior force was the only realistic alternative. The Czechs could find only small consolation in their malicious joy over the plight of the very Poles who had behaved so despicably toward them at the time of Munich. Commenting about the gloomy mood in the Protectorate, Robert Gies, Frank's closest adviser, noted that "some time has to pass so that we may clearly see the future course of the Czech opposition. For the time being, the opposition is shattered and unable to act."[4]

The Germans did their best to deter possible opposition. On the eve of the war, the Protector issued special ordinances against sabotage. Public posters warned that not only individual offenders but the entire population would be held responsible for subversive acts.[5] The style of this outrageous notice suggested Frank's authorship, but it was Neurath who signed it. He thus earned a doubtful distinction as the first official to proclaim the principle of collective responsibility in Nazi-controlled Europe. Then followed the earlier-mentioned ordinances about the structure of the German administration, particularly the police.[6] Listening to foreign radio broadcasts became a criminal offense. Persons guilty of subversion in the broadest sense of the word were threatened with severe sentences, including death. The Germans took full control over censorship.[7] Most important, the Gestapo—following the blueprint already prepared in August—rounded up prominent Czech politicians, intellectuals, priests, Social Democrats, and Communists and shipped them to concentration camps. Their total number has been estimated at several thousands.[8]

While such measures were unprecedented in the Protectorate, they were not significantly harsher, at this time, than those imposed by the Nazis upon their own people. Since most of the special ordinances applied to the entire Reich, arrests in Germany and Austria were similar in pattern and scope to those in Bohemia and

[4] Gies to Raschhofer, September 12, 1939, quoted in K. Fremund (ed.), "Z činnosti poradců," p. 9. Cf. report about the September 23, 1939 conference in the Interior Ministry, September 25, 1939, R 43 II/1325, BA.

[5] *VOB*, 1939, pp. 83–84. *Trial*, XXXIX, pp. 535–36.

[6] See Chapter 5, footnote 21, above.

[7] *RGB*, 1939, I, pp. 1679, 1681, 1683. Pasák, "Problematika protektorátního tisku," pp. 66–68.

[8] H. Krausnick et al., *Anatomy of the SS State*, pp. 464–65, 470–71. *Zpověď K. H. Franka*, p. 58. *Trial*, XVI, p. 662.

Moravia. The laws which were specific for the Protectorate, such as the administrative ordinances, had been scheduled for promulgation for several months before the war began, and their timing to coincide with it was largely accidental.[9] The notice about collective responsibility, though far-reaching in its implications, had no immediate practical consequences. For the time being, there was no subversion calling for reprisals.

The overwhelming need for domestic peace in wartime caused the Nazis to shelve some of the drastic plans which the SS had prepared in August. Neurath, undoubtedly acting upon higher instructions, ordered Gottberg to delay the sequestration of ecclesiastical property indefinitely.[10] The Gestapo postponed the forced concentration of the Jews from the provinces to Prague. The contemplated mass evictions of Czech farmers and the settlement of the South Tyrolians in the Protectorate never took place. With an unusual display of politeness, Gottberg now addressed Neurath as "His Excellency" and promised to heed his orders.[11]

Having suspended the radical experiments planned by the SS, the Germans tried to make political capital of the stability and material prosperity of the Protectorate. They publicly emphasized that the war had hardly affected the course of life in the country. The Czechs were not being forced into military service. Few German troops were stationed in Bohemia and Moravia. By wisely accepting Hitler's protection, Hácha had presumably saved his people from the fate of the Poles.[12] In late September, the Nazis invited newsmen from neutral countries to tour the Protectorate. The propaganda move almost misfired when in Prague unknown culprits tried to stuff the visitors' pockets with anti-German leaflets which were discovered only at the last moment. Even the President hinted sarcastically in his interview with the journalists that not he but Neurath was the real "boss." But such incidents did not mar the overall peaceful aspect of the country.[13]

[9] R 43 II/1325, BA.

[10] Pancke to Pohl, January 15, 1940, NS 2/140, BA. Report on the Reich Association for Welfare and Settlement Assistance, March 1–5, 1940, RFSS, T-175, 188, 2726181–82, NA.

[11] Gottberg to Neurath, September 9, 1939, NS 2/165, BA.

[12] Cf. Neurath's September 29 address at the Prague Fair, *Der Neue Tag*, September 30, 1939. E. Moravec, "Ernüchterung," *ibid.*, September 19, 1939.

[13] Braun von Stumm, "Aufzeichnung über die Reise der Auslandsjournalisten in das Gebiet des Protektorats," September 27, 1939, AA, T-120, 1279, 484579–83, NA.

The invitation to the foreign newsmen indicated that the Germans were taking pains to impress foreign rather than domestic public opinion. The demonstration that the Czechs were satisfied was conceived as part of Berlin's "peace offensive" in late September. In launching this campaign, Hitler was undoubtedly more interested in international recognition of his conquests than in genuine peace. But the extent of the German propaganda activities suggests that they may have been intended as an overture to serious negotiations. In such negotiations, however, Germany's claim to Bohemia and Moravia was not to be open to question.

The Hácha administration was sensitive to the resurgence of Nazi interest in public demonstrations of Czech solidarity with Germany. Anticipating possible German concessions in return for such demonstrations, the cabinet resisted Neurath's pressure and issued only vague and non-committal statements in support of Hitler's war. At the same time, the President and the government, "aware of their responsibility for the fate of the Czech people," reassured the nation that they "were defending its guaranteed rights within the limits of existing opportunities." [14]

Hitler's quick victory in Poland and the inactivity of the Western powers apparently persuaded the Czech leaders that the German power would last and that concessions should be exacted before it was too late. They decided to claim a share of prostrate Poland. Hácha intimated to Neurath his desire for the return of Teschen, the territory which the Poles had so ignobly pilfered at the time of the Czechs' distress in October 1938. The Protector gave his initial blessing to the request. [15] On September 30, Hitler discussed it with Chvalkovský in Berlin. According to rumors in Prague diplomatic circles, the Führer, too, viewed the return of Teschen favorably and had even hinted at a possible extension of the Protectorate's autonomy. [16]

Encouraged by this start, the government prepared a comprehensive statement of grievances for submission to Hitler. Its

[14] *Der Neue Tag*, September 8, 1939. Note in Hácha's office, September 9, 1939, *DHCSP*, II, p. 447.

[15] Neurath to Lammers, October 3, 1939, AA, T-120, 1027, 405559–62, NA. Central Office for Ethnic Germans to Lammers, October 7, 1939, *ibid.*, 405533–34.

[16] *Der Neue Tag*, October 1, 1939. Caruso (Italian Consul in Prague) to Ciano, October 9, 1939, *I Documenti Diplomatici Italiani* [*DDI*], series IX, I, p. 418. Cf. report of the Deutsches Auslands-Institut, October 23, 1939, T-81, 504, 5267127, NA.

drafting revealed significant differences of opinion between the President and the cabinet.[17] Hácha, the lawyer, wished to call attention to violations of the "Czech liberties" supposedly guaranteed in the decree of March 16 which established the Protectorate. Prime Minister Eliáš, on the other hand, feared that such reasoning would amount to acceptance by the Czechs of Hitler's arbitrary act. But President Hácha's version was finally approved and dispatched to Berlin on October 13.[18] In addition, however, the government elaborated a more detailed list of grievances which the President was to discuss with the Führer personally. Here the emphasis was on natural rights rather than on the letter of the March decree.[19]

In the meantime, prospects diminished considerably for a negotiated settlement of the war. Britain and France were rightly reluctant to recognize Germany's recent conquests without guarantees against further aggression. Hitler's formal "peace offer" of October 6, primarily intended to shift the responsibility for continued war upon the enemy, was no longer meant seriously.[20] The changed international atmosphere also determined the fate of the Teschen project. In the meantime, the plan had met with opposition among the Nazi radicals. The Central Office for Ethnic Germans, an SS agency, was appalled that the few Germans in Teschen would have had to live under a Czech government of any kind. Henlein pressed for the annexation of the territory to the Sudetenland. By October 10, Hitler had already decided against returning Teschen to the Czechs but he did not notify them of his decision.[21]

The same uncertainty temporarily surrounded Hácha's *cahier des doléances*. The document reportedly put the Führer into a rage. Yet rather than rejecting it outright, he wished to use it to elicit from the President a major pro-German gesture. On October 15, Heinrich Lammers, the chief of the Reich Chancellery, arrived in

[17] Eliáš to Havelka, October 11, 1939, *DHCSP*, II, p. 454. Cf. Feierabend, *Ve vládě Protektorátu*, pp. 98–101.

[18] Hácha to Hitler, October 11, 1939, *DHCSP*, II, pp. 451–53. Cf. *DDI*, series IX, II, pp. 609–14.

[19] Memorandum of October 14, 1939, *DHCSP*, II, pp. 454–69.

[20] Cf. Bullock, *Hitler*, pp. 554–58.

[21] Henlein to Lammers, October 11, 1939, R 43 II/1324a, BA. Woermann's note, October 12, 1939, AA, T-120, 1027, 405571, 405558, NA. On November 20, 1939 Teschen finally became part of the newly created administrative district of Katowitz; cf. Broszat, *Nationalsozialistische Polenpolitik*, pp. 38, 40.

Prague to extend an invitation for talks in Berlin. There, he hinted, Hácha would be expected to take a ceremonial oath of allegiance (*Treugelöbnis*) to the Führer. We know little about the subsequent deliberations of the Protectorate government except that it was in a perplexing quandary. On October 21, Völckers, Neurath's secretary, stunned the President by telling his *chef de cabinet* that everything was ready for departure to Berlin in four days.[22] The proposed program included the *Treugelöbnis* but little else. After consulting with his advisers, Hácha refused to go until his complaints had been considered. The Germans did not insist, although Neurath reaffirmed the President's obligation to take the oath sometime in the future.[23] The project was thus shelved, as was the Teschen question and the letter of grievances. Hitler, who on October 9 had already issued his first instruction for an attack in the west, was no longer in a bargaining mood.[24]

There was an air of unreality in this top-level maneuvering between the Germans and the Czechs. Both parties acted upon assumptions which failed to materialize. The Nazis misjudged the chances for an international confirmation of their conquests. Hácha and his colleagues overestimated their German partners' willingness to make concessions which would facilitate such a confirmation. As a result, the bargaining between Berlin and the Protectorate government ended before it had even gotten under way.

The majority of Czechs, unaware of the moves behind the scenes, did not give serious thought to the possibility of a compromise peace. Despite the inactivity on the fronts, they soon recovered their optimistic belief that Germany would soon be defeated. On September 30, the anniversary of Munich, an effective boycott of Prague's public transportation indicated the resurgence of opposition.[25]

The people awaited with growing excitement National Independence Day, October 28, which for the first time was not going to be officially celebrated. Never before or after did so many handbills and mimeographed leaflets circulate in the Protectorate. They

[22] Popelka's note, October 22, 1939, *DHCSP*, II, pp. 469–72. Cf. Ripka to Beneš, October 27, 1939, *ibid.*, p. 475.
[23] Neurath to Hácha, October 25, 1939, *ibid.*, 473–75.
[24] H.-A. Jacobsen, *Fall Gelb*, p. 14.
[25] Janáček, *Dva smery*, p. 279. Kropáč and Louda, *Persekuce*, p. 29.

called for mass protest demonstrations: "Since Hitler proclaims our passivity abroad, mistaking it for peaceful and joyful acceptance of his protection, it is necessary to show to the world that this criminal lies again." [26] The authors of the underground appeals urged the people to wear their best clothes with the national tricolor on October 28. One proclamation suggested a repeated boycott of public transportation, another proposed sit-in strikes. Except for a leaflet of apparently Communist origin, which advocated a general strike but failed to give specifications, all of them emphasized silent protest. [27] They cautioned against insults and violence which would give the Germans a pretext for using force: "Your duty is to protest silently but proudly against the Teutonic criminals . . . . At 6 P.M. sharp all patriotic Czechs will meet in the upper part of Wenceslas Square and at the stroke of six they will remain silent for two minutes . . . ."[28]

The Hácha government viewed the approaching anniversary with anxiety. Still awaiting Hitler's reply to the President's letter, it feared that disturbances would endanger the prospects, already diminished, of winning any concessions from the Germans. On October 23, the Minister of the Interior, Josef Ježek, conferred with Walter Stahlecker, the Prague chief of the Security Police. He minimized the significance of the leaflet campaign, misrepresenting it as a primarily Communist undertaking. He reaffirmed the responsibility of his government for the preservation of public order and asked that the Nazi official permit the Czechs themselves to handle any possible disorders. [29] Stahlecker gave no clear reply, especially concerning the role of the German police.

Although abundant evidence suggested that disturbances might take place, the Nazis took no measure to prevent them. Some German officials may have been reassured by the people's quiescence up to that time. In a public speech shortly before the Czech national holiday, the Protector spoke in glowing terms of the peace

---

[26]"Brothers and Sisters!" AA, T-120, 1443, 587141, NA. Cf. the leaflet in W 08-122/1, BA, MA. Cf. the files of indictments "against unknown" by the state prosecutor in the Berlin People's Court, R 60 II, BA.

[27]Report by the Protectorate Ministry of the Interior, November 16, 1939, *DHCSP*, II, pp. 480–81. Cf. the sentence of the leadership of the "Nation's Defense," October 1942, Nur. NG-1909, IfZ.

[28]"Brothers and Sisters!"; see note 26 above.

[29]Cf. Král, *Otázky*, III, p. 89.

which pervaded the country.[30] On the critical day itself, he preferred being absent from the capital, where he admittedly felt like a "captive in a golden cage."[31] In contrast to Neurath's attitude, however, the apparent lethargy of such radical Nazis as Frank or Stahlecker hardly resulted from indifference. They awaited an opportunity to reassert their power.

After the failure of the peace plans, the radicals' influence in Nazi Germany had increased. The "pacification" of Poland enabled the SS to expand the scope of their activities, and having postponed the resettlement projects in the Protectorate, they began to implement these projects in the newly conquered territory. On October 7, Hitler appointed Himmler as Reich Commissioner for the Strengthening of Germandom, an assignment which implied supreme authority over ethnic and racial affairs in the whole of German-dominated Europe.[32]

In the Protectorate, a drastic action foreshadowed the new ascendancy of the radicals. On October 17 and 26, the Gestapo rounded up 1291 Jews from northern Moravia and transported them to the Polish Government-General. According to the plan submitted by Heydrich, the chief of the Reich's Security Police, the deportees joined those from Germany and Austria, to be settled in a "reservation" near Nisko in Galicia.[33] The Nazis also contemplated repression of the Czech intellectual elite, as practiced in Poland. In early October, Frank privately stressed the urgency of this undertaking.[34]

Frank hoped that the suppression of the resurgent Czech opposi-

---

[30] "Aufbau in Böhmen und Mähren," in the daily *Kölnische Zeitung*, October 24, 1939. The Italian Consul in Prague, Caruso, commented in his report to Rome on October 25: "In what His Excellency von Neurath said is surely an excessive amount of optimism and not much truth. The restlessness of the Czech population and its desire to act to bring about an end to a situation which it considers more and more painful every day are incontestable facts."; *DDI*, series IX, II, p. 11.

[31] Neurath to Koepke, October 14, 1939, Nur. Neu-150, CU.

[32] Decree of October 7, 1939, *Nazi Conspiracy and Aggression*, III, pp. 496–98.

[33] The Gestapo records concerning the deportations from Moravia, R 70 Böhmen-Mähren/9, BA. Cf. Lagus and Polák, *Město za mřížemi*, pp. 300–301. For lack of basic facilities to receive the settlers, the Nisko project was abandoned in April 1940. Cf. P. Friedman, "Aspects of the Jewish Communal Crisis in the Period of the Nazi Regime in Germany, Austria and Czechoslovakia," in *Essays on Jewish Life and Thought*, ed. by J. L. Blau, pp. 216–17.

[34] Gies's memorandum, October 7, 1939, in K. Fremund (ed.), "Dokumenty o nacistické vyhlazovací politice" [Documents of the Nazi Extermination Policy], *Sborník archivních prací*, XIII, 1963, No. 2, p. 13.

tion would enable him to outdo Neurath in efficiency and justify his claim for primacy in the Protectorate. Thus the conflict which opened in Prague on October 28 was more than a struggle between the subject people and the occupation regime. It was also a confrontation between the SS and the moderate Nazis to determine which was to play the decisive role in the country. Although the radicals apparently possessed no clear plan of action, they were determined to exploit any opportunities available while the moderates remained inactive.

On Czech Independence Day the behavior of the population did not at first meet the expectations of the underground organizers. In a few Prague factories partial strikes did take place but they were quickly ended after German supervisors intervened with the management. Since the national holiday fell on a Saturday when working hours were shorter anyway, the slowdown in offices and factories was hardly noticed.[35]

The demonstration was more successful in the streets. Many people wore the national colors and some of them allegedly pinned their National Solidarity badges upside down. The initials "SN" instead of "NS" were understood to mean "Smrt Němcům"— "Death to the Germans." German civilians and soldiers insulted and assaulted such persons and the Czechs retaliated in kind. Yet these were only isolated clashes between individuals or small groups, resulting from tension rather than from any deliberate provocation. Although Czech policemen intervened in several cases of disorderly conduct and although their German counterparts made several arrests, nowhere was public order significantly threatened.[36]

By late afternoon nothing really serious had happened. Nonetheless, Frank appeared at Hácha's summer residence at Lány shortly after five o'clock and described the situation as critical. He threatened to use German forces if the Czech police would not preserve order. Hácha and his ministers promised to comply.[37]

[35] Armament Inspection Board Prague to War Economy and Armaments Board, November 8, 1939, W 08-122/24, BA, MA.

[36] Report by the Protectorate Ministry of the Interior, November 16, 1939, *DHCSP*, II, pp. 481–88. Stahlecker's report quoted in Kropáč and Louda, *Persekuce*, pp. 37–38. Cf. J. Polišenský, "28. říjen a 15. a 17. listopad 1939, perzekuce českého studentstva" [October 28 and November 15–17: The Persecution of the Czech Students], in *Sedmnáctý listopad* [The Seventeenth of November], pp. 33–34.

[37] Polišenský, "28. říjen," p. 34. Havelka, "*Vzpomínka*," p. 41.

Frank had deliberately dramatized the situation. In Neurath's absence he was in command of the entire German administration, and he apparently hoped to impress Berlin with his decisive handling of this challenge. He left Lány just in time to reach downtown Prague by six o'clock, when the silent demonstration was expected to begin.

The crowd which gathered in the streets represented various classes of the city's population. Students were especially numerous, although they participated as individuals rather than groups. They were joined by large numbers of people who had arrived from the industrial suburbs. The Security Service later noted that the persons arrested or wounded included students, workers, and even a high-ranking civil servant who reportedly incited the demonstrators.[38] Their feelings surfaced in such cries as "We want freedom," "Long live Beneš," "Long live Stalin." The last slogan, not necessarily inspired by Communists, expressed the sentiments of many nationalist Czechs who welcomed the westward advance of Russian power as a deterrent to Germany.[39]

Frank personally supervised the suppression of the demonstration. Heavily armed Nazi security forces began to brutally disperse the crowds and make arrests. In the ensuing melee, a few policemen received light injuries and several Czechs were hit by gunfire. German bullets killed a young worker and seriously injured a medical student, Jan Opletal.[40] Only as a result of the police intervention did the disorders assume a really serious character. This was undoubtedly Frank's purpose. Himmler promptly expressed his appreciation by promoting him to *SS-Gruppenführer* two days later.[41]

The provocation, however, was not quite successful. Berlin hesitated in deciding whether unrest in the Protectorate should be exploited politically or hushed up. The official press agency, Deutsches Nachrichten-Büro, at first released the news, but upon receiving higher instructions immediately retracted its report.[42] Consequently the German-controlled mass media did not mention

[38] *Meld. Reich*, October 30, 1939, pp. 4–5, R 58/144, BA.

[39] Cf. Caruso to Ciano, October 25, 1939, *DDI*, series IX, II, p. 12.

[40] *Meld. Reich*, see note 38 above. "Mitteilung OKW-Ausland," October 29, 1939, AA, T-120, 1279, 484588, NA. Cf. Polišenský, "28. říjen," pp. 34–35.

[41] Frank file, BDC.

[42] Report of October 28, 1939, Brammer collection, fol. 132, Z Sg 101/14, BA. Cf. W. A. Boelcke (ed.), *Kriegspropaganda, 1939–1941*, p. 215.

the event. In a letter to Hácha on October 31, Neurath regretted his own absence from Prague three days earlier, and noted that if he had been present everything would have gone more smoothly.[43] The demonstrations had no further repercussions, indicating that in the first round Neurath had prevailed over Frank.

In late October and early November tensions continued high. On November 4, the German University in Prague was transferred to the jurisdiction of the Reich.[44] Although this act had been prepared long in advance and its timing was merely accidental, the nationalist fanfare of the ceremonies nevertheless aroused Czech feelings, particularly among the students. Neurath feared new demonstrations on November 8, the anniversary of the 1620 battle of White Mountain, but this time the population remained calm.[45] On the same day, however, an abortive attempt on Hitler's life took place in Munich's Bürgerbräu beer-hall, and Nazi propaganda emphasized that the incident justified a more reckless suppression of all enemies of National Socialism.[46]

On November 15, the funeral of Jan Opletal, the student whose wounds of October 28 had proved fatal, was held in Prague. About three thousand of his colleagues participated. After the ceremonies, they gathered in small groups and sang patriotic songs. Czech police dispersed them without German assistance. This was all that happened, according to the report which Heydrich dispatched on the same day to the Reich Chancellery.[47] The report, based upon information the Nazi security chief had received from his agents in Prague, did not play up the importance of the incident. Its tone hardly suggests that Berlin wished at that time to blow it up. The initiative for further action emanated from Prague.

On November 16, Neurath and Frank flew to Berlin to meet Hitler. No documents have been found to explain who inspired their trip. The two men were accompanied by General Friderici

---

[43] Neurath to Hácha, October 31, 1939, quoted in Kropáč and Louda, *Persekuce*, p. 55.

[44] Ordinance of August 2, 1939, *RGB*, 1939, I, p. 1371. *Der Neue Tag*, November 5, 1939. Cf. R 43 II/1324, BA.

[45] Neurath to Hitler, November 9, 1939, AA, T-120, 1505, D 632595, NA.

[46] After the war, a prominent member of the Protectorate underground claimed that the attempt on Hitler's life had been the work of a Czech resistance organization. There is no other evidence to verify this assertion. Cf. V. Krajina, "La résistance tchécoslovaque," *Cahiers d'histoire de la guerre*, III (1950), p. 43.

[47] Heydrich to Lammers, November 15, 1939, AA, T-120, 1505, D 632599–600, NA.

and Völckers, who were both personally close to Neurath. The Protector probably took them along, anticipating a hard debate in which he might need help against Frank. On the same day the four officials, joined by Chvalkovský, conferred with Hitler.

How they met, whether together or separately, and what exactly was on the agenda, will perhaps never be known. Our main sources of information are Neurath and Frank themselves.[48] The value of their testimony, given later in their trials for war crimes, is slight. According to Chvalkovský's report to the Hácha government, written shortly after the conference, Hitler was in a rage. He "regretted that [he] had not destroyed Prague on March 15. But if the smallest thing ever happens again, [he would] have the Germans evacuated and blow it to pieces."[49] Chvalkovský reportedly heard the Führer announce that the Czech universities would be closed for three years but beyond this no other repression was mentioned.

Hitler, however, also authorized executions and deportations to concentration camps. If Frank was not the person who actually suggested it, he was at least the most eager to jump into action as soon as the Führer had approved these measures. He is said even to have availed himself of the official plane, forcing Neurath to return to Prague by train on the next day. From the airport Frank drove straight to the Gestapo headquarters in the Petschek Palais. Shortly afterward, about 9 : 30 P.M., the German police raided a committee meeting of the National Student Union where budgetary matters were being discussed. Several officials of the union were arrested on the spot, others at their homes. During the night, the Nazi security forces brutally attacked the university dormitories, not only in Prague but also in Brno, where no demonstrations had taken place. About 1200 inmates were arrested and sent to concentration camps. At dawn on November 17, nine students died before a firing squad, apparently without previous trial, and their bodies were burned.[50]

It is a melancholy fact that their death was not a sacrifice for a cause. It was merely an ironic and tragically wasteful twist of fate.

---

[48] Testimony by Neurath, *Trial*, XVI, p. 664. Testimony by Frank, Nur. PS-3801, IfZ. Testimony by Völckers in support of Neurath, *Trial*, XVII, pp. 131–32.

[49] Kropáč and Louda, *Persekuce*, p. 67. Cf. Beran, *Die Tschecho-Slowakei*, p. 34.

[50] *Zpověď K. H. Franka*, p. 62. "Bericht zur innenpolitischen Lage Nr. 19," *Meld. Reich*, November 22, 1939, p. 17, R 58/145, BA. During the raid on the dormitories one student was shot to death; Polišenský "28. říjen," pp. 39–41.

Of the nine murdered victims, eight had recently pledged to work for Czech-German understanding and for this very reason had received posts in the student union. One of them was the deputy chairman of the Union for Cooperation with the Germans. The only person in the group who held no post was a Slovak-Jewish student with left-wing sympathies who was only formally registered at the University while preparing for his doctorate.[51] The Gestapo had obviously not made the selection on the basis of any previous investigation, but had chosen at random the currently known student officials, or anyone who was immediately at hand. Their purpose was intimidation, not the punishment of culprits.

Late on November 17, the Nazis publicized their action by red placards posted in the streets. They asserted that "in spite of repeated warnings, a group of Czech intellectuals has been attempting for some time . . . to disturb peace and order in the Protectorate of Bohemia and Moravia through greater or smaller acts of resistance. It has been possible to ascertain that ringleaders of these acts of resistance are to be found particularly in the Czech universities."[52] All Czech institutions of higher learning were closed officially for three years, although in reality they were never reopened until after the liberation. The poster bore Neurath's signature.

At the Nuremberg trial, Neurath emphatically denied that he had ever signed this announcement. He pleaded ignorance about the plans for the reprisals. Only after they were over did he supposedly learn with horror that Frank had attached his name to the text of the public notice.[53] Of course, it hardly seems possible that after his conference with Hitler Neurath was still in the dark about what was under way. Yet many high-ranking members of his staff were genuinely surprised at learning what had happened. *Oberlandrat* Westerkamp of Brno was outraged that the Police had acted without even letting him know. He wrote to Prague: "Under these circumstances it seems like a joke that . . . the *Oberlandräte* are responsible for peace and order in their districts . . . . An organ

---

[51] Kropáč and Louda, *Persekuce*, pp. 81–84. J. Strnadel, "Marek Frauwirth a 17. listopad" [Marek Frauwirth and November 17], *Plamen*, V (1963), No. 11, pp. 135–36.

[52] *Trial*, XXXIX, p. 534.

[53] *Ibid.*, XVI, p. 664. Cf. testimonies by Irene Friedrich and Theda von Ritter, *ibid.*, XL, pp. 538, 448–49. According to Frank, Neurath signed the announcement; *Zpověď K. H. Franka*, p. 68.

of the Reich Protector . . . cannot responsibly perform its duty if it is not notified in time or at least kept informed about what has already taken place."[54] As late as November 21, Wilhelm Dennler, a high-ranking official in the Office of the Protector, was unable even to obtain information about the number of arrested students and had to base his estimates on press reports.[55]

This time Frank's triumph seemed complete. While Neurath was still in Berlin, unable or unwilling to go to Prague, and while the German civilian administration was at a loss about what was going on, the police ruled the country. For the following four weeks, the Protector all but disappeared from the scene. He may have left Prague shortly after his return from Berlin on November 17 and retired to his country seat in Württemberg. In any case, he took no part in public affairs and let Frank govern alone.

The repression of the students did not appease Frank's desire for vengeance. On November 19, a newspaper notice announced that "three Czechs had been executed by shooting for having violently assaulted a German. The persons shot included two police officials."[56] After an unidentified attacker had fired upon an SS platoon at Zdice, near Prague, the Gestapo retaliated by wholesale arrests in the town and by selecting ten hostages. The Hácha administration wished to investigate the incident itself and proclaimed a state of emergency in the whole of central Bohemia.[57] The quick capture of the offender settled the affair, but Frank's display of power continued. On November 21, he reviewed a newly arrived regiment of the Regular Police. Two days later, SS Death's-head detachments (*Totenkopfstandarte*) paraded before him in downtown Prague.[58] On December 2, the State Secretary delivered an especially virulent speech at the dedication of the Nazi party headquarters. He warned the Czechs that now was their last chance and that any opposition would be crushed brutally.[59]

---

[54]Westerkamp to Burgsdorff, November 17, 1939, quoted in S. Biman, "17. listopad" [November 17], *Dějiny a současnost*, VIII (1966), No. 11, p. 18.

[55]Dennler to Burgsdorff, November 21, 1939, *Trial*, XXXIII, p. 250.

[56]*České slovo*, November 19, 1939.

[57]*Zpověď K. H. Franka*, p. 65. Cf. Č. Amort, *Partyzáni na Podbrdsku* [Partisans in the Brdy Hills], p. 21.

[58]*Der Neue Tag*, November 22–23, 1939.

[59]K. H. Frank, *Ansprache des Staatssekretärs und SS-Gruppenführers Karl Hermann Frank anlässlich der 1. Kundgebung der NSDAP auf dem Altstädter Ring zu Prag*, pages not numbered.

The persecution in Bohemia and Moravia aroused indignation abroad and had a staggering impact upon the Czechs. During the weeks immediately following November 17, their fears grew to unprecedented proportions. In several districts around Prague mothers refused to let their children be vaccinated. They were afraid that German doctors would inject substances causing illness, sterility, or death. Rumors circulated that chlorine and lead were being added to cigarettes in order to implant tuberculosis. People suspected that women in hospitals were being forcibly sterilized and that the Germans would soon forbid all Czech marriages for four years.[60] Although false, these rumors anticipated with remarkable accuracy what the Nazis were indeed soon to do elsewhere.

The Security Service noted that the psychological climate in the country had become markedly unfavorable. The Czechs boycotted German shopkeepers and German customers had difficulty getting service in Czech stores. The Germans were concerned about the survival of their retail business in ethnically mixed areas. General Ernst Udet, who was in charge of the Reich's aircraft production, saw the military contracts in the Protectorate endangered.[61] Volkmar Hopf, the *Oberlandrat* at Zlín, commented that the gap between the two nationalities in Bohemia and Moravia was disastrously widening: "The aftermath of the October and November events showed an extraordinarily deep and stubborn hatred between the local Germans and the Czechs. This hatred gives time and again the impression . . . that [their] coexistence presents at least in this generation insoluble problems."[62] The opinion of the Nazi official seemed to confirm the prediction George F. Kennan had already made half a year earlier, that "if the tide ever turns, Czech retaliation will be fearful to contemplate."[63] In particular, the Czechs desired more intensely than ever the summary expulsion of the Sudeten Germans, whom they blamed most for their misfortunes.[64]

---

[60] *Meld. Reich,* November 24 and December 6, 1939, pp. 6–8, R 58/145, BA.

[61] *Ibid.,* pp. 5–7, and *Meld. Reich,* January 8, 1940, p. 7, R 58/147, BA. Cf. Caruso to Ciano, November 21, 1939, *DDI,* series IX, II, p. 243. Udet to Milch, December 1939, FD 5590/45, S 391, IWM.

[62] Hopf to the Protector, January 2, 1940, Král (ed.), *Die Deutschen,* p. 398.

[63] Kennan to State Department, May 23, 1939, Kennan, *From Prague after Munich,* p. 178.

[64] Report to Beneš from the Protectorate, end of October 1939, quoted in E. Táborský, *Pravda zvítězila* [The Truth Has Prevailed], p. 422.

Frank's critics in the army and the civil service resented his abuse of power and saw little justification for his measures. Their opportunity came after the SS had become involved in an embarrassing scandal. On November 13, Commissioner Gottberg of the Land Office was summoned to his Berlin superior, Günther Pancke, demoted, and reprimanded in no uncertain terms. Pancke told him:

You are obliged to report yourself immediately sick because of a severe heart attack and to actually *behave* before all people as if you were sick .... You are obliged to avoid any further official contact with any organs of the party, the state, the armed forces, and free business .... You make yourself liable to the heaviest penalty, including especially assignment to a concentration camp, if you bring other explanations into circulation .... If you disregard this order, you will be found guilty of an act against the state of which the consequences in time of war are known to you.[65]

The reason for this spectacular showdown was Gottberg's quite extraordinary haughtiness which had made him neglect the most elementary rules of bureaucratic in-fighting. In the pursuit of his ambition to become the head of the SS Central Land Office for Poland, he had antagonized almost everyone around him. Darré and Pancke himself had grown to hate him. Moreover, his rude manners and drinking habits caused embarrassment even among the hardened SS. Most significant, Gottberg had misappropriated over a million marks of Land Office money. He was stupid enough to have invested it in the manufacture of a new drug fraudulently promoted as a cure for foot-and-mouth disease. Since his subordinates had embezzled additional funds, the activities of the SS under his leadership in the Prague Land Office had finally produced a deficit of 1,340,000 marks.[66]

[65] Note by Pancke and Hofmann, November 13, 1939, Gottberg file, BDC.

[66] Pancke to Pohl, January 15, 1940, NS 2/140, BA. Note on conference, March 1–5, 1940, RFSS, T-175, 188, 2726184–90, NA. Report on revision in the Land Office, October 18, 1939, NS 2/139, BA. In the Berlin Document Center and in the Federal Archives at Coblenz, extensive documentary material has been preserved showing the continuation of the story. Gottberg appealed the verdict, and achieved rehabilitation in April 1942. Pancke, who by taking action against Gottberg had also tried to camouflage his own unsavory financial operations, was reprimanded by Himmler. But Himmler did not renounce the services of either of the two men. Gottberg was appointed in September 1943 as Commissioner-General for Belorussia in Minsk and became notorious for reprisals against the population in partisan areas. Pancke was given the post of Higher SS and Police Leader in occupied Denmark, Cf. A. Dallin, *German Rule in Russia*, pp. 221–25.

Frank's rivals capitalized on the disrepute that befell the SS in the Protectorate. The opposition against him seems to have centered around Burgsdorff.[67] The Assistant State Secretary pressed for the appointment of a civilian as Gottberg's successor and was pleased when Theodor Gross, an agricultural expert, assumed the post. "This measure," Frank commented angrily, "delivers the land policy in the Protectorate definitively into the hands of the bureaucracy and removes it from the control of the SS.[68]

The repression in the Protectorate had coincided with a similar terror campaign on a much larger scale in neighboring Poland. In both countries the intellectual elite was the special target. The persecution of the professors of the Łódź and Cracow universities took place at that time.[69] The Germans also tried to coordinate their policies of land seizure and resettlement in the two nations. In November, these issues were again discussed in the SS headquarters in Berlin.[70] But the position of the radical Nazis was not yet strong enough to determine the course of policy. In Poland, the newly established German civilian government had curbed the worst excesses by late 1939, and in Bohemia and Moravia Frank's methods ran into difficulties at about the same time.

Besides the approval of Gross's appointment, a more comprehensive policy revision was on the agenda of Neurath's conference with Hitler in mid-December. The Führer confirmed that the Protectorate should be treated more leniently than the Government-General of Poland and that in the realization of such drastic projects as forced resettlement of population, Poland held priority. He decided that in Bohemia and Moravia "the German authorities are to avoid anything that is likely to provoke . . . mass actions." At the same time, however, he emphasized that "any Czech defiance must be crushed with the harshest means from the onset."[71]

While the military situation remained undecided during the

---

[67] Heydrich to Lammers, December 19, 1939, NS 2/139, BA.

[68] Frank to Himmler, December 18, 1939, *ibid.*

[69] Cf. Broszat, *Nationalsozialistische Polenpolitik*, pp. 41–51. C. Madajczyk, "Okupační politika třetí říše vůči polskému národu" [Occupation Policy of the Third Reich toward the Polish People], in *Nacistická okupace Evropy*, I, part 1, p. 255.

[70] Pancke's note, November 7, 1939, and note about conferences with Pancke, November 11, 1939, NS 2/139, BA.

[71] Ziemke to Foreign Office, December 15, 1939, *DGFP*, D, VIII, p. 538. The Land Office was ordered not to acquire any more land in the Protectorate without Himmler's special permission. Pancke to Land Office, December 22, 1939, NS 2/139, BA.

"phony war" at the western front, in Germany itself the radical and moderate Nazis maintained an uneasy balance. This determined a relatively lenient course for the German authorities in the Protectorate, as all major decisions were postponed until the outcome of the military confrontation. But although Frank had suffered a rebuff, his repressive policies had a lasting impact. After the experiences of October and November 1939, the Czechs abstained from similar manifestations of defiance. They became more cautious and avoided challenging the Nazis by open mass action.

7 *THE CZECHS ASSIMILATED*

NAZI RACIAL THEORY AND PRACTICE

IN 1945, after the war was over, Frank characterized the attitude of the Czechs during the occupation as that of "realistic politicians who firmly stuck to their national existence." [1] In describing them as "realistic," he was especially alluding to the fact that the overwhelming majority of the people had too much to lose materially by getting involved in resistance activities. He further implied that if only their national identity had been safeguarded under the Protectorate, the Czechs would have willingly accepted political union with Germany. Whether such a conjecture was justified or not, Frank—who was eminently well qualified to judge—pointed out the crucial importance of nationality in a country with a long and turbulent history of ethnic struggles.

In the past, the Germans, like many other peoples, had often tried to impose their culture wherever they were the ruling nation. They used both inducements and force to win the members of subject nationalities to their own values and also to outward conformity with German ways. All willing converts were welcome. Such was, for example, the pattern of Prussia's policy in Poland before 1914. This "traditional" concept of Germanization had grown out of the actual conditions in such ethnically mixed areas as the Poznań region or Upper Silesia.

In contrast, the Nazis' racial concept of nationality—though prepared by nineteenth-century Social Darwinism—was an artificial product of the post-Versailles frustrations in Germany proper. The arguments about the presumed superiority of the German race were intended to bolster the self-confidence of the defeated people and justify Germany's renewed bid for a great-power position. Unlike the older Germanizers, the Nazis stressed the insuperable obstacles that presumably stood in the way of assimilating racially

---

[1] Frank's interrogation at Wiesbaden, June 10, 1945, p. 6, Nur. PS-4079, IfZ.

alien peoples. Once Hitler's conquest of Europe had started, this attitude created formidable problems in the annexed foreign territories.

In Bohemia and Moravia, the Nazis did not initially have a ready answer to the cardinal question of what should be done with the eight million Czechs in the area. Various proposals, such as emigration, assimilation, and forced resettlement had been put forward by various groups within the Nazi hierarchy.[2] Yet Berlin did not officially endorse any one of them. As late as August 1940, Kurt Ziemke, the Wilhelmstrasse representative in Prague, observed that "nothing is known here about what final line is to be adopted with regard to the Czechs . . . [or] whether any fundamental political principle is to be commonly applied in all occupied and incorporated countries."[3]

The top Nazi leaders were notably reluctant to make up their minds about such fundamental issues. On previous occasions, Hitler himself had demonstrated his preference for improvisation rather than for a blueprint of clearly defined long-term policies. By keeping ultimate objectives vague, the leaders could better avoid commitments and preserve their freedom of action. In his secret speech before German journalists in April 1940, Goebbels left no doubt that such vagueness was deliberate: "If somebody asks today, how do you visualize the new Europe, we must say that we don't know . . . . Once we have power, . . . we shall see what we can do about it . . . . Today we say: living space. Everybody can imagine what he wants. At the right time, however, we shall know what we want."[4]

The specific policies concerning race and nationality were neither premeditated nor promulgated upon the initiative of Hitler or his closest associates. Their formulation in the Third Reich did not significantly differ from the decision-making processes characteristic for all modern bureaucratic states. The leaders provide only general inspiration, subordinates take the initiative, and bureaucrats are responsible for the elaboration and implementation of policies. Thus after the collapse of France in June 1940, Germany's leaders spoke grandiloquently of the New Order in which all the promises and aspirations of the Nazi movement would finally be realized. But the pressure for the specific decisions and

2 See Chapter 5, notes 3, 4, 19, 20, 43.
3 Ziemke to Foreign Office, August 30, 1940, Nur. NG-5173, CU.
4 H.-A. Jacobsen (ed.), *Der Zweite Weltkrieg*, p. 181.

actions which were supposed to lead to that goal emanated from the intermediate echelons of the hierarchy, rather than from the summit.

In Bohemia and Moravia, the lower-ranking Nazis were the first to observe that the protectorate status had become obsolete and should therefore be abolished. Ziemke found little expediency in preserving the existing form of autonomy in a situation so radically different from that of March 1939.[5] At the same time, Berlin officials, to whom the phenomenal extension of German influence in Europe gave a new taste for power, hoped to extend their control over territories—like the Protectorate—which had so far escaped their direct jurisdiction. The ministries of the Interior, Economics, Finance, Post, Food, and Transport advanced proposals for the direct administration of Bohemia and Moravia from Berlin.[6]

The abolition of the Protectorate was also strongly advocated in the Sudetenland, though for different reasons. There the local Nazis regarded it as a solution to their own serious problems. Having been catapulted into prominence in 1938, they now ruled merely one of the Reich's many provinces, which other Germans tended to regard—somewhat condescendingly but not incorrectly —as a preserve of parochialism and narrow-mindedness. Most frustrating, the Sudetenland, a separate administrative unit for the first time in history, did not seem to be a viable entity. Franz Künzel, Henlein's aide in charge of ethnic affairs, deplored its frontiers, drawn as they had been in 1938 to divide predominantly Czech territories from those with German majorities. He observed that "the German-Czech ethnic border in most cases bisects areas which are homogeneous units because of their geography, transportation system and economy."[7] Ironically, this opinion vindicated the Czechs' traditional insistence upon the natural unity of their "historic provinces," an interpretation which, having been endorsed by the Versailles conference, had so much irritated the Sudeten Germans before Munich.

---

[5] Ziemke to Foreign Office, August 30, 1940, Nur. NG-5173, CU.

[6] K. H. Frank, "Denkschrift über die Behandlung des Tschechenproblems und die zukünftige Gestaltung des böhmisch-mährischen Raumes," August 28, 1940, *Trial*, XXXIII, p. 264. Cf. Ohnesorge to Neurath, September 10, 1940, R 43 II/1326b, BA.

[7] F. Künzel, "Vorschläge für eine Neugliederung des böhmisch-mährischen Raumes," July 25, 1940, in Král (ed.), *Vergangenheit*, p. 51. A similar proposal was submitted by Rudolf Staffen, another of Henlein's associates: "Böhmisch-mährische Raumgestaltung," September 30, 1940, *ibid.*, pp. 90–93.

Künzel proposed to unite western Sudetenland with Bohemia. The "*Gaufürst* of Reichenberg," as Henlein was sarcastically called by his critics, would move to Prague as chief of the new *Gau* Bohemia.[8] Such an arrangement would also have had the advantage of eliminating Richard Donnevert, Henlein's deputy and principal rival. Donnevert not only scandalized his boss by disgraceful conduct, and especially by his alcoholic parties; he also schemed against Henlein, disseminating slanderous stories in Party and SS circles. The deputy hoped to become a *Gauleiter* himself and rule the eastern Sudetenland, which would be enlarged by the neighboring parts of Moravia, in particular around Ostrava.[9]

Similar ambitions motivated the most ardent advocate of partition for the Protectorate, Hugo Jury, who was in charge of *Gau* Lower Danube. A native of southern Moravia, a graduate of the German University in Prague, and once a physician at St. Pölten, Jury was another chauvinistic product of the ethnically mixed borderland. Since the city of Vienna constituted a separate administrative unit, he was the chief of a *Gau* without a capital. He therefore hoped to unite the Lower Danube region with most of Moravia, making Brno the capital.[10] Jury held an influential position as head of the Party Liaison Office in Prague, an agency which coordinated the relations between the Nazi party and the Protector.

The partition plans alarmed Frank and other "particularists" especially. These were mostly officials established in the occupation administration for whom the disappearance of the Protectorate would mean the loss of good jobs. They understandably favored the preservation of the *status quo*. As the partition projects proliferated, Neurath and Frank found it necessary to solicit support in Berlin. They each sent a memorandum to the Chancellery to be submitted to Hitler.[11]

The two documents differed in emphasis: Neurath stressed the expediency of the existing regime, while Frank devoted more space

[8] Cf. Brehm to Jung, February 5, 1941, Rudolf Jung file, BDC.

[9] Donnevert file, BDC. Cf. *Oberlandrat* Ostrava to Burgsdorff, September 6, 1940, in Král (ed.), *Vergangenheit*, pp. 78–82.

[10] Jury file, BDC. Cf. report to Frank on conference with Jury, August 1940, quoted in K. Fremund (ed.), "Dokumenty," p. 8. *Meld. Reich*, July 7, 1941, p. 18, R 58/162, BA.

[11] K. von Neurath, "Aufzeichnung über die Frage der zukünftigen Gestaltung des böhmisch-mährischen Raumes," August 31, 1940, *Trial*, XXXIII, pp. 253–59. Frank's "Denkschrift," *ibid.*, pp. 260–71.

to the future ethnic transformation of Bohemia and Moravia. Yet they both agreed that Germanization of the country was a highly desirable ultimate goal. The striking common feature of both these memoranda was their cynicism, not surprising in Frank's case but rather shocking in Neurath's. They discussed with remarkable detachment the elimination of the racially unsuitable part of the population. Neurath vaguely mentioned "casting them off" (*abstossen*), without specifying what he had in mind. Frank recommended "special treatment" (*Sonderbehandlung*) which he understood as outright physical liquidation.[12] They agreed, however, that this elimination should concern only a minority. Neurath was impressed by the unusually "high number of fair-haired people with intelligent faces and well-shaped bodies, who would not stand out unfavorably even in central and southern Germany."[13] Frank even ventured the estimate that five-eighths were actually of German origin.

Both authors concluded that the majority of the Czechs, being racially close to the Germans, could be assimilated. For the time being, the abolition of the Protectorate would impede rather than promote this end, because partition into several *Gaue* would make a uniform policy more difficult. Furthermore, separation would intensify Czech nationalism, generating a desire for reunification. The existing regime should therefore be preserved at least until the expected German victory in the war.

The memoranda created a minor sensation in Berlin. Heydrich commented sarcastically that "*SS-Gruppenführer* Frank who has so far advocated a policy of radical destruction of the Czechs, suddenly—granted in a modified form—adopts Neurath's point of view: the most complete, though not total, assimilation possible."[14] Although Frank's "vested interest" in the preservation of the Protectorate can partly explain this switch, his argument rested primarily on ideological grounds. So far as there was any logic in Nazi racial dogma, his recommendations followed logically from its premises. The same approach characterized Hitler's response to the memoranda. His earlier contemptuous statements about the "so-called Germanized Czechs" showed his aversion to any mixing

---

[12] *Ibid.*, pp. 256 and 266.

[13] *Ibid.*, pp. 255–56.

[14] Heydrich's note, September 11, 1940, original reproduced in *Zločiny nacistů za okupace a osvobozenecký boj našeho lidu* [Nazi Crimes during the Occupation and the Liberation Struggle of Our People], following p. 156.

with the hated race.[15] Yet even he was willing to subordinate his prejudice to doctrine. Although he personally detested the Czechs intensely, they were to fare incomparably better in the New Order than other Slavs. As Frank recommended, the Führer ruled during a conference with Neurath on September 23 that the assimilation "of a greater part of the Czech people is possible for historical and racial reasons, provided that those Czechs who are racially useless and hostile to the Reich will be eliminated, *viz.*, subjected to special treatment."[16]

Hitler's decision was not intended to be fully implemented until after the war. He estimated that the process of assimilation would require at least a hundred years. But preparations were to start immediately. In a private interview on October 12, the Führer placed Frank in charge.[17] This assignment notably enhanced the State Secretary's prestige and power at Neurath's expense. Various Nazi agencies concerned with racial affairs jumped into action to lay "scientific" foundations for the ethnic reshaping of Bohemia and Moravia.

In October 1940, Himmler conferred with Heydrich about how the percentage of the assimilable could be ascertained or—as he put it—how a "racial inventory" could be made. The conclusions were typical of Himmler's simplistic thinking and his crude manipulation of human beings as inanimate objects. He ordered the Race and Settlement Head Office to draw up a questionnaire to be completed by Czech doctors during routine medical checkups of school children. Besides "innocent" items, such as weight, vision, or urinalysis, the form included data considered crucial for the determination of race: size and shape of the body, color of the eyes, hair, and skin, form of the occiput. One photograph of the profile and another showing the face were to be included. Forwarding the questionnaire to Frank, Himmler confidently added

[15] *Hitler's Secret Book*, p. 45. Cf. minutes of a meeting attended by Hitler, General Reichenau, and von Tschammer und Osten, June 20, 1939, R 43 II/1327, BA.

[16] Neurath's note, September 25, 1940, AA, T-120, 1505, D 632627, NA. Accounts of Hitler's decision corresponding to that given in Neurath's note were recorded by Ziemke on October 5 and by Friderici on October 15, 1940, *DGFP*, D, XI, pp. 266–67. *Trial*, XXVI, pp. 375–77.

[17] Ziemke to Foreign Office, October 14, 1940, in Král (ed.), *Vergangenheit*, p. 95. Cf. Král, *Otázky*, I, p. 40.

that its results would enable the experts to obtain for the first time the desired "racial inventory."[18]

Having secured the cooperation of the Office of the Protector, the RuSHA (Race and Settlement Head Office) launched the project in March 1941. Four months later, the checkups were already under way.[19] Although the completed questionnaires were presumably later sent to Berlin, we have no evidence about their fate. The mass of meaningless data must have puzzled even the race experts. The Nazis soon tried other methods, in their further attempts to collect information. In May 1941, they contemplated drafting two age groups of the Czech population into compulsory labor service; during this process the draftees would undergo thorough racial examination.[20] Misgivings about the political effects of such a drastic project seem to explain why it was not put into practice at that time. Meanwhile German researchers studied old conscription records, paying special attention to the physical characteristics of the recruits. An anthropologist of some distinction professed to make serious conclusions about race from the incidence of recruits over 5' 8" tall in various districts.[21] In 1942, mobile X-ray units conducted mass screening in the Protectorate under the pretext of preventing the spread of tuberculosis. We do not know what portion of the population was examined, whether the campaign was brought to an end, or whether it yielded the desired racial information. From an interim report dated July 1942, the percentage of the assimilable appeared high, though lower than originally expected.[22]

If the effort to collect useful data through these "objective" techniques was dubious, other proposed methods were outright farcical. The Office of the Protector, for example, elaborated the following guidelines for determining race:

[18] Himmler to Hofmann, October 9, 1940; Hofmann to Himmler, October 24, 1940: RFSS, T-175, 26, 2531948–52, NA. Himmler to Frank, January 1941, *ibid.*, 2531947.

[19] In Fremund (ed.), "Dokumenty," pp. 22–23, 25. Hofmann's note about conversation with Frank, May 24, 1941, NS 2/127, BA. Besides school children, physicians, policemen and civil servants were to be examined later.

[20] In Fremund (ed.), "Dokumenty," p. 23.

[21] K. V. Müller, "Grundsätzliche Ausführungen über das deutsche und tschechische Volkstum in Böhmen und Mähren," *Raumforschung und Raumordnung*, V (1941), p. 494.

[22] Heydrich to Bormann, May 18, 1942, in Král (ed.), *Vergangenheit*, p. 152. Hussmann's address at Wasserburg, June 20, 1942, *Trial*, XXXIX, pp. 362, 365.

Racially valuable are those inhabitants of the Protectorate in whom or in whose ancestry Slavic racial characteristics do not predominate . . . . Slavic racial characteristics, apart from Mongol types, are for instance a markedly disorderly and careless family life, demonstrating a complete lack of feeling for order, for personal and domestic cleanliness, and of any ambition to advance oneself.[23]

By comparing the neat German farms with the less attractive appearance of Slavic villages, the Nazis had deduced the racial qualities of their inhabitants. The prosperous and stately homesteads in the fertile plain of central Moravia supposedly indicated the Germanic origin of their Czech-speaking owners.[24] It was equally ludicrous to single out lack of ambition as a typically Slavic trait, especially since the Germans frequently complained about fierce business competition with the Czechs in ethnically mixed areas. The "guidelines" were too obviously products of primitive prejudice, thinly veiled in respectable, pseudo-scholarly language.

Not all the studies about race conditions in Bohemia and Moravia were entirely worthless. At least some of the Nazi scholars were despite their prejudices conscientious researchers, and their findings cannot be dismissed lightly. This applies especially to Karl Valentin Müller, a Dresden anthropologist, who came to Prague to become Frank's special adviser in race affairs. In the summer of 1940, he toured central and eastern Bohemia with twenty assistants, studying archeological excavations, parish records on births, marriages, and deaths, and inscriptions in village cemeteries. Frank hailed these studies as being "of considerable importance for the destiny of the Bohemian and Moravian area."[25]

Müller reinterpreted the history of Bohemia and Moravia from the point of view of race.[26] The local Slavs of the prehistoric period,

[23] Hufnagel, "Vorschläge zur Vorbereitung der Germanisierung (Umvolkung) im Protektorat Böhmen und Mähren," November 30, 1940, in Král (ed.), *Vergangenheit*, p. 113.

[24] Cf. special "Moravian" issue of *Böhmen und Mähren*, October 1940. Frank to Weizsäcker, June 9, 1941, AA, T-120, 1279, 484620–21, NA. Karmasin to Himmler, October 30, 1941, in Král (ed.), *Die Deutschen*, pp. 461–62.

[25] Frank to OKW, October 10, 1940, in Fremund (ed.), "Dokumenty," pp. 18–19.

[26] Cf. his studies: "Die Bedeutung des deutschen Blutes im Tschechentum," *Archiv für Bevölkerungswissenschaft und Bevölkerungspolitik*, IX (1939), pp. 325–58, 385–404. "Grundsätzliche Ausführungen . . . ," pp. 488–96; see note 21, above. Müller and Heinz Zatschek, "Das biologische Schicksal der Premysliden," *Archiv für Rassen- und Gesellschaftsbiologie*, XXXV (1941), pp. 136–52. "Die Bedeutung des deutschen

as seen from archeological evidence, appeared to have been a fair-haired people with elongated skulls, quite different from the supposedly inferior "Easterners" (*Ostmenschen*). Among the Czechs around the year 1000, there were astonishingly many "Nordic" types. The medieval Bohemian dynasty of the Premyslides, though originally Slavic, had gradually become German through intermarriage. All its outstanding members had either great-grandmothers or mothers of German origin. In the thirteenth and fourteenth centuries, thousands of German colonists brought a further influx of "superior" blood. Müller estimated that after the Thirty Years' War, the ratio of the two races in Bohemia and Moravia had been 1 to 2 in favor of the Germans, only the lower population strata remaining predominantly Slavic. In the late eighteenth century, intellectuals of German ancestry, motivated by sentimental interest in the language, customs, and traditions of the peasant folk, gave impetus to the growth of Czech nationalism. The low birth rate in the upper classes accounted for the gradual recession of the German element. The 1 to 2 ratio was finally reversed in favor of the Czechs. According to Müller, however, this transformation applied only to language, not to race. The impressive Czech national revival was the result of the high percentage of German blood in the veins of its leaders. Müller concluded: "About half of that portion of Bohemian and Moravian population who declare themselves Czech today are products of German blood-admixture. The percentage is even higher in the strata of high achievement." [27] The present task therefore consisted in remaking these people into Germans (*Rückdeutschung*).

Only Müller's contention about the correlation between Germanic blood and achievement can be safely relegated to the realm of myth. Otherwise there is little doubt that Bohemia and Moravia were a melting pot for centuries. Nationalist Czechs frequently denigrated past contributions by the Germans, but they were usually philosophical about their own German ancestries. The Nazis, on the other hand, were caught in the strait jacket of racial dogma, and the German blood-admixture in the country unexpectedly

Leistungserbgutes im tschechischen Volkstum," *Forschungen und Fortschritte*, XVII (1941), pp. 335–37. "Deutschtum und Tschechentum in rassen- und gesellschafts-biologischer Betrachtung," *Rasse*, VIII (1941), pp. 303–307. "Zur Rassen- und Volksgeschichte des böhmisch-mährischen Raumes," in *Das Böhmen und Mähren-Buch*, ed. by F. Heiss, pp. 127–34.
27 *Ibid.*, p. 134.

proved to be a real embarrassment for them. They engaged in the hopeless task of disentangling the ethnic components which centuries had firmly woven together. To make things even more difficult, the Czechs, by a particular irony of fate, seemed to possess "better" racial characteristics than the Sudeten Germans, the vanguards of the Nazi cause in the area. Having been commissioned by Heydrich to study this problem, Walter König-Beyer of the Race and Settlement Head Office (RuSHA), concluded: "A rough estimate of the racial structure of the Sudetenland . . . shows that from the purely numerical point of view the racial picture of the Czech people is considerably more favorable today than that of the Sudeten German population."[28] König-Beyer's estimate concerning the incidence of the main racial types happened to conform with the results of the investigation of old conscription records mentioned earlier. (See the statistics based on König-Beyer's estimate in Table 7).

TABLE 7. *Race Structure of Bohemia and Moravia*

(*in per cent of population*)

	Czechs	Sudeten Germans
Nordic, dinaric, westic	45	25
"Unbalanced" racial mixtures	40	55
Racially alien	15	20

The theme of the biological decline of the Germans in Bohemia and Moravia recurs time and time again in Nazi documents. *Oberlandrat* Möller of Jičín, for example, considered them "sickly" (*angekränkelt*) and therefore unable to contribute fresh blood.[29] Himmler's confidential *Reports from the Reich* described the critical situation in the ethnic enclaves in Moravia, which he had envisaged as the bases for the expansion of Germandom. Their population had preserved its homogeneity by close intermarriage, which often resulted in degeneration manifested by the high incidence of congenital diseases. The average age in the enclaves was extraordinarily high. In one district 23.7 per cent of the inhabitants were over fifty, and only 4.7 per cent under five.[30]

[28] Memorandum by Walter König-Beyer, October 23, 1940, in Král (ed.), *Vergangenheit*, p. 76.

[29] Note on conference of *Oberlandräte*, August 15, 1940, in Král (ed.), *Die Deutschen*, p. 416.

[30] *Meld. Reich*, April 22, 1941, p. 10, R 58/159, BA.

Although this gloomy picture did not apply to the Sudetenland proper, where the birth rate was high throughout the war, the demographic situation there, too, alarmed the Nazis. During the two years after Munich, an estimated 160,000 Sudeten Germans emigrated to other parts of the Reich.[31] During the same period, many Czechs who, fearing persecution, left the area in 1938, had later returned. In addition, workers from the Protectorate moved there, attracted by better jobs and higher wages. Sudeten German men were drafted into the army, leaving their places to be filled with Czechs, who, as Protectorate nationals, were not liable to conscription. The prosperity of Czech artisans, storekeepers, and farmers in the Sudetenland caused much local resentment. Not surprisingly, the strongest opposition to assimilation came from the Sudeten Nazis. In their opinion, political attitude counted more than race. For the purpose of assimilation, the Czechs should therefore be judged according to their "worthiness" rather than their "capability" (*Eindeutschungswürdigkeit* rather than *Eindeutschungsfähigkeit*).[32]

All the debates about the ethnic transformation of Bohemia and Moravia were held in deep secrecy. Only exceptionally did an impatient Nazi let his tongue slip sufficiently to elaborate in public upon that subject. In August 1941, for example, a speaker at a rally in Jihlava hinted at the possibility of shipping the Czech "Wenzels" beyond the Urals.[33] The local *Oberlandrat*, upset about this indiscretion, complained to the Protector, who then tried to hush up the incident. Still, rumors about various plans for assimilation and "special treatment" leaked out. The Czechs, suspecting a sinister design, viewed German policies with profound mistrust.

The initial Nazi measures in nationality matters had already

---

[31] *Ibid.*, June 9, 1941, p. 14, R 58/161, BA. Cf. J. Orlík (ed.), *Opavsko a severní Morava za okupace* [The Troppau Country and Northern Moravia during the Occupation], esp. p. 58.

[32] Schulte-Schomburg to Heydrich, March 11, 1942, in Král (ed.), *Vergangenheit*, pp. 150–51. Künzel's Carlsbad address of October 17, 1940, in Fremund (ed.), "Dokumenty," pp. 19–24 and 3–4. Cf. Z. Antoš, "Blut und Boden—ke konečnému řešení národnostní otázky v sudetské župě," [Blut und Boden: The "Final Solution" of the Nationality Question in the *Gau* Sudetenland], *Slezský sborník*, LXIV (1966), pp. 28–59.

[33] *Oberlandrat* Jihlava to the Protector, August 11, 1941, in Král (ed.), *Die Deutschen*, p. 448. Cf. Neurath's instruction, June 27, 1941, *Trial*, XXXIII, pp. 271–73. ("Wenzel" [Wenceslas] was a name used in derisive references to the Czechs.)

given offense to Czech feelings. These measures included, for example, ordinances about the priority of the German language and school restrictions in ethnically mixed areas. The closing of the Czech institutions of higher learning further strengthened the impression that the Nazis were striving to obliterate the Czech national identity. Yet these measures still followed the "traditional" rather than the racial Germanization pattern. Frank, their chief instigator, was at that time motivated primarily by his primitive Czechophobia of the Sudeten variety. Only later did he begin to turn toward dogmatic racism, with its emphasis upon biological criteria of assimilation relatively favorable to the Czechs—the change which had elicited Heydrich's surprise and sarcasm in September 1940.

The transition from the traditional to the racial approach was also reflected in Protectorate marriage and citizenship legislation. Shortly after March 15, 1939, all former Czechoslovak nationals had to decide for either Reich or Protectorate citizenship.[34] The Germans, aware of their own uncomfortably small proportion in the alleged *Reichsland,* hoped that at least some Czechs of mixed ancestry would opt for Reich citizenship. But despite their efforts, only about 200,000 Germans were registered in Bohemia and Moravia, compared with over 8 million Czechs. This outcome prompted Hitler to cancel Reichstag elections there, so that voters' registration might not reveal the scarcity of Germans.[35]

The marriage laws of the Third Reich did not originally discriminate against the Czechs, who were not distinguished from other foreigners. Many German soldiers and officials in the Protectorate married Czech women. Of the 2956 marriages concluded there before a German magistrate in the year following August 1, 1939, 593 were mixed. This worried the Nazis. In strange contradiction to the notion of racial superiority, they believed that in such marriages the Czech component usually prevails, causing the children to be lost to alien nationality.[36]

The introduction of the racial principle into marriage legislation was another bizarre example of Nazi decision-making. The process

[34]Cf. ordinances of March 29 and May 25, 1939, *Ministerialblatt des Reichs- und Preussischen Ministeriums des Innern,* 1939, pp. 786 and 1233–40.

[35]Examination of Stuckart, *U.S. v. Weizsäcker, Proceedings* (in English), p. 24559, CU.

[36]*Meld. Reich,* April 22, 1941, pp. 9–14, R 58/159, BA. Frank to Ministry of Interior, November 16, 1940, R 43 II/1325a, BA.

in all its incredible detail can be traced from documents. On April 4, 1940, Martin Bormann, the liaison man between Hitler and the Party Chancery, informed the Ministry of the Interior in Berlin: "The Führer has instructed me to notify you that officials who become sexually involved with Polish or Czech women are to be dismissed at once and without pension from state service."[37] The force which set the legislative machinery in motion had apparently been Hitler's sudden indignation, probably aroused by a scandalous report from Poland or the Protectorate. Despite the informal character of the directive, the legal experts of the Interior Ministry promptly drafted an ordinance. In their eagerness they extended the threat of dismissal to officials in the broadest sense of the word, including soldiers, SS men, and indeed all members of the Party. A "privy councillor" in the Reich Chancellery, who had received the draft for comments, noted its deficiencies and urged that the law also define "what is to be understood by the term 'become sexually involved,' whether, *e.g.*, a visit to a brothel in the respective areas is also to be covered."[38] This involved basic questions concerning race and the work on the proposed law was suspended, pending their clarification. But, in the meantime, the intriguing subject was being debated in Party circles. In August 1941, the journal *Der Parteirichter* published an article entitled: "Is Sexual Intercourse of Party Men and Women with the Members of the Polish and the Czech Ethnic Groups Liable to Prosecution by Party Courts?"[39] In his zeal for racial purity, the author, a certain Wendel, answered in the affirmative.

Unfortunately for him, however, a different official decision had already been made. By that time, Frank's and Neurath's memoranda on the Czech question had already reached Berlin, causing Hitler to change his mind in favor of assimilation. While no such revision applied to the Poles, the provisions about intermarriage with Czechs were adapted accordingly. Hans Globke, the Interior Ministry's expert in race legislation, drew up the new regulations.[40]

[37] Bormann to Frick, April 4, 1940, R 43 II/423a, BA.

[38] Note by Busch, August 12, 1940, *ibid.*

[39] "Ist der geschlechtliche Umgang von Parteigenossen und Parteigenossinen mit Angehörigen des polnischen und tschechischen Volkes parteigerichtlich zu verfolgen?" *Der Parteirichter*, August 15, 1941, pp. 1–3.

[40] Circular of April 3, 1941, Nur. NO-2580, IfZ. Ordinance of June 6, 1941, *RGB*, 1941, I, p. 308. Cf. "Neue Veröffentlichung über Globke," in the daily *Stuttgarter Zeitung*, February 7, 1961.

Mixed marriages were allowed, though they henceforth required special authorization by the *Oberlandrat*. Applicants had to submit to racial investigation. According to an original provision, they were obliged to furnish nude photographs, a requirement later changed to pictures in bathing suits. If the examination did not bring conclusive results, as presumably in a majority of cases it did not, the authorities decided whether the alien candidate represented a "positive addition" to Germandom.[41]

With the question of mixed marriages settled, that of extra-marital sexual intercourse still presented a challenge. The Nazis believed that the problem involved not only "protection of German blood" but also "avoidance of public disturbance" and preservation of "peaceful working conditions."[42] Consequently, it became the subject of confidential police directives by the Reich Security Head Office. The male offender of Czech nationality was first to be examined for his political views. If these were hostile to the Reich, he was liable to immediate shipment to a concentration camp. The same treatment applied in case of rape or of intercourse with a married German woman, especially the wife of a serviceman. In all other cases, the culprit's racial qualities were to be investigated. If he was found fit, the authorities tried to persuade the couple to marry. If the verdict was negative, the male offender went to a concentration camp. With characteristic pedantry, the Nazi bureaucrats crowned their achievement with the following proviso: "In cases of sexual intercourse between Protectorate citizens and German prostitutes investigation as to fitness for Germanization is superfluous. Since German blood is not imperiled, nor is there any danger to public order and peaceful working conditions, state police measures are as a rule unnecessary in such cases."[43]

Striving for fictitious racial purity, the Nazis did not win many converts to Germandom. Even after the fall of France, when more Czechs than ever before or after considered acquiring Reich citizenship, the total number of applicants was negligible.[44] Those

[41] About the grotesque elements in these examinations, see the affidavit by Karl Schoepke, August 4, 1942, Nur. NO-5112, CU. Cf. "Die Tätigkeit des RuSHA-SS auf dem Gebiet des Staatsangehörigkeitswesens in Böhmen und Mähren," January 25, 1944, Nur. NO-4122, CU.

[42] Decree of June 13, 1942, Nur. NO-1391, IfZ. Cf. circular of May 10, 1944, Nur. NO-1388, IfZ.

[43] *Ibid.*

[44] Cf. Král, *Pravda*, p. 160.

who did apply hardly represented a desirable addition to the German nation. The Security Service had a gloomy view of their qualities:

Criminals with Czech names and without the slightest knowledge of German have recently reported themselves as Germans in order to avoid prosecution by Czech courts . . . . In the provincial prison at Pardubice, all fourteen inmates professed German nationality, some of them reporting voluntarily for military service. All have previous conviction records—some over twenty and one of fifty-four previous convictions.[45]

Oberlandrat Krohmer from Klatovy commented that "so far decent and respectable Czechs have not presented themselves, only rubbish (*Gesindel*) has."[46] During the entire occupation, the number of Germans in the Protectorate increased by no more than 70,000.[47] Since this figure included officials on tour of duty and immigrants from other parts of the Reich, the actual number of converts was considerably lower, well under one per cent of the total population.

Rather than the lower classes, where the percentage of the racially unacceptable was presumably highest, the Nazis were interested in assimilating the Czech intellectual elite. But among these very intellectuals opposition to Germanization was particularly strong. Indicative of their attitude was the fate of a plan to recruit Czech students for German universities. The first announcement of this plan, published on March 1, 1941, cautiously limited the proposed fields of study to such "non-political" disciplines as medicine, engineering, and forestry. The choice was further limited to universities in solidly German areas, excluding such "frontier" places as Strasbourg, Vienna, and Königsberg. Admission depended upon a high racial rating. Out of an undisclosed total number, thirty-three candidates were accepted. After the first semester, one of them applied for German citizenship, another expressed the wish to join the *Waffen-SS*, but a third proved to be a fanatical Germanophobe. The behavior of the rest was "politically

[45] Report of Security Service Prague for June 1940, Král (ed.)., *Die Deutschen*, p. 410.
[46] Note on conference of *Oberlandräte*, August 15, 1940, *ibid.*, p. 416. Cf. Bosák, "Germanizační úloha německých škol na Českobudějovicku za okupace" [The Germanization Task of the German Schools in the Budweis Country during the Occupation], *Jihočeský sborník historický*, XXXIII (1964), pp. 70–72.
[47] Král, *Otázky*, I, p. 45.

extremely cautious."[48] The experiment was repeated in the fall of 1941. Out of 20,000 eligible students, only fifteen applied on the first two days. On the third day, the number of applications dropped to ten and on the fourth day to two.[49]

The arrogance of the Nazi rulers discouraged the little social contact that had existed between the two nationalities at the beginning of the occupation. The Czechs were initially less hostile to newcomers from the Reich who lacked the prejudices of their Sudeten German compatriots, and thus compared favorably with the stereotyped conceptions about Germans prevalent in Bohemia and Moravia. Upper-class Czechs, particularly aristocrats, were not averse to educated Germans, many of whom were critical of the Nazi excesses. For political reasons as well, high officials of the Protectorate government sought the company of the conservatives around Neurath.[50] In Bohemia and Moravia, however, formal social life had never been extensive, and mixing with Germans on other than a strictly business level soon became tainted with treason in the minds of the Czechs. For their part, the radical Nazis wished their compatriots always to behave like "masters from top to toe" and viewed the socializing between Czech and German aristocrats with particular apprehension.[51]

In contrast to their economic policies in the Protectorate, the Nazis' approach to the nationality question was singularly inept. Grotesque rather than brutal, their effort to implement this policy was half-hearted and inevitably ineffective. On the one hand, the Czechs were not being forced to become Germans by such drastic methods as those applied—with a measure of success—in the incorporated Polish territories. On the other hand, the doubtful privileges of Reich citizenship—which included liability to draft and Party interference in private life—failed to appeal to most people in the Protectorate. Moreover, the Germans continually revealed a great propensity for petty-minded insults to the Czechs'

[48] *Der Neue Tag*, March 2, 1941. Note by Kritzinger, June 27, 1941, R 43 II/132b, BA. Frank to Lammers, October 21, 1941, AA, T-120, 1505, D 632713–14, NA.

[49] *Brünner Tageblatt*, September 14, 1941. Report of Security Service Prague, September 19, 1941, in Král (ed.), *Die Deutschen*, pp. 454–55.

[50] H. Masařík, "Poslední měsíce s generálem Eliášem" [The Last Months with General Eliáš], *Reportér*, III (1968), No. 21, p. ii.

[51] Heydrich's speech of October 2, 1941, in Král (ed.), *Vergangenheit*, p. 130. Heydrich's speech of February 4, 1942, in Č. Amort (ed.), *Heydrichiáda*, pp. 140–42. Cf. Burgsdorff to Interior Ministry, March 8, 1941, R 43 II/1325a, BA.

national feelings. They carried the overwhelming responsibility for generating an atmosphere of national hatred in Bohemia and Moravia which would cost them dearly at the end of the war, and preclude the possibility of further coexistence between the Germans and the Czechs in that area.

8 *POLITICS—OFFICIAL AND UNDERGROUND*

T HE MOST influential Czech politician in occupied Bohemia and Moravia was a person who did not even live in the country. He was Edvard Beneš, who had left Czechoslovakia for voluntary exile shortly after he resigned the Presidency in October 1938. Aware that his presence represented at that time an insuperable obstacle to Czechoslovakia's good relations with Germany, he took this step admittedly "of [his] own free will and in accordance with [his] personal conviction."[1] He even congratulated his successor, Hácha, on having been elected President.[2] But Beneš's departure from the country and from politics was at most a vacillation, not the result of firm conviction. By the time Hitler entered Prague in March 1939, Beneš was already actively working on behalf of the Czech cause abroad. He toured the United States, explaining his policy during the Munich crisis and mobilizing sympathy for his people. In Beneš's home country, hostility against him diminished considerably, although it had not disappeared altogether, and most Czechs viewed the activities of the former President with hopeful approval. He was, after all, a statesman of international stature and none of his compatriots could even remotely compare with him in political skill and experience.

Apart from the Munich fiasco, Beneš's credentials as leader of the liberation movement were impressive. Once before—during World War I—he had directed Czech diplomatic activities with striking success. As Czechoslovakia's Foreign Minister for twenty years, he had established excellent contacts in both the West and the East. He was thoroughly at home in the lobbies of great international conferences and in the anterooms of high foreign officials. As a scion of a small nation, he had a sure instinct for approaching the powerful of the world. And, as a man who—in Beneš's own

[1] Beneš's radio address of October 5, 1938, *Memoirs of Eduard Beneš*, p. 292.
[2] Beneš to Hácha, November 30, 1938, *ibid.*, pp. 96–97.

words—was "always ready to deny and humiliate himself if it was in the state's interest," he was well qualified to win their sympathetic attention.[3] His patience and his influential acquaintances were the keys to his success.[4]

Beneš had the skill of a great diplomat but not the wisdom of a great statesman. Often vainglorious and dictatorial in his dealings with subordinates, he was unsure of himself when great decisions were at stake and when the eyes of millions were turned toward him—as in the Munich crisis. He was not an inspiring national leader. His people respected but never loved him, a significant contrast to their feelings about his predecessor, Tomáš Masaryk. First and foremost a servant of the state, Beneš did not aspire to a place in the hearts of his people. Politics was for him not a vocation but a profession where expertise mattered most. Jaromír Smutný, one of his closest aides and admirers, wondered at "the absence of everything human in his character. He is a machine for thinking and working, without human feelings, though with human weaknesses . . . . He has lost contact with people. Therefore he often misjudges them if their motives are other than political."[5]

One of the last great practitioners of the "old diplomacy," Beneš was not an ideal leader in the age of mass politics and ideologies. His very realism was likely to become a weakness in dealing with such adversaries as the Nazis or the Communists, whose behavior often defied the traditional norms. Yet in 1939, Beneš was still concerned mainly with the Western governments. His principal ambition was to win their diplomatic recognition, and this task suited him perfectly.

In Beneš's opinion, Hitler's occupation of Bohemia and Moravia and the failure of the French and British to uphold Czechoslovakia's Munich frontiers invalidated the fateful agreement of September 30, 1938. He now felt "freed from all earlier obligations which [he] had temporarily imposed" upon himself as a result of

[3] Smutný's note on conversation with Beneš, April 2, 1941, *DHCSP*, I, p. 196.

[4] Beneš's complex and elusive personality still awaits a balanced historical judgment. P. E. Zinner's excellent essay, "Czechoslovakia: The Diplomacy of Eduard Beneš," in *The Diplomats*, ed. by G. A. Craig and F. Gilbert, covers only Beneš's career before Munich. Křen's short evaluation of Beneš's 1938–1939 policies (*Do emigrace*, pp. 242–65) is an intelligent though heavily biased account by a leading Czech Marxist historian. The same applies for his "Dr. Beneš za války" [Dr. Beneš during the War], *Československý časopis historický*, XIII (1965), pp. 797–826.

[5] Smutný's note, March 22, 1940, *DHCSP*, I, pp. 91–92.

Munich.[6] Although not explicitly stated, this interpretation also implied that his resignation from the Presidency was in abeyance. "The so-called First Republic again existed legally!"[7] In May 1939, he formally notified Paris, London, and the League of Nations that despite the Nazi occupation Czechoslovakia continued to exist.

Beneš's act was an important political gesture but he hardly presented a convincing legal case. No foreign government endorsed his position. Both France and Britain condemned the occupation, and Prime Minister Chamberlain had harsh words to say about Hitler's disregard for solemn promises, but neither government viewed the Munich agreement as defunct.[8] They did not withdraw recognition from Hácha. Unable to maintain diplomatic relations with his administration without German permission, France and Britain preferred to liquidate their legations in Prague. While this act at least denied legitimacy to Hitler's *fait accompli*, most other governments, including those of the United States and the Soviet Union, complied with German wishes and transformed their diplomatic missions in Prague into consulates, thus recognizing the Protectorate *de facto*.[9] Several of them, however, gave expression to their disapproval of the Nazi aggression by tolerating the continued existence of Czechoslovak legations in their capitals. Thus—in defiance of instructions from Prague and Berlin—these legations remained open in London, Paris, Washington, Moscow, and other cities as token vestiges of Czechoslovak statehood.

The ambiguous international response to the occupation did not completely extinguish Beneš's hopes for recognition but neither did it greatly improve the case for the restoration of national independence. In fact, no other victim of Hitler's aggression—with the possible exception of Austria—had poorer prospects for regaining freedom than did Czechoslovakia in 1939. Even the outbreak of the war did not change this unfavorable situation significantly. The French allowed the Czechs to establish a separate military unit but not a government-in-exile. Only on October 17, 1939, did they

---

[6] *Memoirs of Eduard Beneš*, p. 64.

[7] *Ibid.*

[8] Cf. Broszat, "Die Reaktion der Mächte," pp. 265–69.

[9] The complex legal and prestige questions involved in the German exequatur to the American Consulate in Prague are evident from the diplomatic exchanges between Washington and Berlin, printed in *Foreign Relations of the United States: Diplomatic Papers*, 1939, II, pp. 457–67.

consent to the creation of a Czechoslovak National Committee, headed by Beneš, without specifying its international status.[10] They still viewed Hácha's position as "a temporary captivity" and calculated that upon the extinction of German rule, he—rather than Beneš, the living reminder of France's disgraceful conduct in 1938 —would resume full governmental powers.[11] The British, too, were reluctant to commit themselves to the restoration of pre-Munich Czechoslovakia, which they recalled as an unhappy amalgam of nationalities, and remained reserved in their response to Beneš's overtures.[12]

Not only were the Czech exiles in an unenviable international position during the "phony war." Their relations among themselves, too, were far from satisfactory. A prominent member of the emigration lamented:

What our resistance movement abroad is lacking especially is atmosphere: that of confidence, friendship, coexistence and collaboration. On the contrary, we live in an atmosphere of constant, general and persisting mistrust, struggle, conflict, controversy, competition for authority, in a war of all against all. It is a fight under the false pretense of cooperation. I have not found even two persons who would agree on a common positive work. Only in criticizing other people, always in a malevolent way, can we agree.[13]

To complicate matters, the ethnic composition of the émigré group made it a poor spokesman for Czechoslovakia as a single entity. There were only a few Slovaks among the exiles—uncomfortable evidence that the old republic's second largest people was significantly less nostalgic for a common state than the Czechs. The core of the liberation movement abroad consisted of the several thousand persons who had escaped from Bohemia and Moravia— usually via Poland or Slovakia and Hungary—before the Germans sealed the frontiers in late 1940.[14] Not all Slovak politicians in

[10] Cf. proclamation by the Committee, October 17, 1939, *DHCSP*, I, pp. 47–48. Note of October 15, 1939, *ibid.*, pp. 41–42.

[11] Cf. reference in Pasák, "Aktivističtí novináři a postoj generála Eliáše v roce 1941" [The Activist Newsmen and General Eliáš's Attitude in 1941], *Československý časopis historický*, XV (1967), p. 175.

[12] Cf. note about press conference in British Foreign Office, December 27, 1939, *DHCSP*, I, p. 66. Halifax's address, March 14, 1940, *ibid.*, p. 86.

[13] Smutný's note, March 22, 1940, *ibid.*, p. 91.

[14] On the escape routes from the Protectorate, see J. Přikryl, "Příspěvek k ilegálním přechodům hranic na jihovýchodní Moravě na počátku nacistické okupace" [Illegal Border Crossings in Southeastern Moravia at the Beginning of the Nazi Occupation], *Odboj a revoluce*, V (1967), No. 2, Supplement, pp. 137–52.

exile recognized Beneš's leadership, and one of them, Milan Hodža —who had been Czechoslovak Prime Minister before Munich— created in Paris a rival Slovak National Council. Štefan Osuský, another Slovak—who served as Minister to Paris—challenged the former President's authority on legal grounds; in his view, active diplomats—like Osuský himself—were more credible representatives of constitutional continuity than a President who had voluntarily resigned his office.[15]

Paradoxically enough, only France's military *débâcle* in June 1940 significantly improved the prospects of the Czechoslovak liberation movement. From doomed France, its headquarters moved to defiant England, where Beneš figured prominently among the many exiled chiefs of state who had flocked to London. In July 1940, the British allowed him to establish a government-in-exile, although they still withheld full diplomatic recognition from it.[16] Beneš triumphed over his rivals and his leadership was no longer seriously contested. At the same time, the newly created Czechoslovak army earned praise for its share in the Battle of Britain. The Czechoslovaks were now co-belligerents with a strong claim for the restoration of their independence. Full recognition of this claim was merely a question of time.

This was a significant success, but Beneš considered it insufficient to assure Czechoslovakia's international status on a firmer basis than in 1938. To achieve this goal, he was willing to sacrifice all other priorities. He was guided by an almost obsessive urge to erase the consequences of Munich, which he had considered a personal humiliation. Although he asserted that in the liberation movement the suffering nation must play the decisive political role, in reality he regarded the domestic front as secondary in importance. As in World War I, Beneš expected that diplomacy alone, strengthened by the military exploits of Czechoslovak troops on the Allied side, would bring freedom. In that case, the politicians at home would merely confirm the deeds of the exiles by proclaiming independence once the enemy had been

[15] The best study on this subject is J. Křen, "Hodža—slovenská otázka v zahraničním odboji" [Hodža and the Slovak Question in the Resistance Movement Abroad], *Československý časopis historický*, XVI (1968), pp. 193–214.

[16] Halifax to Beneš, July 21, 1940, quoted in *Memoirs of Eduard Beneš*, p. 301. The basic facts about the Czechoslovak liberation movement abroad during World War II are summarized in G. Skilling, "The Czechoslovak Struggle for National Liberation," *The Slavonic and East European Review*, XXXIX (1960), pp. 174–97.

defeated.[17] Consequently, Beneš tried to subordinate the resistance movement in the Protectorate to his personal authority and to the requirements of his diplomacy.

As in most countries of occupied Europe, the underground in Bohemia and Moravia grew from informal discussion groups attended by persons of similar political opinions and professional background.[18] Such gatherings took place soon after March 15. By the summer of 1939, three groupings, not counting the Communists, had crystallized. Convinced of an early end to Nazi rule, their members were primarily concerned with political arrangements after the liberation. Farthest to the right stood the "Nation's Defense" (*Obrana národa*, ON), organized by former Czechoslovak military officers to provide the framework of a future secret army.[19] It consisted of a "staff," "territorial commands" and special services, such as intelligence, communications, sabotage, and others.[20] The ON, though it did not explicitly repudiate Beneš, initially tended to prefer a temporary military dictatorship after the expected defeat of Germany. The "Political Center" (*Politické ústředí*, PÚ), which included some of the former President's closest associates, envisaged a system of government closely resembling the pre-Munich model: besides a strong President, there should be a coalition government by five major parties.[21] The left-wing "Committee of the Petition 'We Remain Faithful'" (*Petiční výbor "Věrni zůstaneme,"* PVVZ), had a following especially among Social

[17] Cf. Beneš's message, November 5, 1939, quoted in Král, *Otázky*, III, p. 214. E. Beneš to Vojta Beneš, end of March 1940, *DHCSP*, I, pp. 96–99.

[18] The Czech literature on the Protectorate underground has grown immensely as the policies of its non-Communist wing have been gradually rehabilitated in Czechoslovakia from the mid-1960's onward. Of the many studies of uneven value, the most informative for the 1939–1941 period is V. Kural, "Hlavní organizace nekomunistického odboje v letech 1939–1941" [The Principal Organizations of the Non-Communist Resistance Movement in 1939–1941], *Odboj a revoluce*, V (1967), No. 2, pp. 5–160.

[19] J. Přikryl, "Vojenská odbojová organizace Obrana národa" [The Military Resistance Organization "Nation's Defense"], *Sborník Matice moravské*, LXXXVI (1967), pp. 43–60. J. Křen, "Vojenský odboj na počátku okupace Československa" [Military Resistance at the Beginning of the Occupation of Czechoslovakia], *Historie a vojenství*, 1961, pp. 271–313.

[20] Kural, "Hlavní organizace," pp. 17–20.

[21] The book about the PÚ by Jaroslav Jelínek, *PÚ—Politické ústředí domácího odboje* [The Political Center of Home Resistance], published shortly after the war, is valuable as testimony by a participant.

Democratic intellectuals and labor unionists.[22] They insisted that reforms in the spirit of democratic socialism must complement national liberation. By the end of 1939, all these groups had accepted Beneš's authority.

The relations between the underground and the exiles were extensive. In June 1939, General Sergej Ingr, a prominent member of the ON, joined Beneš in London.[23] Although Ingr's mandate as delegate of the underground was later contested, his arrival provided the first vital link between the resistance movements at home and abroad, and reinforced Beneš's claim for leadership. From March 1939 to October 1941, over fourteen thousand messages are said to have been exchanged between the Protectorate and the exile centers in Paris and London. Courier services were performed by Czechs travelling on business missions to neutral countries and by diplomats from these countries. Secret radio stations operated from September 1939 onward. The Czechoslovak intelligence officers, who had escaped from Prague on the eve of the German invasion, restored their "Second Bureau" in London to gather military information and relay it to their British colleagues.[24] In the Protectorate, a remarkable network, created by the chief of the official

[22] The peculiar name of this group referred to a committee which had conducted a campaign for national defense during the 1938 crisis. About the program and ramifications of the PVVZ, see the accounts by the Gestapo in the sentence of Oleg Procházka *et al.*, October 7, 1942, Nur. NG-1909, IfZ; and indictment of Fischer and Pešek, September 6, 1944, Nur. NG-1897, IfZ. The article on the PVVZ by V. Vrabec is informative but it lacks references to sources: "Petiční výbor 'Věrni zůstaneme' [The Committee of the Petition "We Remain Faithful"], *Odboj a revoluce*, V (1967), No. 2, Supplement, pp. 21–37.

[23] There are conflicting interpretations of the motives for Ingr's departure: Stránský's memorandum, October 5, 1939, *DHCSP*, I, p. 24. Note on conference at the Czechoslovak Legation in Paris, October 7, 1939, *ibid*, p. 26. F. Machát, "Vzpomínky na spolupráci s generálem Bílým" [Reminiscenses about Collaboration with General Bílý], *Odboj a revoluce*, V (1967), No. 2, Supplement, pp. 8–9. T. Pasák, "Nekomunistický odboj a jeho spolupráce s protektorátní vládou" [The Cooperation of the Non-Communist Resistance Movement with the Protectorate Government], *ibid.*, pp. 71–72.

[24] Notes about a conference between Beneš and Czechoslovak Communists, December 13–20, 1943, in *Cesta ke Květnu* [The Path of May], I, p. 41. Beneš to Stránský, August 1, 1945, *DHCSP*, II, p. 752. Cf. "Zásady organisace spojovací služby" [Organizational Rules of the Communication Service], April 2, 1940, *ibid.*, I, pp. 99–100. The article by V. Kahan contains a mass of plausible information but no source references: "Úloha a úroveň zpravodajství v nekomunistickém odboji" [The Role and Quality of Intelligence in the Non-Communist Resistance Movement], *Odboj a revoluce*, V (1967), No. 2, Supplement, pp. 87–112.

Czech censorship bureau, supplied them with the desired news. It employed former army officers who had been placed as district censors throughout the country. This network was destroyed by the German police as early as August 1939.[25] But the ON continued to relay other valuable news, especially information from Paul Thümmel, the double agent working in the German counter-intelligence agency.

These early activities of the underground compared favorably with those in other European countries at the onset of the Nazi occupation, an evidence of the Czechs' recovery from the post-Munich malaise. But by late 1939 the resistance organizations began to suffer extensive persecution. It started with the decimation of the ON after a Gestapo raid in December. Radio contact with London was then interrupted for four months. By April 1940, the police had arrested fifteen hundred persons suspected of resistance activities. The German State Prosecutor anticipated at that time a further fifteen hundred to three thousand arrests.[26] Some of the surviving members of the underground blamed the Czech broadcasts of the Paris radio for having inadvertently given hints to the Gestapo. A more plausible explanation for the disaster, however, was given in a message dated March 1940: "Due to the clumsiness of our people, pogrom after pogrom has been directed against us with the result that now we remain merely a handful."[27]

The resistance strategy was adjusted only slowly to these harsh conditions. At the outbreak of the war, a London directive urged "armed resistance and sabotage on a mass scale, to start simultaneously over the entire territory, upon signal by the British radio . . . which will be given shortly."[28] The German victory in Poland had a sobering effect upon such calculations. By September 29, Ingr, now Beneš's chief military aide, had rescinded these instructions and sensibly recommended that the underground postpone a general uprising until Germany's weakness warranted its success.

[25] Sentence of Eliáš, October 1, 1941, Nur. NG-147, IfZ. Cf. A Bareš and T. Pasák, "Odbojová organizace Zdeňka Schmoranze" [Zdeněk Schmoranz's Resistance Organization], *Historie a vojenství*, 1968, pp. 1003–1033.

[26] Lautz to Ministry of Justice, April 4, 1940, Nur. NG-682, IfZ. Engert to Ministry of Justice, January 12, 1940, Nur. NG-791, CU.

[27] Message to Beneš, March 1, 1940, quoted in Křen, "Vojenský odboj," p. 284. PVVZ message to Beneš, December 28, 1939, *DHCSP*, II, p. 499.

[28] Message from London to Prague, September 8, 1939, quoted in Kural, "Hlavní organizace," p. 49.

He instead requested continued intelligence activities and inconspicuous subversion.[29]

Shaken by the German executions of students in November 1939, the underground warned against "unnecessary sacrifices."[30] Beneš expressed the same opinion in a broadcast from London on December 3.[31] He continued to believe with his people that the collapse of Germany was imminent, thus making superfluous any further confrontation with the occupation power. The preparation of measures to be taken after liberation seemed more pressing. So optimistic were Beneš's followers in Prague that they urged him to have new currency notes printed quickly, so that they could be flown in promptly as soon as German rule had ended.[32]

Despite persecution, the underground consolidated its ranks. It created the Central Leadership of Home Resistance (ÚVOD) as a shadow government for the future. This body was to step in to prevent continued exercise of power by men who had compromised themselves by collaborating with the enemy. Although the term *ÚVOD* appears in documents from early 1940 onward, its actual role as the supreme resistance organ is questionable. Only in the fall of that year did the PÚ, ON and PVVZ profess adherence to it.[33] We do not know whether the ÚVOD consisted of a definite number of persons with clearly defined functions. It is certain, however, that it acted as the principal clandestine intermediary between Beneš and the Protectorate. Despite further arrests, the ÚVOD continued to exist until 1941.

In contrast with the ÚVOD, which owed allegiance to London, another significant segment of the underground, the Communist party (CPC), depended exclusively upon direction from Moscow. The party's peculiar position on the Czech political scene before 1938 and the subsequent vicissitudes of Soviet foreign policy explain the ambiguous role of the Communists in the Protectorate. Two characteristic features of the pre-1938 CPC were crucial for its later destinies; its devotion to legal methods of political struggle

[29] Ingr's message to Prague, September 29, 1939, *ibid.*, p. 50.

[30] Message from Prague for Beneš, December 1939, *DHCSP*, II, p. 497.

[31] Beneš's radio address, December 3, 1939, *ibid.*, pp. 489–91.

[32] Summary of messages received from the Protectorate, March 14, 1939, *ibid.*, p. 512.

[33] Kural, "Hlavní organizace," pp. 69–72. A. Polavský's *V boj* [Into Combat], is an account of the principal underground newspaper which includes extensive, though not reliably documented information about the ÚVOD.

and its intense loyalty to Moscow.[34] Throughout the period of the pre-Munich Republic, the party was active in parliamentary politics. It used to poll almost a million votes—the strongest legal Communist party in Europe outside the Soviet Union and France in 1938. It seldom had to deal with heresy or deviation from the Moscow line. In conformity with Comintern strategy, the Czech Communists tried—though never successfully—to form a Popular Front government, and they strongly advocated the defense of the Republic in 1938. Their strong indentification with the national cause at that critical time and their tradition of legal struggle proved a temporary liability after the party had been officially banned in December 1938. Its rank and file shared political apathy with the rest of their compatriots, making little progress in building an underground organization. After March 15, they became an easy prey of *Aktion Gitter*, the Gestapo roundup which immediately followed the invasion.[35]

The recovery of the CPC paralleled the revival of Czech national spirit in the summer of 1939. The clandestine Central Committee of the Communist party established radio contacts with Moscow. Some of its members left for the Soviet Union, others went to Paris—a latter-day manifestation of their persistent hopes for an East-West alliance against Nazi Germany. In Paris, the party issued its first public program, whose tenets were echoed in leaflets distributed in the Protectorate.[36] The Communists continued to profess adherence to the concepts of the Popular Front and collective security. Thus they stood for the restoration of Czechoslovakia and, though refusing to recognize Beneš's leadership, they proclaimed readiness to cooperate with anyone opposed to Nazism. In the Protectorate, Beneš's followers viewed the

[34]The best history of the CPC between the wars is the doctoral dissertation by M. P. Mabey, "The Origin and Development of the Communist Party of Czechoslovakia, 1918–1938." Cf. H. G. Skilling, "Communism and Czechoslovak Traditions," *Journal of International Affairs*, XX (1966), No. 1, pp. 118–36.

[35]Cf. J. Kmoníček, "Ilegální činnost KSČ na Královéhradecku, 1938–1941" [Underground Activities of the CPC in the Hradec Králové Country], *Odboj a revoluce*, IV (1966), No. 4, Supplement, pp. 42–43. L. Klimešová and B. Pekárek, "Ilegální tisk" [The Underground Press], *ibid.*, p. 31.

[36]Manifesto of July 10, 1939, *Za svobodu českého a slovenského národa* [For the Freedom of the Czech and Slovak Peoples], pp. 31–33. Cf. O. Janeček, "K programové činnosti zahraničního vedení KSČ v první polovině roku 1939" [Programs of the CPC's Foreign Leadership in the First Half of 1939], *Odboj a revoluce*, IV (1966), No. 4, Supplement, pp. 154–59.

activities of the Communist party favorably, and abroad, the former President himself even contemplated inviting its exiled representatives into his proposed "parliament" in exile.[37]

The Nazi-Soviet pact of August 23, 1939 ruthlessly destroyed such hopes, dramatizing the Communists' conflict between patriotism and obedience to Moscow.[38] Immediately after the incredible news had become known, the underground leadership issued leaflets, trying desperately to reassure the rank and file: "Await quietly the news from the Soviet Union . . . . Remember how many dirty campaigns have been led against the Soviet Union, and at the end [it] alone was always right. Stick faithfully to the Soviet Union!"[39] While the Central Committee was still awaiting new directives from Moscow, the war broke out. The directives finally started coming via secret radio from September 8 onward.[40]

The Czech Communists—like their colleagues elsewhere in Europe—were asked for a heartbreaking *volte face* for the exclusive benefit of the Soviet Union. Moscow, jealously guarding its fresh territorial acquisitions in eastern Europe, did not wish to see these gains jeopardized by an overwhelming victory of either belligerent group. Hoping for a military stalemate which would confirm the *status quo* created by the extinction of Poland, the Kremlin ordered the Communist parties to interpret the war as imperialist on both sides. Such reasoning was difficult to accept

[37] Message from Prague to Beneš, August 19, 1939, *DHCSP*, II, p. 444. Cf. E. Táborský, *Pravda zvítězila*, p. 294. Cf. *DHCSP*, I, p. 17.

[38] Although the Comintern archives remain closed, the tortuous course of Communist policies can be reconstructed from information made available by Czechoslovak historians from their own party archives. Besides the highly selective *Za svobodu českého a slovenského národa*, the following editions of sources are indispensable: J. Radimský, "Letáky z počátku druhé světové války" [Leaflets from the Beginning of World War II], *Sborník Matice moravské*, LXXXIV (1965), pp. 258–77; M. Pravdová, "Soupis nejvýznamnějších komunistických letáků rozšiřovaných ve středních Čechách v letech 1939–1941" [A List of the Most Important Communist Leaflets Distributed in Central Bohemia in 1939–1941], in *Středočeské kapitoly z dějin okupace*, pp. 157–94. Only a few accounts of the CPC's wartime activities meet scholarly standards; the most reliable are: F. Janáček, "Linie a ideologie KSČ, 1939–1941" [CPC's Line of Policy and Ideology, 1939–1941], *Odboj a revoluce*, IV (1966), No. 4, pp. 5–64; J. Novotný, "Činnost KSČ v letech 1938–1941" [CPC's Activities 1938–1941], *ibid.*, pp. 65–114.

[39] Č. Amort (ed.), *Na pomoc československému lidu* [To the Aid of the Czechoslovak People], p. 198.

[40] G. Bareš and O. Janeček (eds.), "Depeše mezi Prahou a Moskvou" [The Radio Messages between Prague and Moscow], *Příspěvky k dějinám KSČ*, VII (1967), pp. 389–90.

unconditionally and the editorialist in the CPC's clandestine news-paper, *Rudé právo*, asked in disbelief: "Doesn't everybody know that there is only one danger and one principal enemy, German Fascism and the handful of traitors, lackeys and cowards allied with it?"[41] Throughout October, contradictory statements still appeared in the Communist press: Beneš was alternately praised for his anti-Communist efforts and abused as a tool of the "Western warlords." Only by November was the victory of the new Moscow line complete, although a purge of several members of the Central Committee may have been necessary to assure this outcome.[42]

Despite the ostensible condemnation of both camps in the "imperialist" war, the Soviet and Communist position was not so non-committal as it may seem. Since the West still appeared to be the stronger party, Moscow found it advisable to encourage a stalemate between the warring imperialists by favoring the Germans. The Comintern's confidential instructions to Prague urged friendship with the "German worker, though today wearing the enemy uniform." Or, in another message: "We stand along with the German working people against England and France as aggressors."[43] In the Protectorate, Communist tracts—pretending to defend the workers' rights—attacked the Czech capitalists more vehemently than the Nazi oppressors, thus diverting attention from the political to the economic struggle. The abstract talk of a proletarian revolution in Europe, including Germany, was obviously merely window dressing.

Just how far the Communists supported Germany's cause during the heyday of the Berlin-Moscow *rapprochement* is very difficult to document. In June 1940, Goebbels indicated that he was using the services of French and German Communists in preparing radio broadcasts which were intended to undermine the morale of the population in France. After its collapse, the French Communist party applied for permission to publish a daily newspaper under

---

[41] Cf. Janáček, "Linie," pp. 27–29. In a message to Moscow on September 6, the Prague Central Committee protested against what it termed "the rotten bureau-cratism" of the Moscow radio broadcasts. Bareš and Janeček (eds.), "Depeše," p. 389.

[42] Cf. underground report to Beneš, October 15, 1939, quoted in B. Lašťovička, *V Londýně za války* [In London during the War], p. 222. Article by Václav Majer, in D. Healey (ed.), *The Curtain Falls*, p. 86.

[43] Cf. Janáček, *Dva smery*, pp. 300, 306. Jelínek, *PÚ—Politické ústředí*, p. 94. Janáček, "Linie," p. 41.

German auspices, an initiative which the Nazis turned down, perhaps because they preferred more discreet forms of collaboration.[44] In the Protectorate, too, there seems to have existed a peculiar kind of symbiosis between the clandestine party organizations and the German police. In any case, the CPC suffered relatively little persecution between August 1939 and May 1940. This was less likely a result of conspiratorial skills—which the Communists were in no better position to acquire than anyone else in the underground—than of deliberate German leniency. Among most Czechs, the Communists enjoyed the reputation of reliable, though politically somewhat naive patriots.[45] But even diligent researchers have not been able to unearth convincing evidence to prove that the party's activities were aimed at harming the occupation power during this period.[46]

Only after the Nazi military victories, which chilled the German-Soviet relationship by mid-1940, were many Czech Communists seriously persecuted. Early in 1941, on the night of February 12–13, the Gestapo arrested almost the entire Central Committee and destroyed its radio communications with Moscow.[47] Quite understandably, the pro-German note of the party propaganda was toned down, although not to the extent of giving up its pathetic "neutrality" completely. And from the Soviet side, as late as December 1940, for example, Moscow was still urging Czech Communists to suspend anti-German criticism, apparently for fear of harming the Berlin negotiations Molotov was undertaking at that time.[48]

By mid-1941, all segments of the underground had been hit hard by police intervention and only a few active new members joined

---

[44] Goebbels's conference of June 2, 1940, in Boelcke (ed.), *Kriegspropaganda, 1939–1941*, p. 375. A. Rossi, *Physiologie du parti communiste français*, p. 18.

[45] Gabriel to Gürtner, January 22, 1940, R 22/3384, BA. Sipo report of December 6, 1939, quoted in Král, *Otázky*, III, p. 220.

[46] For example Kmoníček, "Ilegální činnost KSČ," pp. 41–82. Z. Jelínek, "Z dějin nacistické okupace a hnutí odporu na Kutnohorsku" [The History of the Nazi Occupation and the Resistance Movement in the Kutná Hora Country], *Středočeské kapitoly z dějin okupace*, pp. 54–99.

[47] Novotný, "Činnost KSČ," pp. 113–14. Cf. "Přehled politické situace v Čechách a na Moravě v červnu 1940" [A Survey of the Political Situation in Bohemia and Moravia in June 1940], July 20, 1940, *DHCSP*, II, p. 549.

[48] P. Stahl, "Niektoré problémy prechodu KSS do ilegality" [Problems Concerning the Passage of the Communist Party of Slovakia Underground], *Odboj a revoluce*, V (1967), No. 1, p. 41.

the depleted ranks. Oppression was harsh enough to deter potential recruits, yet not so harsh as to drive any substantial number of persons underground out of desperation. In late 1940, the authors of the secret messages to London complained that most people condemned the cowardice of others but were extremely unwilling to risk themselves.[49] The circulation of clandestine periodicals kept declining after 1939.[50] Reliable evidence of organized acts of sabotage is extremely scarce. Only in June 1940 did the Germans record the first proven case in the armament industries.[51] This was followed only sporadically by similar incidents. Thus the principal function of the resistance movement remained its ability to provide the vital link of communication between the Protectorate and the headquarters of the liberation movement abroad.

Prime Minister Eliáš played a key role in establishing contact between London and Prague. He may have solicited Beneš's approval before accepting his office in April 1939, and may have tried henceforth to develop his policies in conformity with those of the exiled leader.[52] Reliable evidence of contacts between the two statesmen dates from the summer of 1939. On June 26, Jan Masaryk, who was in London as the former Czechoslovak Minister to Britain, reported to Beneš:

Eliáš has just sent a message saying that he was placing himself entirely at my disposal, that he had taken the government job only in order to protect the nation against Frank, and that he and the entire cabinet were ready to resign if we should desire it. Even Hácha indicated that he would like to quit. I have strongly advised them not to do it: the Germans would definitely appoint Gajda and worse.[53]

Although no specific agreement between Beneš and Eliáš was probably ever concluded, a basic understanding existed between them. The exiles would work for liberation abroad while the Prague

[49] ÚVOD to London, July 1940, *DHCSP*, II, p. 553.

[50] For the entire occupation period, about 120 titles have so far been registered in the Protectorate, as compared with 1100 in Poland, 1000 in France, and 500 in Denmark. Klimešová and Pekárek, "Ilegální tisk," p. 39.

[51] A machine in the Explosia ammunition factory was damaged by sand and pieces of glass. Armament Inspection Board Prague, "Kriegstagebuch Nr. 4," folios 5, 88, 99, W 08-172/4, BA, MA. This war diary did not take into account a similar incident which occurred before the beginning of the war. W 01-8/295, BA, MA.

[52] Fierlinger to Pasák, November 28, 1966, quoted in Pasák, "Aktivističtí novináři," p. 176.

[53] Quoted in Křen, *Do emigrace*, p. 177.

government would protect the nation's interests at home. The cabinet would stay in office only as long as it was able to perform this function and it would resign as soon as the Germans began to benefit from its activity more than the Czechs. Such a moment was of course difficult to determine and the fear of reprisals was also likely to deter the ministers from resignation. Yet at the beginning, the unwritten agreement provided at least the basis for a working relationship between Prague and London.[54]

Despite the ambiguity of Beneš's Presidency, there was no disagreement between him and Hácha when the occupation started. Beneš avoided attacks against Hácha, and although he emphasized that the Protectorate had been imposed upon the Czechs illegally and against their will, he did not question the legitimacy of its government. For his part, Hácha refrained from statements which could be interpreted as acceptance of the present status of the country. He did not embarrass Beneš in his public pronouncements and carefully avoided mentioning him by name.[55]

The events of November 1939 created a painful dilemma for the Protectorate government. The cabinet contemplated resigning in protest against the persecution of the students. Since Frank made it clear, however, that he would consider such a move a provocation, and since Neurath appeared unable to restrain him, the resignation plan was shelved.[56] Alarmed by the growing number of arrests, the government decided that the time was not favorable for gestures of defiance. It apparently reached this conclusion independently, since the radio contacts with London were interrupted from December 1939 until late March 1940 and Eliáš had no possibility of quick consultation with exile headquarters. Only after the decision had been made did he send a note asking for Beneš's approval of "whatever opportunistic policy would prevent national and economic losses."[57] On the same day, the Prime

[54] Beneš to Stránský, August 1, 1945, *DHCSP*, II, pp. 751–53. Cf. J. Eliášová and T. Pasák (eds.), "Poznámky k Benešovým kontaktům s Eliášem ve druhé světové válce" [Beneš's Contacts with Eliáš during World War II], *Historie a vojenství*, 1967, pp. 108–40.

[55] Beneš's message to State Council, November 25, 1941, quoted in Lašťovička, *V Londýně*, pp. 225–26. Cf. Eliášová and Pasák (eds.), "Poznámky," p. 122. Hácha's declaration of September 7, 1939, *Der Neue Tag*, September 8, 1939.

[56] Message to Beneš, December 22, 1939, *DHCSP*, II, pp. 496–97. Examination of Havelka, news item in *Svobodné noviny*, February 6, 1947.

[57] Beneš to Stránský, August 1, 1945, *DHCSP*, II, p. 752. Message of December 8, 1939, quoted in Pasák, "Aktivističtí novináři," p. 175.

Minister stated in an interview with the correspondent of the Deutsches Nachrichten-Büro, the official German press agency, that he welcomed his country's association with Germany and condemned the claims of the exiles to speak in the name of the Czech people.[58] Other Czech spokesmen echoed this view, eliciting sarcastic comment by the Prague representative of the Wilhelmstrasse, Ziemke: "They probably take comfort in the thought that these declarations compromise no one because they will be regarded abroad as having been made under coercion. But there is no question of any coercion; the people have actually made these declarations voluntarily since they are fully aware that it is in their own interest to do so."[59]

In early 1940, the government had additional reasons for conciliating the Germans. Its contacts with the enemy appeared to have become known to the Gestapo, probably from the interrogations of arrested underground members. In January, two cabinet ministers who were deeply involved in these contacts escaped abroad with Eliáš's approval. They soon emerged in London as members of the Czechoslovak National Committee in exile. In March the Hungarian Minister to Berlin submitted information to the Nazis about a Czech escape-network supposedly protected by Prime Minister Eliáš.[60] By that time the Germans already knew that he was playing a double game. Ziemke reported to the Foreign Office in reference to Eliáš: "His anti-German attitude and his contacts with the émigré circles have already been confided to us by a reliable Czech source of information."[61]

But despite this evidence, Hitler decided to keep Eliáš in office "for the time being." His decision conformed to the relatively moderate course of German policy after Frank's independence had been curbed in December 1939. Possibly upon Neurath's prodding, the Führer may have agreed to experiment with leniency in order to cultivate the gratitude of the Czech officials. Thus the Protector also made no move to play up the affair of the fugitive ministers and let Hácha choose their successors.[62]

58 Press interview of December 8, 1939, *DHCSP*, II, pp. 493–94.

59 Ziemke to Foreign Office, December 15, 1939, *DGFP*, D, VIII, pp. 538–39.

60 Foreign Office to RSHA, March 29, 1940, Nur. NG-3051, IfZ.

61 Ziemke to Foreign Office, April 3, 1940, Nur. NG-2641, IfZ. Cf. Feierabend, *Ve vládě Protektorátu*, pp. 136–38.

62 Ziemke to Foreign Office, April 5, 1940, Nur. NG-2641, IfZ. Ziemke to Foreign Office, January 31, 1940, *DGFP*, D, VIII, p. 724. Neurath to Hitler, February 5, 1940, AA, T-120, 1505, D 632562, NA.

The President appreciated such magnanimity and on the first anniversary of the Protectorate he responded to a polite German request by sending an unusually obsequious telegram to Hitler:

The present day brings into my memory the time, one year ago, when I found with Your Excellency full understanding for the then severely tried Czech people. Taken by you under the protection of the Reich, they received a share in valuable advantages; in particular, they were spared the horrors of war, though themselves participating in the war within the Greater German Reich. Today, I feel an urge to call *Sieg und Heil* upon the glorious German weapons which also protect the Czech people.[63]

Undoubtedly delighted by the concluding sentence, which had been suggested to Hácha by Völckers, the Führer replied in a friendly and generous tone:

Thank you, Mr. President, for your wishes in the great struggle which our common Reich is forced to wage today. I do wish that the final victory would bring the Czech, no less than the German people, lasting peace, prosperity and great social benefit.[64]

Even Frank, inaugurating the new official magazine *Böhmen und Mähren* at a special ceremony, refrained from his usual threats and elaborated instead upon the advantages of the Protectorate for the Czechs.[65]

For a short period in the spring of 1940, the relations between the Hácha administration and the Germans seemed to be improving. In a conversation with Lammers, the chief of the Reich Chancellery, Hácha's envoy Chvalkovský learned that there was a good chance for the release of the students who had been detained in concentration camps since November. On March 20, the President brought up this question at a conference with Neurath. The Protector's reply was encouraging and soon afterward the first two-hundred students returned home from Sachsenhausen. Others followed at irregular intervals.[66]

[63] Popelka's note, March 14, 1940; Hácha to Hitler, March 15, 1940, *DHCSP*, II, pp. 521–23.

[64] *Der Neue Tag*, March 16, 1940.

[65] "Presseempfang der Zeitschrift 'Böhmen und Mähren' in Berlin," *Böhmen und Mähren*, May 1940, pp. 62–65. Cf. Caruso to Ciano, April 11, 1940, *DDI*, series IX, IV, pp. 35–36.

[66] S. Biman, "17. listopad," pp. 19–20. Hácha's notes for conference with Neurath, March 20, 1940, *DHCSP*, II, pp. 523–25. Neurath's note on conference with Hácha on March 20, 1940, March 26, 1940, *Trial*, XXXIX, pp. 353–54. Cf. Hácha to Lammers, May 22, 1940, AA, T-120, 1505, D 632565, NA.

But beyond the gradual release of the students, the Nazis granted no significant concessions. In June 1940, Hitler's spectacular victory in France dispelled for the time being any doubts about the continuation of the German rule in Bohemia and Moravia. The Nazis' arrogance rose to new heights while the Protectorate government "succumbed to outright panic." The ministers "tried to outdo themselves in assurances of loyalty."[67] They emphasized the need for a transition from "passive" to "active" loyalty and Deputy Prime Minister Havelka inspired the offer of a hospital train for the German army. In reply to the Protector's criticism, the President dismissed the Central Committee of the official National Solidarity Movement and promised to replace it by more "actively loyal" appointees. He professed readiness to make the *Treugelöbnis* to the Führer, which he had withheld in October 1939. In a radio broadcast on June 19, Hácha congratulated the German troops on their victory at the western front.[68] In a message to London, Eliáš explained this declaration as a result of German blackmail, but in reality the President himself had originally approached Neurath with a suggestion that it be made.[69]

Rather than Nazi pressure, the renewed agitation of the Czech Fascists had elicited Hácha's professions of loyalty to Germany. Although the Vlajka group could claim no more than 13,000 adherents, a negligible 0.16 per cent of the population, it conducted a noisy campaign to attract German attention and demanded a share in the government. The Vlajkaists assailed the cabinet and President Hácha personally, accusing them of incompetence and political duplicity, and spoke openly of a violent seizure of power. At a Vlajka rally, a speaker boasted that its special "four-to-five-man squads would do anything. They'll rough up the bosses of the National Solidarity with cowhides and sticks . . . . If any one of those skunks is killed, there won't be any harm since those skunks are much too many anyway."[70]

[67]SD report quoted in Král, *Pravda*, p. 202. Cf. *Meld. Reich*, June 13, 1940, pp. 28–32, R 58/151, BA.

[68] *Der Neue Tag*, June 20, 1940. Note about Hácha's conference with Neurath on July 16, 1940, *DHCSP*, II, p. 548.

[69]Message to Beneš, July 15, 1940, in Eliášová and Pasák (eds.), "Poznámky," p. 125. Note about Hácha's conversation with Neurath, July 18, 1940, *DHCSP*, II, p. 542.

[70]T. Pasák, "Vývoj Vlajky," pp. 862–65.

On August 6, the Protector dissolved the Prague chapter of the NSM, giving rise to speculations about an imminent Fascist resurgence. Two days later, about three hundred Svatopluk Guards, Vlajka's "direct-action" squads, attacked the NSM headquarters. In the ensuing clash, thirty-four policemen were wounded. SS detachments, having arrived on the scene with machine guns, took the side of the rioters and pushed the Czech police back. They were the first to enter the building, followed by the Svatopluk Guards. That evening, about seven hundred Vlajkaists, protected by the SS, paraded through downtown Prague, demanding the resignation of the cabinet.[71]

Yet the episode was more bizarre than serious. As before, the Nazis merely used the Czech Fascists to frighten the Hácha administration but had no intentions of bringing them to power. They preferred a respectable government to that of the Vlajkaist thugs whose "moral qualities [Neurath himself] amply appreciated."[72] The SS soon vacated the NSM headquarters and the Czech police detained the ringleaders in the riots without German interference. After August 8, the Vlajka's influence declined rapidly. It maintained a precarious existence tolerated by the Nazis with the suspicion they reserved for all nationalist movements—including those of congenial Fascist variety—in the occupied countries. A few pig-headed devotees of a Czech brand of Fascism were even sent to concentration camps.

The majority of Vlajka's adherents, however, adjusted to the changed circumstances and joined a new group of collaborators which had been emerging since mid-1940. These so-called "activists," though numerically even weaker than the Vlajkaists, were more sophisticated and, because of their jobs in the official press and radio, more effective. Most prominent among them was Emanuel Moravec, a former colonel in the Czechoslovak General Staff. Ambitious, intelligent, and lax in morals, he had changed from an ardent strategist of anti-German defense in 1938 to a complete renegade by 1940. He viewed the failure of the Czechs to fight for national independence as evidence of their inferiority as a people. By contrast, the Nazis' ruthlessness, which made possible their conquest of most of Europe, convinced him of the superiority of the German cause. In his opinion, the Czechs should

---

[71] *Ibid.*, pp. 867–68.
[72] Neurath's note, March 26, 1940, *Trial*, XXXIX, pp. 353–54.

best be transformed into Czech-speaking Germans. An aggressive publicist and a brilliant stylist, Moravec urged unconditional collaboration more persuasively than the standard voices of the German propaganda. He attained notoriety as the most hated but also the most influential of the Czech quislings.[73]

Because of their indifference to nationalism Moravec and his like were more welcome than the Vlajkaists as allies to the Nazis. At a Berlin reception of the Czech cultural delegation in September 1940, Goebbels lavished praise on the "activists."[74] President Hácha did not resist appointing several of them to the reconstituted Central Committee of the NSM. Instead, in a desperate effort to forestall their further advance, the government adopted some of the "activist" ideas for its own program. It initiated a lecture campaign for the "re-education of the Czech people in the spirit of the Reich idea" and the President used the inauguration of the customs union as an occasion for extolling the presumed advantages of integration with Germany.[75]

In retrospect, the official Czech representatives can easily be castigated for preaching acceptance of the German New Order. But in the few months after the defeat of France, when the Nazi power seemed impregnable, their attitude corresponded to the feelings of a considerable portion of the citizenry. Although the outspoken advocates of collaboration were still generally despised, "activism" was nevertheless beginning to make some inroads. In December 1940, for example, the German army sponsored a contest with prizes for Czech school children. Its aim was to enhance the public image of the German soldier. The sponsors were astonished at having collected some twenty-seven thousand entries, two-thirds of which—undoubtedly encouraged by parents and teachers—included unrequested descriptions of friendly encounters with German servicemen. The army propaganda department also noted a marked increase in the demand for German

---

[73] Moravec's address to Czech journalists, January 26, 1942, *DHCSP*, II, pp. 662–63. Cf. Pasák, "Problematika protektorátního tisku," pp. 73–74; and *idem*, "Aktivističtí novináři," pp. 177–86.

[74] "Rede des Herrn Reichsministers Dr. Goebbels beim Empfang der tschechischen Journalisten und Kulturschaffenden," *Böhmen und Mähren*, October 1940.

[75] Cf. Hácha's memorandum for conversations with Neurath and Frank, September 3, 1940, *DHCSP*, II, pp. 563–65. "Přehled politické situace v Čechách a na Moravě v letních měsících 1940" [A Survey of the Political Situation in Bohemia and Moravia in Summer 1940], October 3, 1940, *ibid.*, pp. 576–77.

language-textbooks and in unenforced sales of political literature, in particular of Moravec's pamphlets.[76]

Such incidents should not be overestimated as evidence that the Czechs might have abandoned their hopes for liberation and were happily embracing the German cause. Yet neither should they be discounted for their apparent triviality. They were indicative of the mentality often associated with the name of the "Good Soldier Schweik." Only a superficial reader of the famous World War I novel by Jaroslav Hašek can consider the behavior of its hero a form of resistance. In reality, "Schweikism," the ostensibly zealous though skeptical compliance often typical in repressive societies, was little more than the sly opportunism of the "little man"— which, however, extended also to the highest ranks. With the especially rapid spread of this attitude during the second half of 1940, the exiles in London had sufficient reason to worry about the state of the nation in the Protectorate.

Although in 1939 Beneš had felt little need for sacrifices and had in fact sanctioned the opportunistic policies of the Hácha government, in 1940 he began to wonder whether these policies had not gone too far. He feared that excessive manifestations of pro-German loyalism might be interpreted abroad as evidence of Czech acceptance of the Protectorate, thus obstructing the diplomatic efforts of the exiles.[77] Almost a year after the establishment of the London government-in-exile, its full diplomatic recognition by the powers, including Great Britain, was still pending.

Beneš was especially alarmed by Hácha's customs union speech, and gave vent to his indignation in a confidential message to Prague:

Telling the people here that it has been enforced, to people who are facing themselves every day the danger of death, whose homes and entire cities are going down in ruins, and who are being threatened with the downfall of a world empire, is neither effective nor advisable, nor possible, nor honest . . . . I am giving my last warning, and if this does not help, the final break will follow.[78]

Pressed by the Germans from one side and by London from the

[76] Armed Forces Propaganda Department, report for December 1940, OKW, T-77, 802, 5534389–94, 5534383, NA.

[77] Beneš's message to Prague, May 1, 1940, in Eliášová and Pasák (eds.), "Poznámky," p. 122.

[78] Beneš's message to Prague, September 28, 1940, *ibid.*, p. 127.

other, the Protectorate government was again in a quandary. Would greater firmness or continued appeasement bring better results? Opposed to the more resolute Eliáš was a cautious faction around Havelka, his deputy. Havelka disapproved when Zdeněk Bořek-Dohalský, a member of ÚVOD and Beneš's principal confidant in Prague, tried to exact from Hácha a firm promise to conform to the London line. As a jurist and civil servant, the President was reluctant and resented such duplicity as being "unfair" to the Germans. How could he honestly ask them for concessions, while entertaining behind their backs contacts with the enemy? In all sincerity, Hácha told Bořek-Dohalský that "he felt very tired and faint." Yet he added: "I am at your disposal whenever you please. I look forward to turning it over. You know to whom . . . ."[79]

At a time when the Nazi armes were sweeping through Europe and Britain was still fighting for its very survival, there was little wonder that the hearts of the Prague leaders sank. Before making further decisions, Eliáš requested Beneš's opinion about the international situation and a prognosis of future developments. The analyses that subsequently reached Prague from London via the ÚVOD radio were amazingly inaccurate.[80] The former President ventured predictions of an impending German collapse and anticipated a peace offer by Hitler—evidence of both wishful thinking and isolation from the realities of power. If Beneš's views in his Protectorate messages had not been confirmed by similar utterances to his associates, we might almost suspect him of deliberately bluffing in order to boost the spirits of his partners in Prague.[81]

The pattern of German policy in late 1940 and early 1941 gave little clue to the Nazis' real intentions. Reflecting Hitler's recent secret decision in favor of a partial assimilation of the Czechs,[82] they vacillated between harshness and moderation. On the one hand, statements by various Nazi leaders visiting Prague could be interpreted as evidence of their interest in German-Czech partnership within the framework of the New Order. On the other hand, the Germans tried more than ever before to suppress Czech

[79] ÚVOD message to London, December 25, 1940, *ibid.*, p. 128.

[80] ÚVOD to Beneš, October 11, 1940, *ibid.*, p. 127. Beneš to ÚVOD, October 7, 1940. *DHCSP*, I, pp. 130–32.

[81] Cf. Smutný's notes on conversations with Beneš, December 15, 1940, and June 2, 1941, *DHCSP*, I, pp. 149, 219.

[82] See Chapter 7, note 16, above.

nationalism; thus, for example, they imposed new restrictions upon secondary education.[83]

The situation was further complicated by the intensified struggle between Protector Neurath and State Secretary Frank, in which the Protector was rapidly losing ground. In January 1941, Frank opened an attack against the Hácha administration, veiled as a campaign against the veterans of the "treacherous" Czech Legion of World War I.[84] Since Prime Minister Eliáš had been a prominent member of the Legion, the real target of the attack was obvious. By that time, the Nazis had enough evidence of his connections with London and in February Frank urged Himmler to have Eliáš arrested. But the influence of the State Secretary was not yet strong enough for this.[85]

The Protectorate government was understandably nervous and debated what steps should be taken to counter Frank's pressure. The cabinet again considered resignation but finally ruled against it. Beneš undoubtedly knew of this decision and approved of it. The scanty source material, however, does not allow us to say with certainty whether postponement of the move had followed advice from Beneš, or whether Beneš's compliance came after the decision had been made.[86]

A new crisis soon developed at the second anniversary of the Protectorate. Shortly before the fateful date, there emerged a proposal for a plebiscite in which the Czechs would symbolically express their support of the Reich. Although we do not know who was the actual instigator of this plan, Havelka's ardent advocacy of it suggests his authorship. If—as seems probable—the idea indeed originated in the cabinet, it was indicative of a growing tendency to conciliate the Germans regardless of the protests from London. At the same time, the tension between Eliáš and Havelka mounted.[87]

---

[83] Cf. public speech by Otto Dietrich, "Geistige Grundlagen des Neuen Europa," in *Böhmen und Mähren*, February 1941. Frank to Eliáš, August 15, 1940, *DHCSP*, II, pp. 560–61.

[84] K. H. Frank, "Tschechischer Legionärgeist—oder Friede im Protektorat?" *Böhmen und Mähren*, January 1941, pp. 12–14.

[85] Frank to Himmler, February 22, 1941, quoted in Pasák, "Aktivističtí novináři," p. 177.

[86] Havelka, "Vzpomínka," p. 42. Masařík, "Poslední měsíce," pp. ii–vi.

[87] Cf. V. Král, "Kolaborace nebo rezistence?" [Collaboration or Resistance?], *Dějiny a současnost*, VII (1965), No. 7, p. 6. ÚVOD to London, May 4, 1941, OKW, T-77, 1050, 6526061, NA.

Informed by the ÚVOD about the planned plebiscite, Beneš took decisive steps to prevent what he feared would deal a serious blow to the reputation of his people abroad. In a long message to Prague, he first painted a rosy picture of the international situation. He claimed to have "absolutely reliable" reports that the German military command had "definitely lost faith" and that "panic and real depression" prevailed in the Berlin government, Nazi party, and armed forces.[88] Beneš regarded the American Lend-Lease Act of March 1941 as the crucial turning point. Interpreting it as a virtual declaration of belligerence, he believed that the war would continue at most three or four months. In his opinion, the opening of a new front in the Balkans was imminent. As in 1918, the German power would start "crumbling from the south." Influenced by these beliefs, he ventured an estimate of Hitler's ultimate designs:

At the time it has to start yielding, Germany will offer the evacuation of western European countries, but it will insist upon the incorporation of Poznania, Polish Pomerania, Bohemia and Moravia, and Austria into the Reich .... The moment will probably come when ... you will be offered concessions: [The Germans] will return universities and schools, free our prisoners, and maybe offer Bohemia and Moravia the status of today's Slovakia. These concessions may well be very attractive ....

The message ended with a dramatic appeal:

I beg and insist that both threats and offers of any kind be resolutely rejected .... Upon our demand President Hácha and the government must be ready to resign their offices immediately in order to manifest the end of their commitment.[89]

This message made a deep impression upon its underground recipients. They did not question Beneš's estimate of the situation—further evidence of his tremendous, though not fully justified prestige as a statesman. After Bořek-Dohalský's conversation with Hácha, the ÚVOD reported to London the following promise from the Protectorate President:

1. I agree with a common course of action and submit to it.
2. I shall not sign any international declaration amounting to constitutional commitment.

[88] Beneš's message to Prague, March 20, 1941, in Eliášová and Pasák (eds.), "Poznámky," pp. 128–30.
[89] *Ibid.*, pp. 130–31.

3. I shall not agree to sign any plebiscite which threatens us and which I consider to be an even more drastic form of constitutional declaration.

4. March 15 will never be repeated.

5. Please make clear in confidential conversations with appropriate persons abroad that that day was not a result of my weakness but rather a result of Munich. I am an old man and wish to die in honor. If I am again forced into a similar situation, I shall follow the example of Count Teleki [and take my life].[90]

This may have been Hácha's finest hour. Never before had he taken such a courageous stand. But this very divergence from the usual pattern is a compelling reason for interpreting his sensational statement with caution. As preserved today, its formulation is not by the President himself but rather by Bořek-Dohalský, who—elated by the success of his mission—may have chosen a considerably more resolute wording.[91] Moreover, Hácha was too unstable and susceptible to pressure to stand by his promise under duress. Finally, Beneš's optimistic prognosis, which had apparently helped to induce the statement, failed to materialize. Rather than starting to "crumble from the south," Germany victoriously swept through the Balkans in April 1941. But Beneš's admonition to Prague—added to the Nazis' coolness toward the plebiscite proposal—at least helped to avert this awkward project.

A third crisis of the Protectorate government followed shortly after the invasion of Yugoslavia, whose fate as a friendly Slavic nation the Czechs watched with great emotional involvement. The trouble started after a pro-German journalist—acting upon Frank's prodding—had submitted insidious questions to Havelka and two other ministers, requesting answers for publication in an official newspaper. Referring to the defeat of Yugoslavia, the questions were formulated in such a way as to necessitate unambiguous answers regarding the recent feats of German arms. It is not altogether clear why the Nazis selected Havelka to answer these questions, along with two other ministers of apparently greater

[90] Bořek-Dohalský to Beneš, April 12, 1941, *ibid.*, p. 134. Pál Teleki, Prime Minister of Hungary, committed suicide in early 1941 after the Germans pressed his country to invade Yugoslavia and thus violate the Hungarian-Yugoslav friendship treaty.

[91] In November 1941, after the Gestapo had captured the records of the messages exchanged between Prague and London and had arrested Bořek-Dohalský, Heydrich asked Hácha whether he had promised in March to abdicate. The President resolutely denied any knowledge of it and Heydrich was satisfied with this explanation. Heydrich to Hácha, November 15, 1941; Hácha to Heydrich, November 17, 1941: *DHCSP*, II, pp. 640–41.

pro-German disposition. For, despite Havelka's loyalist maneuvers, Frank never revised his early estimate of him as the "evil spirit" among the Czechs.[92] If the purpose was to promote a split within the cabinet, the scheme misfired; the ministers refused to answer, contending that in such important matters the cabinet as a whole must reply.[93] But, of the three ministers, only Havelka suffered as a result. Neurath forced his dismissal by Hácha, explaining confidentially to Berlin that the activities of the Deputy Prime Minister "had become politically intolerable."[94] It is difficult to believe that the Protector had suddenly found any imperative reasons for doing this, after he had tolerated Havelka and the entire cabinet for the period of almost two years since Hácha's April 1939 reorganization of the cabinet. The explanation of the episode is rather to be sought in the growing influence of Frank, who may have wished to warn the Czech representatives that they could not continue much longer to avoid an unreserved commitment to the Reich.

The subtlety of Czech political maneuvering during the first two years of the occupation defies easy classification in terms of resistance to the Nazis. The frontiers between collaboration and resistance were fluid and often the same persons participated in both. As of May 1941, there was still a basic understanding among the Protectorate government, the pro-Beneš underground, and the exiles. The few "activists" and misguided Communists did not seriously disturb this extraordinary political consensus. The relatively benevolent Neurath regime enabled the politicians to fluctuate between expediency and cautious opposition. Mounting Nazi pressures, however, were likely, in time, to make this maneuvering more and more difficult, and finally force both Prague and London to adopt unequivocal positions.

[92] Stuckart to Lammers, May 2, 1939, *Trial*, XII, p. 895.

[93] Krychtálek to Havelka, Krejčí and Ježek, April 7, 1941; Havelka *et al.* to Krychtálek, April 9, 1941; Ježek to Hácha, April 20, 1941: *DHCSP*, II, pp. 603–607. Cf. Havelka, "Vzpomínka," p. 42.

[94] Neurath to Lammers, May 12, 1941, AA, T-120, 1505, D632632, NA. ÚVOD to London, May 4, 1941, OKW, T-77, 1050, 6526061, NA.

9 *TURNING EAST*

CZECH HOPES AND GERMAN ARMS

D ESPITE its cramped neutrality, Russia loomed large both in the calculations of the belligerents and in the hopes of the defeated peoples now relegated to the sidelines as anxious spectators. For the besieged British, the Russians were the only potential allies of any value on the continent. Hitler had been preparing a military campaign against the Soviet Union from the late summer of 1940, in the mistaken belief that this would solve his strategical problems and at the same time help to fulfill the old Nazi dreams about an empire in the East. Although the German preparations proceeded in secrecy, the steady deterioration of the relations between Berlin and Moscow was evident. More and more people were becoming convinced that rather sooner than later the Soviet Union would be drawn into the war and they had little doubt that, if this happened, the Russians would get involved on the anti-German side.

If other subject peoples were heartened by this prospect, the Czechs looked forward to it with impatient enthusiasm. Hardly anywhere in Europe could more ardent believers in a future British-American-Russian coalition be found than in the Protectorate. Although Westerners at heart and by tradition, the Czechs also nourished a sentimental admiration for the Great Slavic Brother. Their historic experience with Russia had been excellent. Unlike the Poles or the Magyars, they lived outside the traditional Russian spheres of interest. The clash between the Czechoslovak Legion and the Bolsheviks in the faraway Urals during World War I was outlandish enough to be discounted as a misunderstanding. Not even Communism represented an insurmountable obstacle to good mutual relations. Prewar Czechoslovakia accommodated the Communist party to its parliamentary system. In 1935, the Prague government followed Paris in concluding a defense alliance with Moscow. In 1938, this alliance was not put to the test, thus enabling the Russians to emerge from the Munich crisis unscathed.

Not even the Hitler-Stalin agreement tarnished Russia's image in Bohemia and Moravia. Many Czech nationalists, who otherwise had little sympathy for Communism, hailed the westward advance of the great Slavic power in 1939. They rationalized the Soviet action as a clever move to preserve strength for the inevitable later confrontation with Nazi Germany. And Beneš, the democratic Machiavelli, privately praised the scandalous pact because it had encouraged Hitler to plunge into the war, thus brightening liberation prospects for the Czechs.[1] The Germans themselves helped to promote the pro-Russian sympathies of their Protectorate subjects by their arrogant disregard of the Czechs' national feelings. Underground reports reached London in 1940 that even some wealthy people "preferred Stalin to Hitler," as the lesser of two evils: "Rather let the Bolsheviks come than lose our own nationality under the Germans. Let the Bolsheviks take everything I own, if only the Germans don't get it."[2]

Nor was the pro-Russian disposition of the Czechs limited to vague sentiments. In late 1939 and early 1940, the Czech industrialists visiting Moscow tried to explore the possible political advantages of the Protectorate's economic relations with the Soviet Union.[3] At that time, the Russians remained reserved; it was the period in which they evicted the Czechoslovak Minister to Moscow, who owed allegiance to Beneš, and invited an envoy of the puppet Slovak government. The Comintern opposed the restoration of Czechoslovakia as an "imperialist and anti-Soviet" trick.[4]

Later in 1940, however, the situation changed significantly. In June, the representatives of the ÚVOD approached the Soviet Consulate in Prague. By the end of July, they had established regular contacts, by which the information the Czechs were receiving through German counter-intelligence channels was supplied to the Consulate.[5] At about the same time, the exiles

[1] Smutný's note, June 23, 1941, *DHCSP*, I, p. 235.
[2] Messages to London, July 1940, and October 20, 1940, *ibid.*, II, pp. 553–54, 578. Cf. *Meld. Reich*, June 27, 1940, pp. 26–28, R 58/151, BA.
[3] See chapter 4, note 26, above.
[4] Janáček, "Linie," pp. 34–40.
[5] J. Křen and V. Kural, "Ke stykům mezi československým odbojem a SSSR v letech 1939–1941" [The Relations between the Czechoslovak Resistance Movement and the USSR in 1939–1941], *Historie a vojenství*, 1967, pp. 732–33. Cf. V. Krajina, "Ústřední vedení odboje domácího" [Central Leadership of Home Resistance], in L. K. Feierabend, *Beneš mezi Washingtonem a Moskvou* [Beneš between Washington and Moscow], p. 139.

introduced a similar initiative and in August they succeeded in inaugurating cooperation with Soviet agents in Istanbul.[6] The two actions may have been coordinated, although it is more likely that the Beneš government wished to concentrate the intelligence exchanges in its own hands, thus eliminating direct contact between the underground and the Soviet Consulate in the Protectorate. In October, a crisis of confidence between the partners in Prague arose, as the Russians were pressing for more information than the ÚVOD was giving them. A few weeks later, the Gestapo arrested several Czechs who had been working with the Soviet diplomats. This aroused suspicion of foul play by Moscow at a time when Foreign Commissar Molotov was in Berlin exploring the chances of a German-Soviet *détente*.[7]

But the mutual distrust was soon dispelled. In the spring of 1941, Beneš, responding to a request from the Soviet government, sent a high-ranking military mission to Moscow in order to expand the promising partnership.[8] It is possible that with the information relayed to the Russians was a warning about the impending German invasion. In April 1941, the ÚVOD reported to London that maps of Soviet territory were being extensively printed in the Military Cartographic Institute in Prague.[9] In any case, the Czechoslovak intelligence center in London was highly esteemed by both the Russians and the British, who allowed it considerable independence.[10] And the secret links between Soviet and Czech

[6] Křen and Kural, "Ke stykům," pp. 750–54. Beneš's instructions for F. Moravec, November 7, 1940, *DHCSP*, I, p. 139. Beneš to Svoboda, March 24, 1941, *ibid.*, p. 191. F. Hieke-Stoj, "Mé vzpomínky z druhé světové války" [My Reminiscences from World War II], *Historie a vojenství*, 1968, p. 599.

[7] Křen and Kural, "Ke stykům," p. 739. Smutný's paper on Czechoslovak-Soviet relations, April 1941, *DHCSP*, I, p. 211. London to ÚVOD, June 21, 1941, OKW, T-77, 1050, 6526085, NA.

[8] Smutný's notes, April 1 and June 4, 1941, *DHCSP*, I, pp. 197, 222. Kural, "Hlavní organizace," p. 152. Hieke-Stoj, "Mé vzpomínky," p. 581.

[9] *Memoirs of Eduard Beneš*, pp. 149–50. ÚVOD to London, April 23, 1941, OKW, T-77, 1050, 6526050, NA. By a fortunate accident, a German transcript of the messages exchanged between ÚVOD and London from April to September 1941 has been preserved in the National Archives in Washington. This document, originally compiled by the Gestapo from the messages seized in late 1941, had been captured along with the OKW papers by the Allied troops after Germany's defeat. Cf. Smutný's note, April 24, 1941, *DHCSP*, I, p. 206.

[10] Smutný's note, August 26, 1942, *ibid.*, p. 280. Information given by F. Moravec to L. Feierabend, March–April 1964, Feierabend, *Ve vládě v exilu* [In the Exile Cabinet], II, pp. 38–39.

intelligence systems enabled Beneš's government-in-exile to establish friendly relations with Moscow at a time when the Soviet Union was still widely ostracized as Hitler's accomplice.

The Czechoslovak Communist party (CPC) did not initially capitalize on Czech pro-Russian feelings. Its awkward propaganda against the "imperialist" war did not appeal to anyone but party diehards, and the leaders were keenly aware of their isolation from the masses.[11] Individual party members may have ingratiated themselves with the ÚVOD by helping to maintain the liaison with the Soviet Consulate, although no reliable evidence of this has been preserved.[12] Among the London exiles the Communists continued to be regarded as black sheep: Beneš was especially angered by their disruptive agitation in the armed forces. But the CPC, while it did not muster much sympathy among the Czechs, did not inspire their active hostility either. And in the long run, the leftward trend of public opinion—in the Protectorate as elsewhere in wartime Europe—favored the Communists.

The political platform of the Czech underground—endorsed by the ÚVOD in 1941—was the work of the left-wing PVVZ. The document, entitled *For Freedom: Into a New Czechoslovak Republic*, professed allegiance to Masaryk's democratic ideas but envisaged a republic with marked socialistic features.[13] It embodied demands for the restriction of the number of political parties and a dominant economic role for the state. The ÚVOD urged the exiles to keep in step with the social radicalization at home.[14] Beneš, always sympathetic to moderate Socialism, approved. He agreed that the new state, though "a logical, clear and conscious continuation of the First Republic," must be "radicalized socially and deeply changed politically."[15] He hoped that the inevitable

---

[11] This isolation was recognized, in retrospect, in a document of the Central Committee dating from the end of September 1941: G. Bareš (ed.), "Dokumenty ze zasedání II. ilegálního ústředního výboru KSČ v září 1941" [Documents from the Conference of the Second Underground Central Committee of the CPC in September 1941], *Příspěvky k dějinám KSČ*, I (1961), pp. 550, 553.

[12] Cf. Pasák, "Aktivističtí novináři," p. 173.

[13] *Za svobodu: Do nové Československé republiky* [For Freedom: Into a New Czechoslovak Republic]. Cf. O. Janeček, "O programu Petičního výboru 'Věrni zůstaneme' z let 1940–1941" [The Program of the Committee of the Petition "We Remain Faithful" in 1940–1941], *Příspěvky k dějinám KSČ*, VI (1966), pp. 481–99.

[14] Messages to London, August 4, October 1, November 23, 1940, *DHCSP*, II, pp. 558–59, 573, 586. ÚVOD to London, April 23, 1941, OKW, T-77, 1050, 6526051, NA.

[15] Beneš's message to Prague, October 7, 1940, *DHCSP*, I, p. 132.

radicalization which would accompany liberation could be channeled into democratic and orderly forms: "You at home and we here must keep constantly in step with the military and later revolutionary events, so that at the moment of Germany's collapse we may be able to strike the right note, both nationally and socially."[16]

Inevitably such a policy further complicated Beneš's relations with the Protectorate government, in which conservative tendencies were strong and the influence of the former party bosses, particularly the Agrarians, was considerable. The growing animosity between the underground and the Hácha administration was an additional reason for Beneš to press the Protectorate President and his government to conform to the London line.

For months, Beneš had been preparing the ground for a Czechoslovak-Soviet partnership. His nervousness grew as the anticipated clash between Russian and Germany was not forthcoming. On the eve of the Nazi invasion of the Soviet Union, he was torn with doubts about the future course of the war. Pursued by the persistent nightmare of a compromise peace, Beneš interpreted the flight to Scotland of Rudolf Hess, Hitler's deputy, as an ominous overture to Berlin's peace feelers. The Czechoslovak President had little confidence in the determination of the British to fight for complete victory.[17] These doubts explain his enormous relief when the news of Moscow's involuntary belligerence arrived on June 22, 1941.

Rarely did Beneš, the cool and calculating politician, appear so emotional and exuberant as in the days following June 22. Jan Masaryk, his Foreign Minister, commented with characteristic bluntness that the President "now has only Russia on his mind. We must hold him, so that he won't fly off to the sky." Masaryk added skeptically that the Russians "will get a sound beating and we'll be stuck with them."[18]

Beneš held that after the Munich experience the Western powers could never again be trusted. He had been desperately searching for another ally, and the Soviet Union, with whom he had signed a treaty of alliance in 1935, was his first preference. Admittedly,

[16]*Ibid.*, p. 131. Cf. ÚVOD to London, April 23, 1941, OKW, T-77, 1050, 6526051, NA.

[17]Smutný's notes, June 2, 4, 7, and 21, 1941, *DHCSP*, I, pp. 219, 221, 225, 232.

[18]Smutný's notes, June 23 and 24, 1941, *ibid.*, I, p. 234, and II, p. 613.

the Russians had been doing "awful things, really filthy," [19] between August 1939 and June 1941, but at least in one respect their dealings with Hitler had been reassuring. Their behavior seemed to indicate that Soviet policy was guided by considerations of power, which Beneš understood well, rather than by inscrutable ideological motives, which were unfamiliar to him. He found Stalin a "reasonable statesman who knew what he wanted." [20] To Beneš's great satisfaction, even Churchill, the old enemy of Bolshevism, announced Britain's full support of Russia's struggle. Finally, the President's confidence in Moscow was in conformity with the sentiments of the majority of his compatriots in the Protectorate. They, too, welcomed Soviet belligerence with "inner satisfaction and unconcealed joy." [21]

To his intimates, Beneš explained that future Russian predominance in east central Europe was not only probable but desirable. He outlined a hopeful vision of postwar developments:

The whole future depends on the victory or defeat of Russia and on its condition at the end of the war . . . . For us this is decisive. After the war, even in twenty years, France will not play a leading role in European politics. After five years, England will retire from Europe and go a different way along with America. In Europe, only Germany and Russia will be left. Germany will be disrupted, and in the East, and, I hope, in central Europe as well, Russia will play the decisive role . . . . [The Russians] will come together with Europe and after the war Bolshevism will not even be remembered. [22]

Acting upon this last assumption, Beneš proceeded unswervingly to promote understanding with Moscow upon the foundations already laid by the Czech-Soviet pooling of intelligence information up to June 1941. His policy seemed to pay off immediately. On July 9, the Soviet Union—as the first of the great powers— announced its willingness to fully recognize the Czechoslovak government-in-exile. Moscow's initiative prompted the long-pending recognition by London, and the two governments made their decisions public on the same day, July 18. The United States

[19] Smutný's note, quoting Beneš, June 23, 1941, *ibid.*, I, p. 234.
[20] Smutný's note, July 18, 1941, *ibid.*, p. 252.
[21] Report of Security Service Prague, June 1941, in Amort (ed.), *Heydrichiáda*, p. 17.
[22] Smutný's note, July 12, 1941, *DHCSP*, I, pp. 241–42.

took a similar step shortly afterward, to be fully implemented on October 26, 1942.[23]

Beneš believed that Communism would not complicate Czechoslovakia's relations with the Soviet Union, although initially he had felt no urge to conciliate the Communist exiles who a short time earlier had abused his "bourgeois" government. But they themselves came to him, "*Feuer und Flamme* for a common front against Hitler."[24] At the first meeting, the President treated them condescendingly. He made it clear that they must submit to his leadership unconditionally and give up any thoughts of seizing power in the future. He hoped that by dealing with their Moscow masters directly, he would be able to keep the Communists under control.

In the Protectorate, the CPC sought collaboration with other underground groups.[25] London advised its followers to establish contacts with the Communists in order to keep an eye on them, assure their subordination to the government-in-exile, and prevent a possible split within the resistance movement. In August, the ÚVOD replied that "we negotiate with the Communists about cooperation. . . . We keep regular contacts with them once a week."[26]

The actual scope of these relations is uncertain. After the war, a prominent veteran of the ÚVOD denied that any cooperation had taken place.[27] The Communists claimed in the fall of 1941 that they had joined with the rest of the underground in creating a Central National Revolutionary Committee. Two proclamations

[23]Jan Masaryk to Hurban, July 10, 1941, *ibid.*, p. 239. Eden to Jan Masaryk, July 18, 1941, *ibid.*, pp. 247–48. *Memoirs of Eduard Beneš*, pp. 156–57, 180.

[24]Smutný's note, July 23, 1941, *DHCSP*, I, p. 254.

[25]ÚVOD to London, July 15, 1941, OKW, T-77, 1050, 6526102, NA. There are indications that the Communist turn toward active opposition to the Germans in conjunction with other resistance groups may have antedated Hitler's invasion of Russia. The CPC had already passed a resolution to that effect in May 1941. It is not clear whether this policy revision originated in the Comintern—perhaps at variance with the Soviet government line—or resulted from an independent decision by the Prague Central Committee, which was unable to maintain radio contact with Moscow at that time. Cf. Janáček, "Linie," p. 58. Novotný, "Činnost KSČ," p. 114. ÚVOD to London, April 23, 1941, OKW, T-77, 1050, 6526051, NA.

[26]London to ÚVOD, August 6, 1941; ÚVOD to London, August 19, 1941; OKW, T-77, 1050, 6526153–54, 6526131, NA. Cf. messages of July 15 and August 7, *ibid.*, 6526102 and 6526119.

[27]Krajina, "La résistance tchécoslovaque," p. 75. Cf. J. Korbel, *The Communist Subversion in Czechoslovakia*, I p. 54.

in the name of this Committee appeared in *Rudé právo*, the CPC's own clandestine newspaper.[28] They abound in Marxist jargon. The existence of the Committee cannot be confirmed from other sources, an indication that it may have been an invention of Communist propaganda, intended to enhance the party's status in the resistance movement.

The Nazi-Soviet conflict had immediate repercussions upon the policies of the Hácha administration. On June 23, the President delivered a radio address in which he praised the German crusade against the Soviet Union, emphasizing that the Czechs, preferring social justice without violence, had always rejected Bolshevism as "negative, destructive and racially alien."[29] Although the Nazis had undoubtedly pressed him to make such a statement, he seems also to have expressed his own genuine abhorrence of Communism, not surprising in a devout Catholic and a conservative. He hardly realized the political implications of his speech and was probably surprised to hear of the furor it had created in London.

Beneš learned of Hácha's address at about the same time the Bratislava government announced the dispatch of Slovak soldiers to the eastern front. He considered both moves as extremely damaging to Czechoslovakia's cause, particularly to future relations with the Soviet Union. The exiled leader gave vent to his indignation in an important message to Prague on June 24 in which he urged that the participation of Czech troops in Hitler's Russian campaign must be prevented at any cost. Beneš further pleaded that the Protectorate government avoid more concessions to the Germans, including loyalist statements. Any such concessions might in the future "give the Communists a pretext to take over power on the justified reproach that we helped Hitler." Hácha and his associates "must re-examine [their] attitude and . . . let [him] know [their] decisions immediately."[30] Although Beneš concluded that he expected their demonstrative resignation shortly, he did not demand it immediately—as he was to insinuate after the war. It is likely that Eliáš, and perhaps other cabinet members as well, were informed about the message but we have no evidence that Hácha was familiar with Beneš's demands.

---

[28] Bareš, "Dokumenty," p. 547. "Společné provolání" [A Joint Appeal], in *Za svobodu českého a slovenského národa*, pp. 212–19. Cf. J. Fučík, *Milujeme svůj národ* [We Love Our People], pp. 210–12.

[29] *Der Neue Tag*, June 24, 1941.

[30] Beneš to ÚVOD, June 24, 1941, *DHCSP*, II, p. 614.

Active participation of the Czechs in the war was urged by the Vlajkaists and a few smaller Fascist groups. Their agitation—rather than Beneš's plea—prompted Hácha to seek out Neurath. The President hoped to convince him that the Reich would be better off if Protectorate nationals continued to contribute by working rather than fighting. But Hácha had not yet presented his argument when the Protector interrupted him to say that the military assistance of the Czechs was not contemplated anyway.[31] Hitler remained steadfast in his determination not to let them fight. Thus the danger Beneš feared most was averted. He could not know, of course, that the Nazis' decision was not made in response to Hácha's intervention; hence Beneš asked the ÚVOD to convey his thanks to President Hácha.[32]

The future policies of the Prague leaders, however, remained an open question. For months, Beneš had supplied them with optimistic estimates of the military situation and with predictions of Germany's bargaining moves. The forecasts had failed to materialize. It is most likely that only the desire to reassure London could have motivated Eliáš's promise that he and the government would abstain from further pro-German declarations and would resign promptly if the Nazis presented intolerable demands. At the same time, he defended Hácha's address of June 23, which had presumably induced the Germans to grant economic concessions. In his message to Beneš, the Prime Minister emphasized the necessity of preserving a smoothly functioning public administration in order to prevent "far-reaching economic disturbances." For the time being, he considered "quiet on all fronts the only reasonable counsel."[33] The ÚVOD, however, strongly disapproved and condemned Eliáš's attitude as a "slippery policy."[34]

The most important decision made under the impact of the Soviet-German conflict concerned the future of the Germans settled in Czechoslovakia. To most Czechs, the Soviet Union appeared to be the safest guarantee that after the war these Germans would be punished as severely as they seemed to deserve. In an emotional exchange of opinion with London, the ÚVOD rejected Beneš's

---

[31] Hácha's note, July 3, 1941, *ibid.*, pp. 623–24. Cf. "Ereignismeldung UdSSR," July 5, 1941, Nur. NO-4532, IfZ; Minutes of a conference in the Foreign Office, June 30, 1941, Nur. NG-4652, IfZ.

[32] Beneš to ÚVOD, July 26, 1941, Eliášová and Pasák (eds.), "Poznámky," p. 138.

[33] Messages for Beneš, July 2 and August 3, 1941, *ibid.*, pp. 137–40.

[34] ÚVOD to London, August 3, 1941, *ibid.*, p. 140.

earlier proposals for only partial expulsion of the Sudeten Germans, self-contained autonomous German districts, and the cession of exposed portions of Czechoslovak territory to Germany.[35] This had been obviously a project tailored to Western sensitivities. It was under pressure from home in August 1941 that Beneš—not unwillingly, to be sure—changed his mind in favor of complete expulsion. Not only was such a radical project likely to please the Russians, but it could only be carried out with their support, thus further strengthening Czechoslovakia's link with Moscow. From the summer of 1941 dated Beneš's break with Wenzel Jaksch, the leading German Social Democrat from the Sudetenland who lived in London as a British protégé, and the beginning of his systematic efforts to secure Soviet help for the drastic plan.[36]

In the critical summer of 1941, the policies of the Czechoslovak government-in-exile changed decisively. They would henceforth be subordinated to Beneš's overriding desire to promote close friendship with Moscow. Inevitably, the days of his collusion with Hácha and Eliáš were numbered. Looking back at that period, Beneš wrote in 1945: "In late summer 1941, I gave up all hope of saving anything at home by further contacts with the Protectorate government and of influencing its activity in our own and the Allies' advantage."[37] In a message to ÚVOD on September 3, 1941, he stated for the first time that after the war all people who held important positions during the occupation would be purged.[38] Still, the link between London and Prague lasted another few weeks before the Nazis enforced a decisive showdown in October.

As the war intensified, both Great Britain and the Soviet Union tried to activate resistance in the Protectorate. The British Special Operations Executive (SOE), the agency for underground warfare, originally hoped to create secret armies in Czechoslovakia and Poland. These were to attack as soon as the Allies started advancing. Moscow urged the Czech Communists to organize resistance

---

[35] ÚVOD to London, August 18, 1941, OKW, T-77, 1050, 6526129, NA. London to ÚVOD, September 10–12, 1941, *ibid.*, 6526177–82. Cf. Smutný's notes, March 1, April 11, June 5, 1941, *DHCSP*, I, pp. 184, 198–200, 224–25.

[36] Cf. W. Jaksch, *Europe's Road to Potsdam*, pp. 364–65. Jaksch interprets the expulsion as a result of Beneš's personal design, rather than as a consequence of the Czech-German confrontation in the Protectorate. On the Beneš-Jaksch controversy, see Luža, *The Transfer of the Sudeten Germans*, pp. 225–34.

[37] Beneš to Stránský, August 1, 1945, *DHCSP*, II, p. 753.

[38] Beneš to ÚVOD, September 3, 1941, OKW, T-77, 1050, 6526173, NA.

efforts on a massive scale: sabotage, guerrilla warfare, and eventually a general strike.[39]

Although the British were the first to begin training airborne agents, the Russians apparently preceded them in dispatching their own commandos to the Protectorate. Between late August and early October, Soviet planes dropped three small parties, probably recruited from the nascent Czechoslovak military unit in Russia. We do not know whether the local Communists—who had resumed radio contact with Moscow early in the summer of 1941—participated in this undertaking. In any case, the Gestapo quickly captured the agents, an outcome which kept the Russians from similar attempts until 1943.[40] The military setbacks of the Red Army, too, had a sobering effect upon the Communists in the Protectorate. By late 1941, their pamphlets no longer advocated an immediate uprising but suggested instead the tactics of "gnat bites" and the postponement of more important actions to an appropriate time in the future.[41]

Because long-range aircraft were in critically short supply, the British abandoned their original plans for underground armies in central Europe. In the summer of 1941, they confined themselves to preparing specific subversive assignments on a smaller scale. By August, 158 members of the Czechoslovak army in Britain were being trained for that purpose in special SOE centers. They were to build up the underground organizations, strike against enemy communications, and attack military targets in Bohemia and Moravia. According to a British source, the first SOE agent arrived in the Protectorate in April 1941. The Czechoslovak documentation gives a more probable date, December 1941. In that month, the SOE also stepped up its activities in other European countries, such as Denmark.[42]

[39] F. W. Deakin, "Great Britain and European Resistance," in *European Resistance Movements*, II, pp. 118–19. "Lide český" [To the Czech People], in *Zločiny nacistů za okupace*, p. 96. "Ve jménu svobody českého národa—do boje!" [For the Freedom of the Czech People—Into Struggle!], in *Za svobodu českého a slovenského národa*, pp. 161–72.

[40] J. Doležal, *Jediná cesta* [The Only Way], p. 130.

[41] "Společně, organizovaně a vytrvale až k vítězství!" [Together, Organized and Unrelenting toward Victory!], in *Za svobodu českého a slovenského národa*, pp. 181–85.

[42] F. E. Keary in "Proceedings of a Conference on Britain and European Resistance Movements Organised by St. Antony College, Oxford, December 10–16 1962," p. Cz. 10. London to ÚVOD, August 6–7, 1941, OKW, T-77, 1050, 6526154, NA. Doležal, *Jediná cesta*, p. 129. Cf. J. Bennett, *British Broadcasting and the Danish Resistance Movement*, p. 45.

In the meantime, the government-in-exile, too, tried to encourage resistance activities. It explained to the ÚVOD that their expansion was badly needed in order to help the Czechoslovak cause abroad:

It is necessary to pass from theoretical plans and preparations to deeds . . . . In London and Moscow, we have been bluntly reminded that the disruption or at least a substantial reduction of the war industry in the Czechoslovak territory would at this very moment hit the Germans severely . . . . Our whole situation would definitely appear in an unfavorable light if we . . . [did not] at least keep in step with the others.[43]

The surviving members of the underground could not be blamed for the poor impression the Czech resistance made abroad. Having evaded the Gestapo for more than two years, they were people of extraordinary courage and dedication. When tracked down, they often opposed the police by force of arms and, if there was no other choice, they preferred suicide to surrender. Those who were captured, especially former army officers, proved to be a hard task for the Nazi interrogators. Several of them did not break down even under severe torture. Some of the arrested Communist functionaries, too—according to the chief of the Prague Gestapo—were "just possessed by fanaticism . . . and refused to talk with the interrogating officer at all."[44]

But such examples of gallantry were deceptive indices of the actual strength of the underground. Perhaps because of the lively exchanges of messages with the ÚVOD, the exiles indulged in wishful thinking about the chances for an organized resistance movement. Their demands were ludicrously unrealistic. On September 5, London inquired about the state of preparations for a military uprising, to be carried out in the final stage of the war.[45] These preparations were to aim at disarming German troops in the Protectorate and dispatching an expeditionary corps for a swift occupation of the Sudetenland. In his reply, General Homola of the "Nation's Defense" (ON) complained bitterly that there were virtually no arms available. Of the original leadership of his

[43] London to ÚVOD, August 30–September 1, 1941, OKW, T-77, 1050, 6526169–70, NA.

[44] Heydrich to Bormann, October 11, 1941, in Amort (ed.), *Heydrichiáda*, p. 90. Geschke to Müller, November 12, 1941, *ibid.*, p. 109. Cf. J. Vozka, *Hrdinové domácího odboje* [The Heroes of the Home Resistance].

[45] London to ÚVOD, September 5, 1941, OKW, T-77, 1050, 6526175–76, NA.

organization, he alone remained.[46] He was a hunted man, high on the Gestapo list of wanted persons.

The ÚVOD nevertheless promised to do its best to step up resistance. It reported to London an impressive number of acts of sabotage which had supposedly taken place during the first eight months of 1941. They ranged from the blowing up of gasoline dumps to the derailing of military trains. From German sources, we have information about further acts of subversion credited to the Communists. These exploits included the secret manufacture of explosives in a small factory whose owner was himself a party member. Documents from the Nazi archives mention frequent fires in railroad freight cars, the destruction of air brakes in trains, and the cutting of telephone wires in the summer of 1941.[47]

The actual extent of these activities is difficult to estimate. Most of the spectacular deeds mentioned in the ÚVOD message have not been confirmed by other evidence. In order to satisfy London's demand for more resistance, the ÚVOD may have included unverified reports. The German data, too, should be treated with extreme caution. Since there was no accepted definition of sabotage, the Nazis also listed mere accidents. In September 1941, for example, the Counter-Intelligence (*Abwehr*) reported 114 cases in the entire Protectorate. In the same month, the Gestapo statistics for Moravia mentioned only 4.[48] It is unlikely that the remaining 110 cases occurred in Bohemia. Most probably, each one of the rival agencies tended to overstate the figures in order to make its own achievements in combating subversion look more impressive.

Even if sabotage may not have been widespread, unrest was clearly evident. Several strikes shortly followed the outbreak of the Soviet-German war, although all of them collapsed within a few hours, after the Gestapo had arrested hostages. The Nazi police discovered Communist networks in several factories but investigation revealed no link with the strikes. The work stoppages were

[46] Homola to London, September 23, 1941, *ibid.*, 6526218–22. Cf. Kural, "Hlavní organizace," p. 143.

[47] ÚVOD to London, September 5 and 8, 1941, OKW, T-77, 1050, 6526196, 6526204, NA. Geschke to Müller, November 12, 1941, in Amort (ed.), *Heydrichiáda*, pp. 108–109. Nolle to Pommerening, November 14, 1941, *ibid.*, p. 118. Armament Inspection Board Prague, "Kriegstagebuch Nr. 8," fol. 128, W 08-122/8, Armament Command Brno, "Kriegstagebuch Nr. 8," fol. 107, W 09-70/6, BA, MA.

[48] Doležal, *Jediná cesta*, p. 61. SD report, September 28, 1941, Nur. NO-3145, IfZ. Cf. Kural, "Hlavní organizace," p. 156.

spontaneous rather than the result of conspiracy. The workers complained above all about their material condition. Their purchasing power temporarily decreased, after the customs union with Germany had upset the stability of the wage and price indices. Partly because of the poor harvest in 1940, food rations had been lowered. Mismanagement of the factory canteens was another reason for frequent complaints.[49]

There were other manifestations of discontent, motivated by political rather than economic causes. During the week of September 14, the Czechs, following instructions on the London radio, staged an effective boycott of the official press. Newspaper sales went down by 25 to 50 per cent, the decline being even higher for those papers which did not sell by subscription.[50] The success of the boycott demonstrated the popularity of the BBC among the masses of people and their willingness to submit to guidance from abroad.

On September 16 or 17, high-ranking officials of the Nazi administration conferred in Prague. According to ÚVOD sources, the principal item on the agenda was the unrest in the Protectorate. An argument reportedly broke out between State Secretary Frank and Protector Neurath.[51] After the war, Frank told his Czech interrogators that soon afterward, "perhaps on September 24 or 25," he and the Protector had been summoned by Hitler for discussions. According to evidence from the Führer's archives, however, Frank had already seen Hitler on September 21, two days before Neurath.[52] The interview may have actually taken place at the request of the State Secretary, who hoped this time to succeed in ousting the Protector. Frank probably described the situation as critical and pointed out to the Führer Neurath's incompetence in coping with it.[53]

[49] Armament Inspection Board Prague, "Kriegstagebuch Nr. 4," fol. 88, W 08-122/4. "Kriegstagebuch Nr. 8," fol. 27, W 08-122/8, BA, MA. ÚVOD to London, September 8, 1941, OKW, T-77, 1050, 6526197, NA. Geschke to Müller, November 12, 1941, in Amort (ed.), *Heydrichiáda*, p. 103. SD report, July 4, 1941, Nur. NO-4529, IfZ.

[50] ÚVOD to London, September 8 and 18, 1941, OKW, T-77, 1050, 6526197 and 6526210–11, NA. "Propaganda-Lagebericht," September 29, 1941, OKW, T-77, 980, 4470545, NA.

[51] ÚVOD to London, September 21, 1941, OKW, T-77, 1050, 6526216, NA. "Proč přišel Heydrich" [Why Heydrich Came], *Hlas revoluce*, September 22, 1961.

[52] *Zpověď K. H. Franka*, pp. 126–27. Hitler's daily activities, p. 78, MA 3 (1), IfZ.

[53] Cf. *Trial*, XVII, p. 16.

In this matter, the Führer did not need much persuading. He no longer considered Neurath suited for the high office. In Hitler's opinion, the Czechs regarded the Protector as "an affable old gentleman and mistook his good heart and leniency for weakness and stupidity."[54] On September 22 and 23, Bormann, Himmler, and Goebbels were called to the Führer's headquarters to discuss the selection of a new ruler in Prague. Undoubtedly to Frank's great disappointment, Bormann suggested Reinhard Heydrich. Hitler approved the new appointment on September 24.[55] Four days later, the Czechs were stunned to learn from an official announcement that because of "failing health," Neurath was being temporarily replaced by the dreaded chief of Germany's Security Police.

The three months between the German invasion of Russia and Heydrich's appointment to Prague had sufficed to transform the Czech political scene. In the last analysis, all the decisive changes originated with Hitler's fateful decision to attack the Russians and the ensuing Soviet involvement in the war. Responding to this development, the Beneš government began to turn decisively toward the East—a re-orientation which also strained its relations with the Hácha-Eliáš administration. Soviet participation in the anti-German coalition helped to radicalize Czech public opinion both socially and politically. The Communist party emerged from isolation to assume a legitimate place in the resistance movement. Efforts to activate resistance were stepped up under pressure from abroad, and although their results remained short of expectations, growing unrest in the Protectorate precipitated resolute German action. With the appointment of Heydrich, Nazi policy hardened significantly. The heavy hand of the new Protector began to reshape the destiny of the Czech people.

[54] Minutes of Hitler's conference with Toussaint, October 7, 1941, in Amort (ed.), *Heydrichiáda*, p. 82.

[55] Hitler's daily activities, p. 85, MA 3 (1), IfZ. Decree of September 30, 1941, *RGB*, 1941, I, p. 591.

PART IV

HEYDRICH AND THE HEYDRICHIÁDA

10 *BREAKING AND BENDING*

REINHARD HEYDRICH, widely regarded as the personification of Nazi ruthlessness, was by no means a primitive brute. His complex, twisted personality was quite unique among the leaders of the Third Reich. There is little doubt today that the German security chief—most notorious as the architect of the extermination of the Jews—was himself one-quarter Jewish.[1] During his lifetime only a few of Heydrich's intimates suspected this embarrassing ancestry, which he anxiously tried to conceal. At the same time, the fanatical Nazi desired almost obsessively to overcome the supposedly crippling effects of the "non-Aryan" blood-admixture. He studiedly maintained a stiff military posture and took pride in his prowess at sports.

If Heydrich's uneasy memory of his Jewish grandmother may have accounted for such traits in his character, the overriding lust for power was peculiarly his own. He was able to put his considerable intellectual capacity to the service of this ambition. But regardless of his unquestionable devotion to the Nazi creed, Heydrich was indifferent to the meaning and justification of power; he worshipped it for its own sake rather than as an instrument for the advancement of a cause. Entirely devoid of moral scruples and capable of using any imaginable means to further his ends, he was overwhelmingly concerned with devising techniques for the control and management of men; in this direction, Heydrich's propensity was phenomenal.[2]

Until 1933, Heydrich's career was undistinguished. After a short period of service as a naval officer he was forced to resign because of discipline violations. The one significant outcome of this episode

[1] The available evidence is convincingly summarized in C. Wighton, *Heydrich, Hitler's Most Evil Henchman*, pp. 21–26.
[2] The best study of Heydrich is the essay by Fest, *Das Gesicht des Dritten Reiches*, pp. 139–55.

was his lifelong rivalry with Admiral Wilhelm Canaris, his former superior in the navy and later his chief competitor for control of the German intelligence service. Whereas Weimar Germany—a civilized country despite its deficiencies—was an unfavorable environment for Heydrich, Hitler's rise to power provided him with unprecedented opportunities. A regime founded upon terror was congenial to his mentality, and he rose quickly through the Nazi ranks, eventually to become the chief of the formidable Reich Security Head Office. By 1939, he combined in his hands the direction of the Gestapo, the Criminal Police, and the Security Service. As the operator of this vast apparatus, Heydrich was the best-informed man in the Reich.

Heydrich's personal power grew along with the expansion of Nazi rule on the continent. His agents were active throughout Europe, and in occupied Soviet territory he claimed jurisdiction over the entire German police machinery. In May 1941, Göring placed him in charge of the "final solution of the Jewish question."[3]

It is possible that the rapid increase of Heydrich's influence began to worry others who were prominent in Hitler's Reich, including his main protector, Himmler. Several authors have suggested that in the reshuffling within the top leadership which followed Hess's flight to Britain, Heydrich was deliberately relegated from Berlin to provincial Prague.[4] Bormann, who as the new supreme boss of the Nazi party benefited most from these shifts, was actually the man who suggested Heydrich's appointment to the Protectorate.

Yet the bulk of contemporary documents gives an impression of unity rather than of discord among Heydrich, Bormann, and Himmler. Their correspondence reveals close personal affinity and, in Himmler's case, undiminished paternalistic feelings for his protégé.[5] While in Prague, Heydrich was not at all isolated. He kept a special plane at hand and used it for frequent commuting to Berlin. He retained all his former functions, adding to them a prestigious title, "Acting Reich Protector." His wife later affirmed that both she and her husband had welcomed the new job with enthusiasm: "It was the first time since my husband joined the SS

[3] On Heydrich's role in the "final solution," see Hilberg, *The Destruction of the European Jews*, pp. 181–82, 262–66, and *passim*.

[4] Cf. G. Reitlinger, *The SS: Alibi of a Nation*, p. 213. Fest, *Das Gesicht des Dritten Reiches*, pp. 151–52. Cf. *The Schellenberg Memoirs*, pp. 243, 246.

[5] Cf. *The Kersten Memoirs*, pp. 91, 97–99. Heydrich to Bormann, September 27, 1941, in Král (ed.), *Die Deutschen*, p. 455.

that he had been well off. Up to that time we had lived a very quiet bourgeois existence in Berlin. Now we began to enjoy the perquisites of high office and for the first time we had enough money."[6]

Rather than as a victim of intrigue, Heydrich came to Prague as one of the chief organizers of the new Nazi empire to be built along racial lines. He became increasingly involved in this task, especially after the invasion of Russia seemed to have opened vast spaces in the East for German exploitation. Heydrich is said to have founded at Wannsee, on the outskirts of Berlin, a large institute devoted to the study of eastern Europe.[7] But elsewhere in Europe, too, he examined the possibilities for expanding the domination of the "master" race. Not only did he oppose the withdrawal of German inhabitants from South Tyrol, but he also hoped to "re-convert" the Italians there into Germans. In September 1941, he had plans prepared for the occupation of Switzerland, which would bring the German-speaking Swiss into the orbit of the Third Reich. Even in Iceland, an informant gathered data for him relating to the future role of the kindred Nordic people.[8]

Heydrich's mission to the Protectorate took place at a time when the plans for the New Order were assuming a definite shape. He devoted to this theme a major part of his inaugural address, delivered at the confidential meeting of high German officials in Prague on October 2, 1941. Rarely were the Nazi designs expressed in such a frank and cynical manner as in this impromptu speech, whose stenographic record has been preserved.[9] The new Protector described a future Europe ruled by the German master race. The role of other peoples would be determined by their presumed racial qualities; it would range from inferior partnership to virtual slavery. In regard to the Czechs, Heydrich explained the long-term plan for their assimilation and for the "special treatment" of their racially or politically unfit minority. He emphasized the vital importance of Bohemia and Moravia for the Reich.

Czechoslovak historians have interpreted Heydrich's mission as the Nazi reply to a critical situation in the Protectorate. It is more

[6] Wighton, *Heydrich*, p. 255.

[7] P. Kleist, *Zwischen Hitler und Stalin*, p. 135.

[8] Cf. Č. Amort, "Švýcarsko zůstalo svobodnou zemí" [Switzerland Remained a Free Country], *Dějiny a současnost*, VIII (1966), No. 12, pp. 10–11. *Idem*, "Z nacistických plánů na zotročení Evropy" [The Nazi Plans for the Enslavement of Europe], *Mezinárodní politika*, 1962, pp. 572–73. Gerlach file, BDC.

[9] Speech of October 2, 1941, Král (ed.), *Vergangenheit*, pp. 122–33.

likely that the Germans—exuberant as they were at the prospect of their impending victory in the war—thought quite differently about the Czech situation at that time. The very stability of Bohemia and Moravia made the country especially suitable as the showplace of the New Order; in that part of Europe the transformation of the continent could be started most easily. Certainly there had been an upsurge of opposition there during the summer of 1941 which might have caused the Nazis to have second thoughts as to whether this favorable situation would last. But in his speech Heydrich greatly exaggerated the extent of the unrest. He spoke of an "obviously large-scale resistance movement" primarily to justify before his audience the use of drastic methods which the building of the New Order inevitably entailed.[10]

During the few days between his appointment and his inauguration, the new Protector had prepared a detailed master plan which he was going to put into effect immediately. He favored calculated terror in carefully administered doses: "At the moment, we must be hard, yet for tactical reasons, we must avoid any actions which would eventually force [the Czechs] into revolt, just because they wouldn't know any other way out."[11] Aware of the limits imposed by the requirements of the war, he reminded his audience that the Czech worker "must be given enough to eat, *fressen*—if I may put it so bluntly."[12]

As the key feature of his strategy, Heydrich proposed preferential treatment for workers and farmers, the two segments of the population indispensable for the proper functioning of the economy. But he stressed that this policy was not merely intended as a temporary expediency. In the short run, it was expected to split the subject nation and weaken its ability to resist. In the long run, the satisfaction of their material needs would neutralize the Czechs, thus politically facilitating the later indoctrination of those earmarked for assimilation.

[10] *Ibid.*, p. 128. Several Nazi documents from the time of Heydrich's Protectorship refer to the danger of a Czech revolt in the summer of 1941—in retrospect; contemporary sources do not suggest such a menacing situation. Cf. RSHA report about Communist activities, end of 1941, J. Křen (ed.), "Nové dokumenty o boji KSČ proti nacistickému panství" [New Documents Concerning the Struggle of the CPC against the Nazi Rule], *Příspěvky k dějinám KSČ*, I (1961), p. 235. Heydrich to Bormann, October 11, 1941, in Amort (ed.), *Heydrichiáda*, p. 85.

[11] Cf. *Zpověď K. H. Franka*, p. 133. Speech of October 2, 1941 in Král (ed.), *Vergangenheit*, p. 129.

[12] *Ibid.*

Although Frank had hinted at a similar approach earlier, Heydrich was the first to develop it into a coherent and systematic policy. His appointment concluded the period of haphazard German improvisation in the Protectorate, with its attendant vacillations resulting from the rivalry between Neurath and Frank. The head of the Reich Security Head Office eagerly seized upon the opportunity to test his talents as a statesman, in addition to those he had exercised as chief policeman.

Still, Heydrich's first act in the Protectorate was a police measure. On September 27, he ordered the arrest of Prime Minister Eliáš, against whom the Gestapo possessed an extensive dossier with incriminating evidence. A substantial portion of it may have come from the files of the Czechoslovak National Committee in exile which Nazi agents had reportedly rifled after the fall of Paris in 1940.[13] In a swift sequence of events, Horst Böhme, the chief of the Security Police in Prague, called upon Hácha at 5:05 P.M., informed him of the arrest, and added that the new Protector would visit him on the following day. At 7 P.M., the radio announced the establishment of summary courts. Soon afterward, martial law and a curfew were proclaimed in most districts, later to be extended to the entire country.[14]

The Nazi offensive took the Protectorate government by surprise. For months the exiles in London had been predicting tempting concessions and bargaining proposals by the Germans. Instead, Heydrich's actions seemed to indicate that Berlin might no longer be interested in any dealings with the official Czech representatives. Fearing an imminent abolition of the Protectorate's residual autonomy, Hácha prepared himself for abdication. In the evening of September 27, he had his office draft a letter of resignation addressed to Hitler. Contrary to Beneš's wishes, however, Hácha did not want this move to appear as a gesture of protest, and consequently took pains in emphasizing ill health and advanced age as its sole causes. He mentioned that he no longer felt himself to be "in possession of full vigor and capacity to work."[15] This was undoubtedly a sincere explanation. The President must have been

[13] Deposition of Karel Werner, August 29, 1946, Nur. NG-050, IfZ. Cf. M. Hanák to London, August 10, 1943, *DHCSP*, II, pp. 720–21.

[14] Note of Hácha's office, September 28, 1941, *ibid.*, p. 625. Decrees of September 27–28 and October 1, 1941, *VOB*, 1941, pp. 527–32. *České slovo*, September 30, 1941.

[15] Hácha to Hitler, September 28, 1941, *DHCSP*, II, p. 626.

convinced that all his efforts to mitigate the rigors of German rule had been in vain.

The Nazis had envisaged the possibility of Hácha's resignation and had prepared for it. A folder from Frank's archives, dated September 26, 1941, concerns the "constitutional settlement after the possible abdication of the Protectorate President and government with the preservation of full autonomy."[16] Still, the Germans, although prepared for Hácha's departure from office, preferred to prevent it. At his first interview with the President at noon on September 28, Heydrich did not mention any projected changes in the status of the Protectorate. He professed regret about the repressive measures which he had inaugurated "with bleeding heart," and indicated that the martial law was only temporary. Stressing his confidence in Hácha's unfaltering loyalty, Heydrich asked him for a formal reply by 2 : 30 P.M.[17]

The encounter with Heydrich sufficed to shake Hácha's will to go through with the abdication. The President may have dreaded personal reprisals against both himself and his compatriots. At the same time, he may have reasoned that there were advantages to his continuation in office, especially since his fears about the abolition of autonomy had apparently been groundless.

A lawyer rather than a politician, Hácha gave too much importance to the formal vestiges of Czech autonomy. He believed that as long as its institutional forms were preserved, German rule would not be absolute. It was possibly in this belief that he shelved the letter of resignation and delivered the desired reply to Heydrich at 2 : 30 sharp. This reply indicated that the President was still clinging desperately to the hope that the Czechs would be allowed to deal with all critical problems themselves. In it, he meekly told the Protector that such efforts would "meet with complete success if you lend us your helping hand whenever I or my government address ourselves to you with suggestions."[18]

Having secured Hácha's compliance, Heydrich had an easier task in dealing with the Czech cabinet two hours later. Referring to Eliáš's arrest, he left no doubts that its remaining members were implicated as well. They had known about the contacts with Lon-

[16]"Staatsrechtliche Regelung bei Rücktritt von Verfassungsfaktoren des Protektorats unter Aufrechterhaltung der vollen Autonomie," September 26, 1941, in Eliášová and Pasák (eds.), "Poznámky," p. 140.

[17]Heydrich to Hácha, September 28, 1941, *DHCSP*, II, pp. 626–27.

[18]Hácha to Heydrich, September 28, 1941, *ibid.*, p. 627.

don and had done nothing to prevent them. Suspecting their innermost thoughts, he warned the ministers not to attach any hopes to the possibility of Germany's defeat in the war. Any military setbacks, if they came at all, would only be the Führer's "creative intermissions." Heydrich bullied the ministers into a promise of unconditional obedience.[19]

On October 1, Eliáš appeared as defendant at an emergency session of the German People's Court in Prague. His was the only case in occupied Europe in which a prime minister stood trial for treason. Heydrich himself had prepared it, deliberately defying the established judicial rules.[20] He had the chief of the Prague Gestapo, rather than the Reich Attorney-General, represent the prosecution. Hand-picked reporters from among the Czech "activist" newsmen attended the proceedings which took place in Gestapo headquarters. The trial lasted a mere four hours.

Eliáš pleaded guilty to charges of maintaining treasonable contacts with the enemy and of abetting subversive activities. He repented these deeds and explained his motives as those of misguided patriotism. As his final defense speech, Prime Minister Eliáš read a prepared statement. He declared that he would willingly accept punishment as a warning to the Czechs if only his sacrifice would lead them toward sincere and loyal collaboration with the Germans. The court condemned the defendant to death.[21]

There is little doubt that the proceedings followed a carefully prepared scenario. There remains only the question of how Eliáš was made to play the pathetic role assigned to him. He was after all a man of integrity and courage, as indicated by his previous liaison with London. He could hardly have hoped that the statement would save him from the death sentence. He must have also realized what a prize his defense speech would represent for the Nazi propagandists.

The German text of the document, written in Eliáš's own hand, has been preserved in a photostatic copy.[22] Some of its features arouse suspicion. It has linguistic irregularities not characteristic of a native Czech. The press accounts of the declaration differ in a

---

[19] Heydrich's declaration to the cabinet, September 28, 1941, *ibid.*, p. 628.

[20] Controversy among Heydrich, Thierack and Schlegelberger, September–October 1941, R 22, Gr. 5/XXVIII-20, BA. Cf. H. Heiber, "Zur Justiz im Dritten Reich: Der Fall Eliáš," *Vierteljahrshefte für Zeitgeschichte*, III (1955), pp. 275–96.

[21] Eliáš's defense speech, October 1, 1941, *DHCSP*, II, p. 629.

[22] Reproduced *ibid.*, following p. 624.

significant passage referring in one version to the defendant's acceptance of the "expiation by death," in another to his "sacrifice." Finally, the newspapers reproduced the three pages of the manuscript partially hidden.[23]

Such incongruities do not necessarily impair the authenticity of the document, but they cast doubts upon it as an expression of Eliáš's free will. His composed appearance during the trial tends to rule out previous physical compulsion.[24] But there are indications of psychological pressure. In a letter to Bormann dated October 1 Heydrich hinted that his victim had been subjected to such pressure by his ex officio defense counsel the night before the trial.[25] A former guard in the prison where the condemned had been held after the sentence later claimed that Frank had secured Eliáš's compliance by threatening to execute 20,000 Czechs. According to his wife, the former Prime Minister mentioned in a message from prison that his statement had been extorted.[26]

On the other hand, the Nazis may have found extortion fairly easy. Apart from the dramatic circumstances, the content of Eliáš's speech did not deviate from his earlier policies. He had always underrated the importance of pro-German statements which—he estimated—all enemies of Germany would dismiss as having been extorted. In a message to Beneš on August 3, 1941, he mentioned that the people in the Protectorate well understood the behavior of their government. This was the same text in which he had argued that "quiet on all fronts was the only reasonable counsel."[27] In the final analysis, his declaration before the court was after all nothing more than a plea to the Czechs to behave in accordance with this counsel.

Eliáš's pragmatic approach points to the difficulties which exist in evaluating collaboration during World War II. The merit of his policies, and of his final advice in particular, can be questioned—his patriotic dedication cannot. During his entire career as Prime Minister, he was inspired by sincere devotion to the interests of his

---

[23] *Der Neue Tag*, October 3, 1941. *České slovo*, October 7, 1941. Cf. T. Pasák, "Prohlášení generála Aloise Eliáše před německým soudem v roce 1941 a jeho rozpornost" [The Disrepancies in the Declaration of General Alois Eliáš before the German Court in 1941], *Československý časopis historický*, XVI (1968), pp. 447–58.

[24] Cf. deposition of Karel Werner, August 29, 1946, Nur. NG-050, IfZ.

[25] Referred to in Pasák, "Prohlášení," p. 453.

[26] *Ibid.*, p. 452.

[27] See chapter 9, note 33, above.

people—as he understood them—and in this pursuit he knowingly risked his life. Shortly after the trial, Hácha pleaded for clemency for Eliáš.[28] The Germans did not grant the request, but Hitler decided to postpone the execution and hold the Prime Minister as hostage for the good behavior of the Czechs.[29] Only in June 1942, when eight months later peace in the country was again disturbed, did Eliáš die before a firing squad—a rare hero among pragmatists.[30]

Along with the termination of the Eliáš government's double game, the solution of the "Jewish question" held a high priority on Heydrich's agenda. The Protectorate was the next country—after Germany and Austria—slated to become *judenrein*. Heydrich began implementing this plan shortly after his arrival. As an example of his efficiency, he ordered that a transport of 5000 Czech Jews be sent directly to the killing centers in eastern Europe.[31] For further transports, he chose Theresienstadt, a fortress town in northwestern Bohemia, as the transition station before their extermination. It also served as a temporary reservation for those Jews from other parts of Europe whose outright physical liquidation the Nazis did not consider advisable for political or other reasons. The Jewish Council in Prague, hoping that deportation to Theresienstadt was an alternative to death, worked feverishly to help organize the shipments there. It submitted to Heydrich specific proposals for the creation of the new ghetto, and many of these proposals were conveniently implemented by the Nazis.[32]

Although not so openly brutal as in eastern Europe, the "final solution" in the Protectorate followed the no less horrifying pattern of bureaucratized extermination. Deprived of their property

[28] Hácha to Heydrich, October 2, 1941, *DHCSP*, II, pp. 630–31.

[29] *Der Neue Tag*, October 8, 1941. Minutes of Hitler's conference with Toussaint, October 7, 1941, in Amort (ed.), *Heydrichiáda*, p. 81.

[30] See chapter 11, note 59. In Czechoslovak historical literature of the dogmatic Marxist variety, Eliáš was classified as a collaborator. More recently, historians have taken a more understanding view, using metaphors of Eliáš as "the Czech Konrad Wallenrod" or "the great Hamlet of Czech history." Cf. Pasák, "Aktivističtí novináři," p. 175, and J. Tesař, "'Záchrana národa' a kolaborace" [The "Saving of the Nation" and Collaboration], *Dějiny a současnost*, X (1968), No. 5. p. 8.

[31] Note on conference with Heydrich, October 17, 1941, Král (ed.), *Vergangenheit*, pp. 135–36. *Der Neue Tag*, October 6, 1941. Lagus and Polák, *Město za mřížemi*, pp. 301–304.

[32] Heydrich to Bormann, October 11, 1941, in Amort (ed.), *Heydrichiáda*, p. 85. Ordinance of February 16, 1942, *VOB*, 1942, p. 38. Friedman, "Aspects," pp. 217–18. Lagus and Polák, *Město za mřížemi*, pp. 61–65.

and of their legal identities, after wearisome and humiliating formalities, tens of thousands of helpless victims reported in selected places at specified times, to be deported and eventually killed. Resigned to their fate, the overwhelming majority of them conformed to the procedure impassively.[33] With dull and deadly accuracy, the monstrous machinery, invented and directed by the Nazis, but run with the help of the victims themselves, continued operating until 1944. In that year, the remaining officials of the Prague Jewish Council, having duly submitted the last reports to their German superiors, were finally shipped to death.[34] By the end of the war, only 3371 of the 93,952 Jews deported from the Protectorate remained alive.[35]

The absence of mass anti-Semitism in Bohemia and Moravia did not affect the progress of the "final solution." Although many Czechs sympathized with the plight of their Jewish compatriots, often accepting "non-Aryan" property for safekeeping, effective help was rare. Only an estimated 424 Jews survived the war in hiding, a figure believed to be proportionately about the same as in Germany, or even lower.[36] For all practical purposes, the Nazis had succeeded in isolating the Jews from other people.

This outcome was decisively influenced by the timing of the deportations. Their beginning in October 1941 coincided with an unprecedented intimidation campaign against the Czechs, which the new Protector masterminded with utmost skill and equal cynicism. His secret speeches, and twenty-two reports to Bormann in which he analyzed his policies, reveal Heydrich as an expert organizer paying minute attention to detail.[37]

He was also very much aware of the possibilities open to an absolute ruler who wishes to mold the will of his subjects. In one

[33]Jewish Council in Prague to the Central Office for the Settlement of the Jewish Question, June 19, 1944, Records of the Eichmann Trial [Eich.], 1237, CU. In a wider context, the agonizing question of the submissiveness of the Nazi victims is discussed in H. Arendt, *Eichmann in Jerusalem*, pp. 11–12, 117–25.

[34]Jewish Council in Prague to the Central Office for the Settlement of the Jewish Question, June 19, 1944, Eich. 1192, CU. Lagus and Polák, *Město za mřížemi*, p. 331.

[35]*Ibid.*, p. 332.

[36]H. G. Adler, *Theresienstadt*, p. 15.

[37]Only a few of these illuminating documents, which are preserved in the Central State Archives in Prague, have been published. Of those cited here some are printed in German in Král's *Die Vergangenheit warnt*, others appear in a Czech translation in Amort's *Heydrichiáda*. Specific page references will be given with citations of individual documents from these works.

of his speeches Heydrich made an important distinction between two techniques of repression—"breaking" and "bending." He considered the latter especially suitable for the Czechs, as for all Slavs. In his opinion, they could not easily be broken because of their ability to bow before force and return to normal as soon as pressure had ceased.[38] In order to achieve optimum results, he hoped first to "break" them by a short spell of terror, in order to make "bending" easier later on.

The summary courts, established in Prague and Brno, were the principal instruments of terror. They handed down only three types of sentences: death, acquittal, and "transfer to the Gestapo," which implied shipment to a concentration camp. During October and November 1941, when they were most active, the courts sentenced 342 persons to death, and 1289 to be turned over to the Gestapo. They released 30.[39] The total number of sentences may seem low compared with the summary "justice" in occupied Poland or Russia, but it was extraordinarily high by Protectorate standards.

The significance of Heydrich's strategy lay less in the number of its victims than in its meticulous organization, which amounted to a perverse virtuosity. Primarily concerned with "optical effect," he used terror not only to eliminate actual offenders, but to intimidate the rest of the population. The radio and the press publicized the sentences, emphasizing that the condemned persons—with the notable exception of Eliáš—had been promptly executed. Since Heydrich hoped to keep repression within strict limits—"in order not to incite the Czechs to white fury"[40]—he was almost embarrassed after the Gestapo had rounded up more candidates for summary trial than he had originally wished to sentence for "optical" reasons. (In early September, the police had conducted especially successful raids: they arrested almost all the members of the ÚVOD and cut off its remaining radio links with London.) Heydrich quickly found the traditional Nazi solution for dealing with an overabundance of offenders. They were to be shipped to concentration camps and shot there during "attempted escape." Thus, he argued, there would be "created an outward impression

[38] Speech of February 4, 1942, in Amort (ed.), *Heydrichiáda*, p. 126.
[39] According to German statistics, *ibid.*, pp. 95–98. The figures 60 and 24 given here as the number of persons released on November 11 seem to be typographical errors.
[40] Speech of October 2, 1941, in Král (ed.), *Vergangenheit*, p. 129.

of complete peace in the Protectorate, which, after all, would conform to reality."[41]

Heydrich's propagandists emphasized that German justice did not distinguish between "the great and the small, the powerful and the weak."[42] In reality, this very emphasis indicated that the repression was extremely selective. Professional people—teachers, civil servants, army officers—were prominent among the victims. The execution of a high official in the Ministry of Agriculture, condemned for alleged abuse of the rationing cards, was given special publicity.[43]

The simultaneous prosecution of political and economic offenders as public enemies was designed to erase the distinction between their motives and to exploit popular feelings against profiteers. Furthermore, these "hyenas of the domestic front" served as scapegoats for current shortages in food supply. Informers were promised rewards if they would report speculators to special Gestapo offices in Prague and Brno.[44] Conveniently enough, the food situation began improving—though less because of these measures than as a result of the harvest. Heydrich nevertheless claimed credit for the improvement, boasting that "we have put things into better order here than [elsewhere] in the Reich."[45]

After ten fearsome days, the new Protector made his first friendly gesture on October 9. He lifted the curfew and had the summary courts suspend their activities for three days. This temporary relaxation was intended to create a favorable setting for Heydrich's approach to the workers. The NOÚZ, the official labor union, organized factory rallies throughout the country, at which the workers were encouraged to state their grievances. The NOÚZ made sure that the grievances expressed would concern only limited material demands, such as higher rations of fats and of tobacco.[46] On October 24, following another five-day respite in the trials, the Protector received with much pomp a delegation of hand-picked labor representatives at Prague Castle. Responding

[41] Note about Heydrich's conference, October 17, 1941, *ibid.*, pp. 134–35.

[42] Radio Prague on October 11, 1941, quoted in J. Hronek (ed.), *Černá kniha Heydrichova režimu* [The Black Book of the Heydrich Regime], p. 46.

[43] "Ost-Südost-Stimmen," October 17, 1941, NSDAP, T-81, 548, 5320975, NA.

[44] "Hyänen der inneren Front," *Der Neue Tag*, October 10, 1941, *České slovo*, October 2, 1941.

[45] Speech of February 4, 1942 in Amort (ed.), *Heydrichiáda*, p. 139.

[46] *Der Neue Tag*, October 10, 1941. *České slovo*, October 21, 22, and 26, 1941. Heydrich to Bormann, October 11, 1941, in Amort (ed.), *Heydrichiáda*, p. 86.

to their declaration of loyalty, he announced a substantial increase in the rations of fats and ordered free distribution of shoes for work. The food confiscated from speculators was assigned to factory canteens.[47]

On December 5, there followed a similar ceremony with Czech farmers. Heydrich gave a last promise of amnesty for those who would correct their earlier understated production figures. This method had already brought "astounding results," making large quantities of previously undeclared produce, especially thousands of unreported hogs, available for distribution. The Protector praised the cautious disposition of the farmers and juxtaposed their "common sense" with the "irresponsibility" of the intellectuals.[48]

Heydrich believed that the best results could be achieved if the Czech workers were treated like their German colleagues. Both received free lunches in the factories and advanced vocational instruction. The NOÚZ—remodeled as the Czech counterpart of the German Labor Front—organized a "Joy of Work" campaign equivalent to Germany's "Strength through Joy." The participants were treated to "unpolitical" entertainment: sport matches, band concerts, musicals, sentimental movies, and theater plays. The Protector also inaugurated the "Heydrich Action," which offered several thousand workers free vacations in well-known resorts. A series of new laws improved health, accident and old-age insurance, providing also for special protection of miners, female employees, and apprentices.[49]

There is little doubt that Heydrich's courting of the working classes was motivated by expediency rather than by genuine concern for their welfare. He remained cool and formal at the meetings with their frightened and servile delegates. They represented, after all, the portion of the population where most candidates for future "special treatment" were to be found. For the time being, however, Heydrich's social measures did offer their recipients tangible advantages. These advantages were of course linked with rigid regimentation and enforced high production-quotas. Still, both sides found the arrangement convenient. By force and by

---

[47] *České slovo*, October 26, 1941.

[48] *A–Zet Pondělník*, December 8, 1941. *DHCSP*, II, pp. 646–50.

[49] Heydrich to Bormann, May 18, 1942, in Amort (ed.), *Heydrichiáda*, pp. 160–61. *Der Neue Tag*, May 1 and 6, 1942. E. Schubert (ed.), *Deutscher Sozialaufbau in Böhmen und Mähren*, pp. 32–33, 45–49.

concessions, Heydrich instilled narrow materialism and obedience into the Czech working classes, thereby further contributing to their political passivity.

Protector Heydrich's one-man show confined the Hácha government to the role of passive onlookers, totally ignored by the Protector despite Hácha's pleas. Heydrich paid no attention to the President's suggestion that he appoint a new prime minister to replace Eliáš. To his own associates he stated bluntly that under no circumstances would he allow the Czechs again to have an "intact and active government."[50] At the same time, Nazi propaganda heaped abuse upon the Czech authorities for their alleged inefficiency and political unreliability.

A curious incident fitted into the German scheme to discredit the Hácha administration. On October 11, Karel Lažnovský, a prominent "activist" journalist, died with symptoms of poisoning. The official press immediately accused a "leading Czech personality" of complicity in his death.[51] The allusion was to Eliáš's meeting with a delegation of pro-German newsmen held three weeks earlier. After the conference, which had taken place upon the former prime minister's invitation, a number of participants had been mysteriously taken ill and Lažnovský had succumbed. Simultaneously with the press allegations, Heydrich ordered an investigation, undoubtedly hoping that the suspicion of murder would be substantiated. The police took great pains in reconstructing the incident, including the preparation of supposedly poisonous sandwiches. But neither these efforts nor the autopsy led to results conclusive enough to justify a criminal charge.

Trying desperately to dissociate itself from the apparent conspiracy for murder, the Protectorate government ordered a main embankment in Prague to be renamed after Lažnovský, assigned a high pension to his widow, and staged a state funeral for the "martyr." But not even the presence of the entire cabinet there seemed to appease the Germans.

They let Moravec use the occasion for a vicious funeral oration, in which not even Hácha escaped accusations of duplicity. More than any previous incident, this performance by the leading

[50] Heydrich to Lammers, October 9, 1941, R 43 II/1324, BA. Note about Heydrich's conference, October 17, 1941, in Král (ed.), *Vergangenheit*, p. 138.

[51] *Der Neue Tag*, October 12, 14, and 15, 1941. Pasák, "Aktivističtí novináři," pp. 185–91.

collaborator—at the time of Heydrich's blatant overtures to "activist" journalists—suggested that the Nazis might be contemplating total replacement of the official Czech leadership.[52] The prospect of rule by Moravec and the like, and the alarming progress of the executions finally persuaded the ministers to act. At a special session on October 22, they urged the President to intercede with the Protector and ask for an end to the martial law proclaimed on September 27. The President only vaguely promised to "think it over."[53] By that time he appeared to be a broken man, frightened at the mere thought of dealing with Heydrich. His contemporary photographs reinforce this impression. Although conclusive evidence is lacking, Hácha probably did not even meet with Heydrich. In the last week of October, the Protector was absent from Prague most of the time.[54]

In late October or early November occurred what Beneš later referred to as Hácha's "complete reversal."[55] The Protectorate President undoubtedly came to the conclusion that the only service he could still perform for his people was to convince them of the futility of all resistance. There was no way of survival but complete submission. Hácha composed an address to the nation and asked Heydrich's permission to read it over the radio.[56] In the broadcast on November 8, he appealed to the Czechs to "fulfill [their] obligations to the Reich completely and sincerely in a manly and determined manner." He continued: "Citizens, do not listen to the heckling talk of the exiles . . . who by asking us to follow their radio allurements can only bring us great catastrophes . . . . At stake is no longer merely the fate of individuals but the fate of your children and of the whole nation."[57] In his earlier public pronouncements in favor of German-Czech collaboration, Hácha had often used ambiguous wording intended to reassure the Germans rather than to convince the Czechs. In contrast, he now abandoned any remaining reserve and used all his persuasive powers to make the people obey his advice and submit.

[52] *Der Neue Tag*, October 16, 1941. Cf. Heydrich's address to newsmen, October 10, 1941, *DHCSP*, II, pp. 632–34.

[53] Minutes of cabinet meeting, October 22, 1941, *ibid.*, pp. 635–36.

[54] Hitler's daily activities, p. 79, MA 3 (1), IfZ.

[55] Minutes from the conference between Czechoslovak Communist leaders and Beneš in Moscow, December 13, 1943, *Cesta ke Květnu*, I, p. 42.

[56] Hácha to Heydrich, November 1, 1941, *DHCSP*, II, p. 636.

[57] Hácha's address, November 8, 1941, *ibid.*, pp. 636–37.

Hácha's address consummated his break with London. It prompted Beneš to declare officially that the Protectorate government no longer held any legal authority.[58] The Czech service of the BBC began denouncing Hácha as a traitor. In a press release on December 7, the Protectorate President replied bitterly:

Mr. Beneš . . . does not see, as I do, the tears of mothers and wives who address their desperate pleas to me because their sons and husbands fell into disaster having been seduced by deceptive radio broadcasts. He is in a position to permit himself illusions, to build castles in the air, and to paint alluring pictures of the future. . . . For us, there is no way but to face reality with resolution and to soberly act in accordance with bare facts.[59]

There is no reason to question the sincerity of Hácha's words and the depth of his despair. Heydrich noticed it promptly and commented to his associates that the President, though with "considerable inner inhibitions," had finally moved over to the German side.[60] From that time onward, he relinquished any policy of his own and slid into the role of a puppet controlled by the Nazis. It is no wonder that Hácha's mental condition deteriorated rapidly, arousing doubts about his sanity in the last two years of the war.

In an article published in *Die Aktion*, the theoretical journal of the Nazi Party, Heydrich explained the two stages of his Protectorate policy: a short "destructive" phase, to be followed by a "constructive" period. "After a necessarily strict rounding up it is easier to be fair and humane."[61] But toward the end of 1941, more plausible reasons than his alleged humane impulse accounted for the slowdown of Heydrich's drive. Frank later recalled that the course of the war had necessitated at that time "a scrupulous revision of political strategy and tactics in the Protectorate."[62] In December, the stalemate in the battle of Moscow frustrated Hitler's hopes for a quick end to the Russian campaign. In the same month, America's entry into the war widened the scope of the world conflict. The Nazis' confidence in victory remained unimpaired but

---

[58] Reported in the news journal *Čechoslovák* (London), November 28, 1941.
[59] *Der Neue Tag*, December 7, 1941.
[60] Speech of February 4, 1942, in Amort (ed.), *Heydrichiáda*, p. 129.
[61] R. Heydrich, "Nationalsozialistische Führung," *Die Aktion*, III (1942), p. 313.
[62] K. H. Frank, "Reichspolitik in Böhmen und Mähren," March 1944, in Král (ed.), *Vergangenheit*, p. 167.

they realized that greater exertion would be needed. In the occupied countries they became much more interested in the war contribution of the subject peoples.

Heydrich now tried above all to commit the Czechs firmly to the German side. He no longer found it advisable to keep the Hácha government paralyzed. On the contrary, its activation appeared to be a desirable counter-move against Beneš's formal declaration of Czechoslovakia's belligerence, made in December 1941. The Protectorate government, to be sure, must never again become the "supreme clearinghouse for Czech complaints against the Reich." Yet it could still be useful if transformed into "an extended arm of the Reich Protector." [63]

The cabinet reorganization took place in January 1942. In consultation with Frank—who had become his fascinated disciple—Heydrich carefully weighed the suitability of possible candidates for ministerial posts. Unlike Neurath, he selected them himself, rather than merely confirming Hácha's nominees. The most important was Walter Bertsch, the former chief of the economics department in the Office of the Protector. As the only German in the cabinet, he was given the vital Ministry of Economics and Labor, with jurisdiction extending over industry, trade, and labor relations. Emanuel Moravec became Minister of Education and the head of the newly-created Office for Public Enlightenment, the Czech counterpart of Goebbels's Propaganda Ministry. The Protector trusted Moravec, whose "healthy ambition" he considered an asset rather than a liability. He had no illusions about the sincerity of the other appointees' pro-German feelings, but considered them acceptable for various other reasons. Jaroslav Krejčí, who in addition to being Minister of Justice became the Chairman of the government, seemed to Heydrich a man "who agreed with the last person he saw." Adolf Hrubý, a former Agrarian who received the post of Minister of Agriculture, advocated collaboration "for realistic reasons." As Minister of the Interior, the Protector had originally wanted to keep Gendarmerie General Josef Ježek, who had held that office since 1939. Heydrich had little doubt about Ježek's compliance, especially after he had hinted at his knowledge of earlier contacts between the Minister's relatives and the underground. However, Ježek showed unexpected courage in refusing a

---

[63] Heydrich to Bormann, January 22, 1942, in Amort (ed.), *Heydrichiáda*, p. 122. Speech of February 4, 1942, *ibid.*, p. 130.

specific promise of allegiance to the Reich in a conversation with Heydrich and left the room with an "insulting remark" about Frank. Significantly, the Protector grumbled but was impressed, and Ježek suffered no harsher treatment than being relieved of his duties. He was replaced by Richard Bienert, the former Provincial President of Bohemia. Although Bienert had been a member of the Czech anti-Austrian underground during World War I, Heydrich thought that in his sixties he had cooled sufficiently. Moreover, Bienert's German ancestry pleased him from the racial point of view. The same consideration played a role in the appointment of the Minister of Transportation and Technology, Jindřich Kamenický. In any case, like his colleague in the Ministry of Finances, Josef Kalfus, Kamenický headed a relatively unimportant department, its duties to be confined to routine tasks.[64]

On January 19, 1942, Heydrich installed the new government. In order to enhance the "optical effect" of this act, he also lifted the martial law and announced that the remaining students had been released from concentration camps. German propaganda hailed the alleged political consolidation in the country and emphasized the Protector's new confidence in the Czech "autonomous" administration.

Although after January 1942 autonomy formally remained, its character changed significantly. In one of his secret speeches, Heydrich appropriately observed that ". . . the Czech minister is actually no minister in our sense; we know quite well that he fulfills orders . . . . I can't put up with any Czech cabinet council deliberating *whether* my instruction should be carried out or not. The Czech ministers can only talk about *how* to carry it out."[65] Moreover, since one of its members was a German, the entire cabinet had to use German as its business language. "Those other gentlemen cannot possibly expect . . . *Parteigenosse* Bertsch . . . to learn Czech."[66] Transformed into a mere council of ministers, the cabinet ceased to function as a collective body. Each minister was now individually responsible for all measures within his department. The council no

---

[64] *Ibid.*, pp. 130–33. Heydrich to Bormann, January 22, 1942, *ibid.*, pp. 123–24. Cf. J. Ježek, "Odchod ministra vnitra z protektorátní vlády" [The Departure of the Minister of the Interior from the Protectorate Cabinet], *Dějiny a současnost*, X (1968), No. 10, pp. 46–48.

[65] Speech of February 4, 1942, in Amort (ed.), *Heydrichiáda*, p. 133.

[66] *Ibid.*

longer deliberated policies at plenary sessions and its chairman merely served as coordinator between the ministers.[67]

The reorganization on the upper level foreshadowed a reform of the entire administration. Originally prepared by Heydrich, this reform was carried out later in 1942. It implemented the concept of "administration by Reich order" (*Reichsauftragsverwaltung*).[68] The German agencies transferred most of the routine business to their Czech counterparts—ministries, provincial governments, and selected district governments. This arrangement finally ended the Protectorate's administrative dualism. Integrated into the bureaucracy of the Reich, the Czech government bodies which received the new assignments were now even formally subordinated to German superiors in all their operations. As an additional safeguard, more Nazi officials were installed directly in the "autonomous" administration. As the work load of the German agencies was cut, many of their employees could be freed for service elsewhere in Europe or for military duty. The new, small *Oberlandräte* merely acted as "inspectors of the Reich Protector," issuing directives and supervising their implementation by the Czech officials.[69]

The Nazis' excellent experience with the local bureaucracy in Bohemia and Moravia justified this experiment, which was unique in Hitler's Europe. By the end of 1942, over 350,000 Czech administrative employees worked under the control of a mere 738 Germans who belonged to the Office of the Protector and of another 1146 who sat in various Czech agencies.[70] Shortly before Heydrich's arrival, the corresponding numbers had been 9362 and 4706. At the same time, the size of the army and police forces remained approximately the same. Consequently, the Germans ruled the Protectorate with less effort, yet with undiminished effectiveness.

[67] Ordinances of January 15, 1942, *SGV*, 1942, pp. 75–80; February 27, 1942, *VOB*, 1942, p. 42; March 4, 1942, *SGV*, 1942, pp. 551–52, and June 15, 1942, *ibid.*, pp. 997–1003.

[68] Šisler, "Příspěvek," p. 55. A. Ševčík, "Příspěvek k dějinám okupační správy v Brně v letech 1939–1945" [The History of the Occupation Administration in Brno in 1939–1945], in *Brno v minulosti a dnes*, VI, p. 135.

[69] Decree of May 7, 1942, *RGB*, 1942, I, p. 329. Ordinance of May 23, 1942, *VOB*, 1942, pp. 118–22. Report of the Office of the Protector, June 11, 1942, EAP 99/1234, Alex. Cf. A. Bohmann, "Die Stellung der Oberlandräte-Inspekteure," *Zeitschrift für Ostforschung*, XV (1966), pp. 118–26.

[70] These figures did not include the police and the military. Report of the Office of the Protector, November 1942, quoted in Král, *Otázky*, I, p. 23. Cf. chapter 5, notes 47 and 48.

From the Nazi point of view, Heydrich's achievement seemed especially impressive since he did not sacrifice long-term goals to temporary expediency. He further accelerated the Germanization program. Under his auspices, mobile X-ray units began touring the country to screen candidates for assimilation. Special identity cards were introduced, in which every head of a family had to give extensive information about its background and present circumstances; this measure was intended not only to tighten administrative control, but also to facilitate racial selection.[71] The first decisive steps towards the Germanization of Czech youth were taken. All Protectorate nationals between ten and eighteen years of age became liable to "service duty." In the future, they were to be indoctrinated in special camps run by Hitler Youth instructors. For the time being, the Board for Youth Education, headed by Moravec, began to organize extracurricular activities for school children in order to counteract the nationalism of their parents and teachers.[72]

Further measures, such as the inauguration of annual "Prague Weeks" of performing arts, were intended to "impress the Slavs with German power and culture."[73] Heydrich converted the former Czechoslovak parliament into a German concert hall and sponsored elaborate celebrations at the anniversary of Mozart's death. The object of his special attention was the German University in Prague. The institution, at that time a preserve of Sudeten German parochialism, had degenerated—as observed in the Berlin Ministry of Education—into a "provincial school of pitiful standing."[74] Intent on restoring its academic excellence (as he understood it), the Protector called in new professors from Germany and Austria, most of them pseudo experts in racial theory and Slavic studies (*Ostkunde*). Along with the German Academy of Sciences in

[71] Speech of February 4, 1942, in Král (ed.), *Vergangenheit*, p. 145. Cf. chapter 7, note 22.

[72] Heydrich to Bormann, May 18, 1942, in Amort (ed.), *Heydrichiáda*, pp. 158–60. Speech of February 4, 1942, in Král (ed.), *Vergangenheit*, pp. 147–48. Ordinances of May 28–30 and August 3, 1942, *SGV*, 1942, pp. 905–913.

[73] Berndt's report about conference with Heydrich, November 15, 1941, Propag., T-70, 94, 3613244–54, NA. E. Schneider (ed.), *Reinhard Heydrich: Ein Leben der Tat*, pp. 33–34.

[74] Harmjanz's note, December 20, 1941, 76/328, GSA. Cf. K. Kučera and M. Truc, "Poznámky k fašizaci německé university pražské" [The Fascist Transformation of the German University in Prague], in *Historia Universitatis Carolinae Pragensis*, I–II, pp. 203–23.

Bohemia and Moravia and the Heydrich Foundation, the Prague University was to focus on studies relating to the ethnic reorganization of east central Europe.[75]

Heydrich's posture as benefactor of the arts and sciences added to his growing power and prestige. Hitler was much impressed with the achievements of the Acting Protector and Himmler took obvious pride in his protégé. Goebbels noted in his diary: "Heydrich's policy in the Protectorate is truly a model. He mastered the crisis there with ease. As a result the Protectorate is now in the best of spirits, quite in contrast with the other occupied or annexed areas."[76]

Although conclusive evidence is lacking, it seems likely that by May 1942, Heydrich considered his mission in Prague completed. He was ready to move on to another country, possibly to France.[77] On May 27 he made preparations for leaving Prague, perhaps to discuss his new assignment with Hitler.

Was the Protectorate really "in the best of spirits," or was it pacified only in the imagination of the Nazi leaders, cleverly

[75] Files of the Reich Ministry of Education, 76/329, 336, GSA. Notes for conversation with Krosigk, April 27, 1942; Heydrich to Krosigk, May 20, 1942, R 2/12465, BA. Cf. K. Fremund (ed.), "Heydrichova nadace—důležitý nástroj nacistické vyhlazovací politiky" [The Heydrich Foundation: An Important Instrument of Nazi Extermination Policies], *Sborník archivních prací*, XIV (1964), No. 1, pp. 3–38.

[76] *The Goebbels Diaries*, p. 3. Cf. Frank's memorandum, May 28, 1942, in Král (ed.), *Die Deutschen*, p. 478. During Heydrich's Protectorship, the discovery of Thümmel's secret contacts with the Czechoslovak intelligence dealt a heavy blow to the *Abwehr*. Heydrich exploited this incident to consummate his triumph over Canaris. At a conference in Prague in May 1942, the chief of the *Abwehr* conceded the Security Service extensive authority over his own agency in the whole of Europe. Heydrich to Bormann, May 16, 1942, in Amort (ed.), *Heydrichiáda*, p. 153. G. Buchheit, *Der deutsche Geheimdienst*, p. 189. Cf. Amort and Jedlička, *Tajemství*, pp. 129, 137–39.

[77] In early May 1942, Heydrich went to Paris to install Karl Oberg as Higher SS and Police Leader. Oberg's appointment marked the successful end of Heydrich's long struggle with the military over influence in occupied France. From Paris, the Protector wrote to Gies, Frank's secretary in Prague, that Hitler might place him "in charge of the occupation administration in France, to act at the same time as the supervisor of the Vichy government." Later in May, Heydrich is said to have been preparing memoranda for Hitler concerning the reorganization of the occupation regimes in Europe according to the experience he had gained in the Protectorate. Heydrich to Gies, May 7, 1942, quoted in Amort (ed.), *Heydrichiáda*, p. 37. Heydrich to Bormann, May 18, 1942, *ibid.*, p. 157. Reitlinger, *The SS*, pp. 207–10. Cf. Amort, "Z nacistických plánů," pp. 572–73.

manipulated by Heydrich? The German Counter-Intelligence records from the period of his Protectorship show that acts of sabotage were not eliminated. A comparison with the previous evidence even indicates their increase immediately after the arrival of the Protector in September 1941. (See Table 8.) Only in the winter of

TABLE 8. *Acts of Sabotage in the Protectorate*[78]

1941	September	114	1941	December	75	1942	March	32
	October	246	1942	January	37		April	34
	November	157		February	19		May	51

1941–1942 did the *Abwehr* counter-intelligence agency record a decline. But a new rise began in March 1942, although on a considerably smaller scale than before.

The contemporary reports by the Reich Security Head Office (RSHA) mentioned distribution of underground leaflets, formation of new resistance groups and attempted industrial sabotage throughout the period.[79] They attributed many such actions to the Communists. Although allowance must be made for the Nazis' sweeping definition of this term, the Communists do indeed seem to have been quite active. Their underground newspaper, *Rudé právo*, appeared regularly and its editorial quality improved significantly. In early 1942, the paper hinted that the party had sponsored new clandestine organizations of intellectuals and of youths.[80] Such claims are difficult to verify, but at least they indicate that the CPC had recovered from the losses it had suffered in early 1942 and had escaped Heydrich's persecution relatively unscathed. In particular, it established a second Central Committee to replace that destroyed by the Gestapo earlier in 1941.[81] The pro-Western underground, which—in contrast to the Communists

[78] J. Doležal, "Diverze a vznik partyzánského hnutí v českých zemích [Sabotage and the Origins of the Partisan Movement in Bohemia and Moravia], in *Z bojů za svobodu* [The Struggles for Freedom], I, p. 114. Cf. J. Doležal and J. Křen, "Český odboj a heydrichiáda" [The Czech Resistance and the Heydrich Terror], *Nová mysl*, 1962, p. 983.

[79] "Meldungen wichtiger staatspolizeilicher Ereignisse," R 58/200–204, BA.

[80] Heydrich to Bormann, November 16, 1941, in *Zločiny nacistů za okupace*, p. 97. Geschke to Müller, November 12, 1941, in Amort (ed.), *Heydrichiáda*, pp. 102, 105, 107–108. "Meldungen wichtiger staatspolizeilicher Ereignisse," January 9, 1942, fols. 16–17, R 58/200, BA.

[81] About its chief organizer, see G. Bareš, *Tři pře Jana Zíky* [Jan Zíka's Three Trials], a glorifying account with extensive but unverifiable information.

—had been hit severely by Heydrich, noted the growing prestige of the CPC: "The intense, almost public activities of the Communist Party might in the course of time convince the masses that it is the only capable force which is afraid neither of sacrifice nor of work. It makes an impression on the people and gains their sympathies."[82]

Whether waged by the Communists or by Beneš's followers, however, the actual extent of resistance activities remained insignificant. The regular internal reports of the Nazi authorities do not reveal any sense of insecurity. Even at the height of terror in the fall of 1941, when the Gestapo was especially busy, the incidence of arrests for political offenses in major cities in the Protectorate did not exceed that in Germany itself.[83] The Protector anticipated that the small minority of irreconcilable Czechs would eventually be extirpated by being "put against the wall."[84] But rather than this minority, his principal target was the masses.

In their hearts, the majority of the Czechs remained hostile. Indeed, the Security Serivce noted in May 1942 that "the recently observed stiffening of the anti-German attitude of the Czech population" continued.[85] For Heydrich, however, inner attitude was of little relevance. He had no illusions about his ability to change it in the short run. In his secret speech of October 2, he admitted explicitly: "We shan't win over the people, we don't want it and we wouldn't succeed in doing it anyway."[86] For Heydrich's purpose, their acts mattered more than their thoughts. He was convinced that "breaking" and "bending" could make men behave in accordance with the ruler's wishes even against their better judgment.

The actual results of Heydrich's policies seemed to confirm his estimate. In the winter of 1941–1942, for example, the Nazis were very favorably impressed by the response of the Protectorate population to the collection of skis and warm clothing for German soldiers at the eastern front.[87] The Czech workers also participated readily in free vacations under the auspices of the Heydrich Action and in return carried out their tasks to complete German

[82] Jindra to London, May 16, 1942, quoted in Lašťovička, *V Londýně*, p. 235.

[83] "Meldungen wichtiger staatspolizeilicher Ereignisse," fols. 58–61, R 58/200, BA.

[84] Speech of October 2, 1941, Král (ed.), *Vergangenheit*, pp. 132–33.

[85] Report of SD Prague, May 19, 1942, in Král (ed.), *Die Deutschen*, p. 472.

[86] Speech of October 2, 1941, in Král (ed.), *Vergangenheit*, p. 131.

[87] Gregory to Propaganda Ministry, January 12–February 16, 1942, NSDAP, T-81, 24, 21286–88, 21307–308, NA. Cf J. Fučik, *Milujeme svůj národ*, p. 231.

satisfaction. In 1944, the armament experts in Berlin estimated that work morale in Protectorate industry was even better than in Germany.[88] The Czech bureaucracy performed faultlessly "by Reich order" until the end of the Reich's existence. In May 1942, Heydrich's record in Bohemia and Moravia elicited the following comment from Hitler:

Recklessly eliminating everything dangerous but otherwise treating them well is the right policy . . . which is naturally suited for the Czechs. It will make the entire Czech population finally adopt Hácha's inner attitude . . . . The Czechs could be made into fanatical supporters of the Reich now, if we give these gourmands double rations and don't send them to fight in the East. Then they will feel morally obliged to work twice as much in the armament industries and elsewhere.[89]

Hitler's remark about "fanatical supporters" was clearly an overstatement. Yet the success of the "breaking" and "bending" was evident. For most people, compliance, though with inner reluctance, grew into a habit, making them behave in the prescribed way even if no threat was immediately present. The Nazis' satisfaction with the conditions in Bohemia and Moravia is the most convincing evidence that the efforts of the underground to wage effective resistance remained inconclusive at best. Both the Czechs' previous record of compliance and Heydrich's adroitness account for this outcome. It is a matter of pure conjecture to speculate whether other nations would have done much better in the face of his calculated ruthlessness. Fortunately, they were spared the test because of the sudden end of Heydrich's career in May 1942.

[88] Minutes of the meeting of the Fighter Staff, June 16, 1944. Nur. NG-1569, IfZ.

[89] Picker, *Hitler's Tischgespräche*, conversation reported in passages on p. 288 and p. 91.

11 *THE DEFEAT OF CZECH RESISTANCE*

H EYDRICH left his country seat near Prague on the morning of May 27, 1942, presumably to confer with Hitler about assignment to France, but he never completed his trip. In the suburbs of the capital, his car was bombed by a group of men. The explosion injured but did not kill him, and the attackers escaped from the scene.[1]

Never before during the war had a Nazi of Heydrich's rank been the target of an assassination attempt. The audacity of the attempt was especially striking in a country with no significant record of violent resistance. The Protector himself felt so secure there that he had dispensed with his bodyguards and had driven alone with his chauffeur in an open car. Now it was the Nazis who were caught by surprise as events took a new turn in Bohemia and Moravia.

The attempt on Heydrich's life had been devised in London. Until the British and the Czechoslovak archives are fully opened to researchers, the motives for the plot can only be surmised from fragmentary evidence. Beneš's desire to demonstrate the strength of the Czech resistance appears to have been the most important motivation. His first determined efforts to promote subversive activities in the Protectorate dated from August 1941. But the ÚVOD soon pointed out the meager prospects of such an undertaking.[2] Perhaps even before Heydrich's appointment Beneš may

---

[1] In the extensive literature about this incident, scholarly studies are still scarce. A good compilation of facts is M. Cygański, "Zamach na Reinharda Heydricha i tragedia Lidic" [The Attempt on Reinhard Heydrich's Life and the Tragedy of Lidice], *Wojskowy Przegląd Historyczny*, 1964, pp. 163–85. Various interpretations are summarized in *Odboj a revoluce* [Resistance and Revolution], pp. 170–77. The following more detailed accounts by journalists are often inaccurate: A. Burgess, *Seven Men at Daybreak*; M. Ivanov, *Nejen černé uniformy* [Not Only the Black Uniforms . . .]; D. Hamšík and J. Pražák, *Eine Bombe für Heydrich*; Amort (ed.), *Heydrichiáda*, pp. 11–78.

[2] See chapter 9, notes 43 and 46, above.

have concluded that only "imported" resistance could produce the desired effect. The decimation of the underground by Heydrich seemed to confirm such a conclusion, providing at the same time an additional reason for striking back.

Contrary to later assertions, especially those popular with postwar German authors, the assassination was not originally designed as a response to Heydrich's successful "pacification" of the Protectorate. The first reference to the plan was made at a conference at the Czechoslovak Ministry of Defense in London only five days after the Acting Protector's September 28 arrival in Prague.[3] At that time *a* political assassination was considered and Heydrich was merely mentioned as one of several possible targets. The government-in-exile justified his selection by the necessity to retaliate with an act which would "make history."[4] Throughout October, a number of Czech and Slovak soldiers underwent training for this mission in special SOE centers. According to the original plan, Heydrich was to die by October 28, the Czechoslovak Independence Day. Jozef Gabčík and Jan Kubiš were eventually chosen for the task, but bad weather and technical difficulties delayed their landing in the Protectorate until December 28, 1941. They were shortly followed by other airborne agents, who succeeded in establishing contacts with the remnants of the underground and also in restoring its radio communications with London.[5]

Despite the exiles' reluctance to claim full credit, the plot against Heydrich seems to have been an overwhelmingly Czech undertaking. The British SOE trained the agents, equipped and transported them.[6] But all other arrangements were probably worked out by the Czechoslovak intelligence department in London which enjoyed a large measure of independence.[7] Beneš, who never fully overcame his bitterness toward the British—the chief accomplices of Munich—may have deliberately kept them in the dark about many of the details.

Once in the Protectorate, Gabčík and Kubiš found local conditions worse than expected. They maintained deep secrecy about

[3] Minutes of the conference of October 3, 1941, quoted in Ivanov, *Nejen černé uniformy*, pp. 35–36.

[4] "Abschlussbericht, Attentat auf SS-Obergruppenführer Heydrich am 27.5.42 in Prag," p. 10, Occ E 7 (a)-5, Yivo.

[5] In Amort (ed.), *Heydrichiáda*, p. 27.

[6] Communication by F. E. Keary, "Proceedings of a Conference on Britain and European Resistance," p. Cz. 10.

[7] See chapter 9, note 10, above.

their assignment, waiting almost five months before its implementation. At last in May 1942, their underground supporters guessed the purpose of the mission. Alarmed at its possible consequences, they dispatched an urgent coded message to London on May 9 and again on May 12. It was an adamant demand that the assassination plan be cancelled:

An attempt against Heydrich's life . . . would be of no use for the Allies, and its consequences for our people would be immeasurable. Not only would it put our hostages and political prisoners into jeopardy, but it would also cost thousands of additional lives and expose the nation to unprecedented suppression. At the same time it would sweep away the last remains of [our] organization, thus preventing any further action here which would be of use to the Allies. We beg your therefore to see that the attack is not carried out. To delay is dangerous. Give the order immediately.[8]

It is interesting that this unfavorable estimate of the situation conformed with the British decision to suspend all offensive operations by the SOE until August 1942—another indication that the government-in-exile acted independently.[9] Beneš avoided a direct reply to the objections raised by Prague. Yet his message of May 15 leaves no doubt that he did not call off the orders given to Gabčík and Kubiš. He defended his policy as follows:

I expect that in a forthcoming offensive the Germans will push with all their forces. They are sure to have some success . . . . In such a case I would expect German proposals for an inconclusive peace. The crisis would be a serious one and it would shake some people even here among the Allies . . . . In such a situation, an act of violence such as disturbances, direct subversion, sabotage, or demonstrations, might be imperative or even necessary in our country. This would save the nation internationally, and even great sacrifice would be worth it.[10]

Regardless of Beneš's earlier fallacies and misconceptions, it is difficult to believe that he still seriously feared a compromise peace as late as May 1942. Deliberately or out of inertia, he used this

[8] Silver-A to London, May 4, 1942, quoted in Frank to Daluege, June 22, 1942 in Amort (ed.), *Heydrichiáda*, p. 236. Silver-A to London, May 12, 1942, quoted in A. Benčík *et al.*, *Partyzánské hnutí v Československu za druhé světové války* [The Partisan Movement in Czechoslovakia during World War II], p. 41. Cf. L. Vaněk, "Atentát na Heydricha" [The Attempt on Heydrich's Life], *Dějiny a současnost*, IV (1962), No. 4, p. 11.

[9] Cf. J. Bennett, *British Broadcasting*, pp. 76–78.

[10] Beneš's message, May 15, 1942, quoted in Král, *Otázky*, III, pp. 242–43.

improbable argument to justify the assassination plan. He seems to have clung to the scheme as the last resort to dramatize Czech resistance, since Heydrich's intervention had made unlikely the demonstrative resignation of the Hácha government and had effectively forestalled manifestations of popular discontent.

Thus Beneš, the statesman who had won fame as a diplomat in the councils of the League of Nations, now found himself resorting to an unfamiliar instrument of national policy—a calculated political assassination. Beneš denied responsibility for it after the war.[11] But his denial is hardly credible against our evidence. It rather suggests that he was not satisfied with the outcome of the plot—and especially that he wanted to escape criticism for the heavy sacrifices which the attack on Heydrich had inevitably entailed.

On May 27, two hours and twenty minutes after the bomb had wrecked Heydrich's car, Hitler issued instructions to Frank by telephone. He entrusted the State Secretary with the conduct of government affairs pending the Protector's expected recovery. The Führer called for "all conceivable" measures to capture the attackers. He wished all persons who knew of their whereabouts and failed to notify the police to be executed, along with their families. As an immediate reprisal, he ordered "10,000 suspect Czechs, from among those who are on the black list, to be arrested, or, if they are already detained, to be shot in concentration camps."[12] To avoid any misunderstanding, Himmler clarified Hitler's instruction in a teletype message, stating that 10,000 persons, primarily intellectuals, were to be taken hostage. One hundred of the most important were to be shot that very night.[13]

At 5:00 P.M., Frank proclaimed martial law. He ordered public transportation stopped and set a curfew until the following morning. His notice included the warning about the execution of accomplices and their families. The Germans offered a million marks for information leading to the capture of the principal offenders and the Protectorate government matched this reward with an additional million.[14]

[11] Feierabend, *Ve vládě v exilu*, II, p. 39.

[12] Frank's note, May 27, 1942 in Amort (ed.), *Heydrichiáda*, pp. 165–66.

[13] Himmler to Frank, May 27, 1942, in Doležal and Křen (eds.), *Czechoslovakia's Fight*, p. 70.

[14] *Der Neue Tag*, May 28 and 31, 1942.

In the late afternoon of May 27, Kurt Daluege, the chief of Germany's Regular Police, appeared in Prague, bringing bad news for Frank. Superseding his previous decision to give Frank the post, Hitler had appointed Daluege as Heydrich's interim successor.[15] The perennial candidate for the Protectorship had again missed his chance. Frank was especially incensed at the appointment of a man whom he rightly considered to be "completely unacquainted with the tricky politics of the area."[16]

Daluege, the son of a minor civil servant from Upper Silesia, was a construction engineer by training. Having joined the Nazi party in 1922, he first organized the SA in Berlin and later switched to the SS. As *Oberstgruppenführer*, he was, after Himmler, the highest-ranking SS man.[17] Hans Bernd Gisevius, his former colleague at police headquarters, who later joined the anti-Nazi opposition, appropriately characterized Daluege: "He was not the type of an utterly lost soul, but rather the model of one utterly corrupted. Stupid, immeasurably vain, but on the other hand neither hungry for power nor steeped in falsehood, his first reaction was usually decent, never malicious . . . . It was only when he had a chance to make calculations that he became a scoundrel."[18]

Hitler's reasons for appointing this rather colorless person are not clear. Daluege may have been chosen not for political reasons but simply to head the police investigation. Himmler later explained to Frank that the Führer had made the decision because of Daluege's accidental presence in Prague.[19] In 1946, Daluege himself told the Czechoslovak court that he had gone there on his own initiative as soon as he had heard of the assassination attempt. He claimed that, in accordance with an earlier promise, he had wanted to offer help to Heydrich's wife.[20] His explanation seems odd, but not altogether out of character with Gisevius's remark about Daluege's "often decent" first reaction.

[15] Hitler appointed Daluege orally; the formal document of appointment was issued only on May 30, 1942: Rk 7699 A, R 43 II/1329b, BA.

[16] Frank's note about visit in Hitler's headquarters, May 28, 1942, in Král (ed.), *Die Deutschen*, p. 475.

[17] Daluege's personal papers, G-96, Yivo. Daluege's background information, DeWitt C. Poole Collection, RG-59, NA.

[18] H. B. Gisevius, *To the Bitter End*, p. 138.

[19] Frank's note, May 28, 1942, in Král (ed.), *Die Deutschen*, pp. 474–75. Frank's postwar interrogation, *Zpověď K. H. Franka*, p. 136.

[20] Daluege's testimony in the Frank trial, quoted in *K. H. Frank, vrah českého národa, před soudem lidu* [K. H. Frank, the Murderer of the Czech People, Facing Trial by the People], p. 41. *Český národ soudí K. H. Franka*, p. 113.

The new chief representative of the Reich in Bohemia and Moravia lived up to his reputation as a vain and indolent simpleton with little interest in power. On his second day in Prague, the *Oberstgruppenführer's* major concern was the publication of his biography in the newspapers. He had his photograph conveniently handy for the chief of the Protector's propaganda department. With a pretense of modesty, Daluege mentioned that he did not want the newspaper account to be too laudatory. Yet in order to "scare the Czechs," he wished to emphasize his being an "old fighter used to hitting hard." The press was also instructed to "appropriately mention" Frank's name, to avoid the "impression that he had been removed."[21] Daluege indeed let him handle all important matters of policy.

Despite these assurances, Frank was deeply worried about his career. Anxious to keep the Führer's continued favor, he flew to Hitler's headquarters on May 28. He was relieved to hear that the function of the Protector was to be, in the future, merely honorific, something like that of the "Viceroy of India." The State Secretary would actually govern, safeguarding political continuity in much the same manner as the top British administrators in the colonies.[22]

Frank had an additional reason to appear before the Führer in person. He had not carried out Hitler's orders as to the seizure and execution of hostages. In order to justify this omission, Frank argued that the attempt against Heydrich's life was an "isolated act engineered by the enemy abroad, rather than the result of a strong revolutionary or resistance movement of the Czech people .... The perpetrators are almost certainly either English parachute agents or Czech parachute agents in English service, or members of a Czech resistance group who cooperate with them."[23] The debris of the British-made bomb found around the wreckage of Heydrich's car seemed to support Frank's conclusion.[24] He estimated that indiscriminate reprisals would drive "fifty- to one-hundred

---

[21] Wolf's note about conversation with Daluege, May 28, 1942, in Amort (ed.), *Heydrichiáda*, pp. 189–90.

[22] Frank's note, May 28, 1942, in Král (ed.), *Die Deutschen*, pp. 477–78.

[23] *Ibid.*, p. 476.

[24] Baldur von Schirach, the *Gauleiter* of Vienna, independently reached the same conclusion as Frank. In a telegram to Bormann on May 28, he warned against "Draconian measures" which would "make the world think that the population of the Protectorate is in opposition to Hitler. [The assassination attempt] must be immediately branded as being of British authorship." *Trial*, XXXIII, pp. 297–98.

thousand" relatives and friends of the victims to adopt an irreconcilable stand. This would also alienate the many Czechs who during Heydrich's Protectorship had demonstrated readiness for cooperation. Frank's reasoning shows that the man who had inspired the wanton persecution of students in 1939 had since that time learned the more subtle methods of limited terror so expertly practiced by Heydrich. Persuaded by Frank's argument, Hitler rescinded his earlier order about hostages and instead approved the proposed course.[25]

According to a proclamation issued after Frank's return to Prague, all persons who had previously failed to report their residence had to do so within twenty-four hours. Failure to report, as well as sheltering unregistered persons, was punishable by death. In the night of May 28, German police, reinforced by armored units from other parts of the Reich, conducted an extensive search throughout Bohemia and Moravia. As in October and November 1941, the summary courts began operating at full speed, announcing their sentences on the radio and in the press. Their victims included persons who were guilty only of "approval of the assassination attempt." At this time, in contrast to the fall of 1941, entire families were sometimes executed under the infamous pretext of shared responsibility.[26]

Frank considered selective rather than indiscriminate intimidation as the most effective method to secure cooperation from the people. He confidently believed that with their help the police would capture the offenders within a month. Frank enlisted the active support of the Hácha government, which he observed was now willing "to do almost anything."[27] Daluege told the ministers that he held the "incorrigible minority" rather than the nation as a whole responsible for the outrage, and insisted that the Czechs themselves bring their wayward compatriots into line. Concerning German intentions, he vaguely but ominously hinted that "the Führer's orders have been issued and will be carried out."[28]

[25] Frank's note, May 28, 1942, in Král (ed.), *Die Deutschen*, pp. 476–77.

[26] Ordinances of May 28, 1942, *Der Neue Tag*, May 29, 1942. Cf. Frank to Böhme, May 30, 1942; Riege to Police Regiment "Böhmen," May 28, 1942; Böhme to Daluege, May 30, 1942: in Amort (ed.), *Heydrichiáda*, pp. 171–73, 196–99.

[27] Frank's note, May 28, 1942, in Král (ed.), *Die Deutschen*, p. 477.

[28] Daluege's address to the cabinet, May 29, 1942, in Amort (ed.), *Heydrichiáda*, pp. 191–93.

With Nazi prodding, the Protectorate government started an intensive campaign of persuasion. Addressing the nation on May 30, President Hácha warned that "whoever works against the Reich in the slightest way will be destroyed."[29] In a dramatic climax to his speech, he labelled Beneš as "Public Enemy Number One." The ministers were developing similar themes at mass rallies across the country. The speech by Moravec, who was rightly be-believed to be the authentic voice of the Germans, attracted the greatest attention. Referring to a recent incident in France, where ten hostages had been executed in reprisal for the assassination of a low-ranking German officer, he suggested to his audience: "Just think a little bit, what would await the Czech people if the culprits were not found."[30]

The first results of this psychological offensive confirmed Frank's expectations. The Gestapo received about one thousand tips, about half of them from the Czechs. In a newspaper notice on June 3, the Gestapo expressed its appreciation for this "extraordinarily active cooperation," and urged the citizens to limit their zeal to reporting only seriously suspicious cases. Although the under-ground may have supplied some of the reports anonymously in an effort to mislead the Gestapo, their overall high number neverthe-less indicated that many Czechs considered the capture of Hey-drich's attackers desirable.[31]

The Protector's wounds proved to be more serious than origi-nally diagnosed. After protracted agony, he died in a Prague hospital on June 4. In the late afternoon his coffin was carried on a gun carriage through streets deserted by the frightened inhabitants. SS, army, and Party formations stood guard along the route. At the Castle the Nazis staged a midnight ceremony with burning torches.[32] Heydrich's funeral took place five days later in Berlin, followed by Hitler's interview with Hácha and the Protectorate government. The Führer threatened drastic measures against the Czechs— particularly mass deportations—if the assassins were not found.

[29] Hácha's address, May 30, 1942, *V hodině dvanácté* [At the Eleventh Hour], pp. 7–9.

[30] Moravec's address, May 31, 1942, *ibid.*, p. 13.

[31] *Der Neue Tag*, June 3, 1942. "Abschlussbericht," p. 31, and appendix F, pp. 6–7, Occ E 7 (a)-5, Yivo. Böhme to Daluege, June 14, 1942, in Král (ed.), *Die Deutschen*, p. 482. Cf. L. Vaněk, "Lidé proti smrti" [The People against Death], *Lidová demokracie*, October 4, 1963.

[32] *Der Neue Tag*, June 6–10, 1942. Timetable of the ceremonies, June 7, 1942, RFSS, T-175, 80, 2600217–21, NA.

After Hácha had pleaded for clemency, Hitler ended the conversation with the ominous words: "We shall see."[33]

Hitler's fury indicated that at that time the Nazis were already contemplating a spectacular revenge. The German population in the Protectorate and in the Sudetenland widely shared this desire. As early as the first days after the assassination attempt, the German authorities had to intervene to prevent lynchings of Czechs in ethnically mixed areas. Party organizations in the Sudetenland and in Vienna demanded mass expulsion of Czechs from their respective territories.[34] According to a Security Service report, Germans in the Protectorate urged that "the strictest measures should be adopted finally. They insist that continued humane and tolerant treatment of the Czechs, as has hitherto been the case, would in the long run only harm the Germans."[35] About an hour and a half after Hitler's interview with Hácha on June 9, Frank telephoned from Berlin to Böhme, the chief of the Security Police in Prague. He stated that "as a result of a conversation with the Führer," the village of Lidice was to be destroyed, its male inhabitants shot and women and children deported.[36]

Why was this particular village chosen by the Nazis? On June 3 a Czech factory owner from Slaný near Prague had intercepted a letter addressed to one of his employees. Since he believed he had found in it references to enemy agents, he reported his discovery to the police. The Gestapo immediately arrested a number of suspects including several from the nearby village of Lidice, one of whose natives was known to be serving in the Czechoslovak army in Britain.[37] Yet the investigation failed to supply any clue about the attack against Heydrich. The chief Gestapo official who had followed the trail to Lidice told the Czech interrogators after the war that by June 9, 1942, the police had found no evidence of subversive activities there.[38] The informers' report about an arms cache and

[33] Frank's note, June 9, 1942, in Amort (ed.), *Heydrichiáda*, pp. 208–11. *Hitler's Table Talk*, pp. 557–58.

[34] *Meld. Reich*, May 28, 1942, p. 6, R 58/172, BA. SD report, June 6, 1942, quoted in Amort (ed.), *Heydrichiáda*, p. 48. Müller to Reichsstatthalter Sudetenland, July 2, 1942, in Fremund (ed.), "Dokumenty," pp. 30–31. Bormann's circular, June 8, 1942, RFSS, T-175, 66, 2582148, NA. Bormann to Goebbels, RFSS, T-175, 139, 2667342, NA.

[35] Report of SD Prague, June 9, 1942, in Král (ed.), *Die Deutschen*, p. 480.

[36] Böhme's note, June 12, 1942, *ibid.*, p. 480.

[37] V. Konopka, *Zde stávaly Lidice* [Lidice Used to Stand Here], pp. 28–33.

[38] Examination of Wiesmann, *ibid.*, p. 55.

an illegal transmitter in the local mill—which the Gestapo had not even bothered to verify before that date—proved to be inaccurate. Only later did the Germans learn that some of the parachutists had been given addresses in Lidice for contacts.[39]

By 10:00 P.M. on June 9, German troops and police, assisted by Czech gendarmerie, had encircled the village. During the night they registered its population, evacuating livestock and other movable property. At dawn on the following day, a special squad of the Regular Police shot 173 male inhabitants in the yard of one of the farmhouses. The women, numbering 198, were transported to the district town of Kladno from which most of them proceeded to the Ravensbrück concentration camp. Of the 98 children, 81 deemed racially unsuitable were later killed, probably in the gas chambers at Chełmno in Poland. The others were placed for adoption in German families. On June 10, army engineers burned down the village.[40]

Unlike similar atrocities committed elsewhere in Europe in the course of military operations, the destruction of Lidice took place in a peaceful country. It was not the work of irresponsible subordinates and retreating desperadoes, like the mass murders in the French Oradour in 1944. The reprisal in the Protectorate was carried out by responsible German officials in a premeditated and systematic manner. They had an additional twenty-six inhabitants of Lidice executed after June 9. These included nine night-shift workers who had been absent from their homes on that date, and a miner who was in the hospital with a broken leg. The Gestapo waited for his recovery and shot him afterward. Another Lidice man was captured and executed after the police had hunted him for three days in the forests. Four pregnant women from the village were sent to a German hospital in Prague, only to be separated from their children after delivery and shipped to Ravensbrück.[41]

The Nazis were fully aware of what they were doing and took pride in their achievement. The Protectorate chief of the German Reich Labor Service, in which Party members were required to

[39] "Abschlussbericht," pp. 20–21, Occ E 7 (a)-5, Yivo.

[40] Král (ed.), _Die Deutschen_, pp. 480–81. Böhme's note, June 12, 1942, in Amort (ed.), _Heydrichiáda_, pp. 212–14. Fischer to Auswanderungszentrale Łódź, June 12, 1942, CCCXXVI-34, CDJC. Krumey's affidavit, June 6, 1961, Eich., _Proceedings_, pp. 5–8, and documents 936–39, CU.

[41] "Nové dokumenty o Lidicích" [New Documents about Lidice], _Hlas revoluce_, XVI (1963), No. 5. Konopka, _Zde stávaly Lidice_, pp. 41, 69.

serve limited terms as workers, commented on the "moral lesson" which the leveling of Lidice gave to his men: "The man who has been assigned to this spot intensifies his feelings, thus contributing to the strengthening of German power. The full effect will be achieved when his work obliterates all traces of the village and on the very spot where the enemy of Germandom used to live the earth is turned under the plow." [42] The Security Service reported that the German population of Bohemia and Moravia welcomed the atrocity with "great satisfaction and in many cases open joy. Local Germans find their constant warnings against the Czechs confirmed; they even say that officials in high places will now perceive how the Czechs should be treated." [43]

This reaction added evidence of the deadlock between the two nationalities. After Lidice, the Czechs still more impatiently awaited the time when they would be able to take revenge on those who had applauded the crime.

In June 1942, the events in the Protectorate made headlines in the world press. The fate of Lidice aroused tremendous indignation on the Allied side, making the name of the village into a symbol of Nazi barbarity. In several countries communities were renamed Lidice to demonstrate solidarity with the Czechs. In his customary cool fashion, Beneš assessed the international impact of the tragedy: "What the Germans are doing is horrible, but from the political point of view they gave us one certainty: under no circumstances can doubts be cast any more upon Czechoslovakia's national integrity and her right to independence." [44]

After more than two weeks of intensive efforts, the Gestapo still had no trace of Heydrich's assassins. The frustrated Nazis tried to bring the search to a successful end by relying upon mass intimidation rather than upon the conventional methods of police detection. With Moravec's help, they proceeded to create in the country an atmosphere of extreme fear and uncertainty. In a major speech in Brno on June 12, the chief collaborator threatened:

If we are faced with the choice of who should perish, whether the Czech nation or a couple of agents sent by Beneš, the archfoe of our people, we

[42] Commichau to Hierl, August 6, 1942, quoted *ibid.*, p. 52.

[43] Report of SD Prague, June 12, 1942, in Král (ed.), *Die Deutschen*, p. 480. The reaction of the Germans in the Sudetenland was similar. Situation report by Hans Krebs, July 3, 1942, *ibid.*, p. 490.

[44] Smutný's note, June 11, 1942, *DHCSP*, I, p. 274.

must save the nation by delivering the scoundrels. Here human feelings end and responsibility for the entire nation begins.

Referring to his conversations in Berlin on the occasion of Heydrich's funeral, Moravec carried his argument to a dramatic climax:

Neither the statesmen in Berlin nor I, here in Brno, can prevent the Czech people from committing its last historical stupidity, in comparison with which the White Mountain [battle of 1620] would appear as a mere mishap. What would befall us tomorrow might be a catastrophe . . . . Woe to the Czech people if the criminals who murdered Herr Acting Reich Protector are not found. Woe, woe, three times woe![45]

Frank appropriately described such tactics as "systematic fraying of nerves" (*planvoll bewegte Nervenmühle*).[46] On June 13, he had Daluege issue an ordinance promising clemency to persons who knew of the assassins' whereabouts, provided that they informed the police by 8 P.M. on June 18.[47] The date immediately took on a fateful meaning. As it was approaching, the Czechs shuddered at the thought of what the Nazis would do if the deadline passed without the desired effect. Rumors circulated about the planned execution of every tenth citizen. On the morning of June 18, the shortening of the deadline by seven hours intensified the agony.

The surviving members of the underground, seasoned by long experience, did not break down. Although fourteen persons had known in advance about Gabčik's and Kubiš's mission and about thirty-five could have given information about their hiding place, none of them talked to the police. This was as much a tribute to the integrity of the individuals involved in the conspiracy as to its skillful organization. The Nazis themselves later expressed admiration in their own way, referring to the people involved as the "racial elite."[48]

Not all the agents parachuted to the Protectorate, however, shared these impressive qualities. On June 16, Karel Čurda, who had landed after Gabčik and Kubiš, voluntarily surrendered to the

[45] Speech of June 12, 1942, *V hodině dvanácté*, pp. 39–40.

[46] Daluege to Hitler, September 1942, Nur. NG-2068, IfZ. Although the report was signed by Daluege, its style points to Frank's authorship.

[47] Ordinance of June 13, 1942, *VOB*, 1942, p. 163. Jacobi to Frank, June 25, 1942, in Amort (ed.), *Heydrichiáda*, p. 258.

[48] Geschke's report, June 25, 1942, *ibid.*, p. 265. "Abschlussbericht," p. 48, Occ E 7 (a)-5, Yivo.

police. Anxiety about the future of his family had supposedly prompted him to take this step despite considerable reluctance. Čurda could only guess that Gabčík and Kubiš were Heydrich's assassins, and he did not know their hiding place.[49] But his confession enabled the Gestapo to arrest persons who knew it and extract from them the desired information. Early on June 18, hundreds of the SS and police surrounded the Orthodox Church of St. Cyril and Methodius in Prague, where Gabčík and Kubiš had been sheltering with five other parachutists. In this hopeless situation they resisted for several hours and finally preferred suicide to surrender.[50]

The dramatic action had taken place a few hours before Frank's deadline of June 18 expired. On the following day, a short official notice announced that Heydrich's assassins had been caught and killed.[51] Their capture was attributed to the successful work of the police, an interpretation which was, because of Čurda's decisive role, something of an overstatement. Apparently because of the small propaganda value of such an announcement, the Nazis issued another communique on June 23 in which they offered a more sophisticated explanation. It referred to the voluntary surrender of several parachutists and mentioned that "numerous Czech informers" had been rewarded.[52] The new version conformed to Frank's instructions that any mention of "resistance to the last breath and heroism" must be avoided and the Czech help given to the police must be emphasized. Significantly, the official story was, until the end of the war, widely considered a face-saving move. Yet Čurda did indeed receive at least part of the reward. From a total of 500,000 marks he was allowed to draw 3000 every month.[53] He was awarded Reich citizenship and lived in Germany under an assumed name until 1945. Extradited to Czechoslovakia after the war, he was sentenced to death and executed.

[49] Report of Gestapo Prague, June 20, 1942, in Amort (ed.), *Heydrichiáda*, pp. 227–28. Čurda landed in the Protectorate on March 28, 1942. A. Šimka, "Chronologie odboje na jihozápadní Moravě" [The Chronology of Resistance in Southwestern Moravia], *Odboj a revoluce*, V (1967), No. 3, p. 178.

[50] Von Treuenfeld to Daluege, June 23, 1942; Geschke to Frank, June 29, 1942: in Amort (ed.), *Heydrichiáda*, pp. 239–44, 292–95.

[51] *Der Neue Tag*, June 20, 1942.

[52] *Ibid.*, June 23, 1942. Frank's note, June 19, 1942, in Amort (ed.), *Heydrichiáda*, p. 224.

[53] *Ibid.*, p. 56.

Once the hunt for Heydrich's assassins was over, Frank recommended a more lenient course. The public announcement of the rewards was to demonstrate that the Germans kept their word. According to his memorandum for Daluege, dated June 19, Frank even favored amnesty for some of the recently arrested persons.[54] Because of his apparent desire to show a friendlier face, a new reprisal on June 24 is difficult to interpret. In pursuing Čurda's hints, the Gestapo found out that some of the parachutists had operated their radio from Ležáky, a hamlet in eastern Bohemia. On June 24 the SS raided the village and shot its twenty-four adult inhabitants, women as well as men. The eleven children suffered the same fate as those from Lidice.[55]

The tragedy of Ležáky conforms to the usual pattern of Nazi retaliation better than that of Lidice. At least some of the inhabitants had indeed given active support to the enemy. The initiative seems to have originated with the local Gestapo chief, anxious to imitate the Lidice example.[56] Although Frank had undoubtedly given his approval and probably also secured authorization from Berlin, he must have realized that this time he had gone too far. The Security Service reported that the Czechs took the reprisal at Ležáky as evidence of continuing resistance and as a proof that German promises of leniency could not be trusted.[57] Probably to avoid such an impression the Nazis dropped plans for a third raid against the small town of Bernartice, where parachutists from England had also found refuge.[58]

In the Czech balance sheet for the events of June 1942, liabilities exceeded assets. A total of 1331 persons died by order of the summary courts. This figure does not include the victims of Lidice and Ležáky. Former Prime Minister Eliáš was shot on June 19. In retaliation for Heydrich's death, the Germans dispatched a transport of 1000 Jews from Prague directly to Majdanek extermination camp. Only one of them survived the war. In October 1942, another 252 persons, including entire families, were massacred in the Mauthausen concentration camp for having directly or

---

[54]Frank's note, June 19, 1942, *ibid.*, p. 223.

[55]L. Šíma, *Ležáky*, pp. 56–88.

[56]Draft press release approved by Frank, June 23, 1942, in Amort (ed.), *Heydrichiáda*, p. 251.

[57]Jacobi's note, June 26, 1942, *ibid.*, p. 254.

[58]"Abschlussbericht," pp. 20–21, Occ E 7 (a)-5, Yivo. Cf. V. Procházka, "Město zemře za svítání" [The Town Will Die at Dawn], *Jihočeská pravda*, June 2, 1963.

indirectly been involved in the assassination plot. The Orthodox priests who had sheltered Gabčík and Kubiš were shot after a public trial. The underground network set up by the parachutists disintegrated completely. The Gestapo arrested the last remaining members of the ÚVOD. This time, the Communists did not fare much better. Almost all their leading functionaries, including the Central Committee, fell victim to the persecution.[59] Despite the heavy toll, Beneš considered the sacrifices worthwhile because they had decisively bolstered Czechoslovakia's position in case of a negotiated peace. Since the threat of such a peace, however, existed only in his imagination, this advantage was illusory.

As far as the enemy side was concerned, the Nazis had lost one of their most capable leaders. Hitler supposedly felt Heydrich's death as "a greater blow than a lost battle."[60] By the time of his assassination, however, Heydrich's mission in the Protectorate had been almost completed, so the Germans' loss was not the Czechs' gain. On the contrary, the Nazis exploited the assassination to their advantage. The very audacity of the challenge gave them a pretext for taking exceptionally drastic measures. Although the efficiency of the police left much to be desired, they achieved what they wanted by political means. Frank's strategy, though appalling in its cynicism and brutality, was successful.

Although brilliantly executed, the assassination of Heydrich was a political mistake. It decimated the Czech underground to an extent hardly paralleled elsewhere in Hitler's Europe. Still more important, the living memory of the *Heydrichiáda*, as the people dubbed the awesome weeks following the tyrant's death, was a powerful deterrent to a revival of active opposition. By his death, Heydrich fulfilled his primary ambition—the pacification of the Protectorate.

[59] "Abschlussbericht," p. 29, Occ E 7 (a)-5, Yivo. Amort (ed.), *Heydrichiáda*, pp. 61–63. Himmler to Daluege, August 16, 1942, RFSS, T-175, 80, 2600224, NA. *Der Neue Tag*, September 5, 1942. Lagus and Polák, *Město za mřížemi*, pp. 310–11. "Meldungen wichtiger staatspolizeilicher Ereignisse," July 1942, fols. 58, 73, 94, R 58/206, BA.

[60] Himmler to Kersten, August 20, 1942, *The Kersten Memoirs*, p. 96. Cf. entry for September 23, 1943, *The Goebbels Diaries*, p. 384.

CONCLUSION

AFTER the *Heydrichiáda*, the occupation of Bohemia and Moravia lasted for almost another three years. Repression continued while further attempts were made to restore the underground. But at no time did the Czechs challenge the Nazis with a significant resistance movement; it is in this sense that the expression "failure of national resistance" has been used for the subtitle of this study. Its second volume will bring the story up to the controversial Prague uprising in the last days of the war in 1945. It will deal with the period which ended with the eventual restoration of Czech national independence—an independence regained, however, in a fashion which made the Czechs exceptionally prone to losing it again in the near future.

Such an outcome testifies to the extraordinary effectiveness of the Nazi occupation policies. Yet this does not imply that the German power was unlimited. In the 1938–1939 period especially, it was significantly less formidable than most contemporaries and subsequent observers were disposed to believe. Only in Heydrich did the Nazis find a man capable of transforming terror into a system both subtle and frightening; his mastery of this instrument of force had few parallels indeed in modern history. But, until Heydrich, the Germans were cautious and vacillating; they lacked a consistent policy of repression. In his gamble for Bohemia and Moravia, Hitler, though willing to take considerable risks, took into account the probable reaction of his adversaries and acted accordingly. Had they only been less impressed by his arrogance, they could have rebuffed him decisively at the outset or at least avoided moves which facilitated the German success. With each new success, of course, the Nazis' self-assurance grew and the chances of defying them kept diminishing.

If determination was in such critically short supply among the established European great powers—such as France and Britain—

its shortage among the Czechs—a small nation with inadequate political experience—need not cause much surprise. Still, the series of their mistakes, mishaps, and miscalculations from Munich onward is well worth analyzing as a warning example. Although the Western statesmen earned the dubious distinction of devising the Munich outrage, the Czechs contributed to their own and Europe's catastrophe by meekly submitting to it. While conditioned by the consequences of Munich, Hácha's trip to Berlin and his resulting semi-voluntary acceptance of German "protection" was still a cardinal mistake; it further undermined his people's will to resist. The subsequent collaboration by considerable segments of the population—the politicians, bureaucracy, business, labor—went to lengths which were both unnecessary and dishonorable, short-sighted despite immediate material advantages, and ultimately damaging to the nation's self-respect. The argument that by meeting or even anticipating German demands the Czech officials were able to uphold their people's interests cannot be seriously defended. Thanks to the attitude of the Czech administration, the Germans could promote their own interests exclusively; at no time were they forced to sacrifice these interests by making concessions.

As far as the resistance strategy is concerned, the assassination of Heydrich was a classic example of an attack against a powerful enemy undertaken with inadequate forces and disastrous consequences. It showed how counterproductive violence can be, when it is employed in the wrong place and at the wrong time. Throughout the entire occupation period, the Czech underground and the exiles in London improvised in a vain search for the right strategy. Their failure makes evident the need for advance planning of underground resistance; such planning should be part of the national defense effort in peacetime.

The particular strategy of the Communists prior to June 1941 was not any more successful. Far from being an exercise in *Realpolitik*, their uncomfortable neutrality poorly served the interests of both the party and the Czech nation. It did not save the Communists from persecution and only the accident of Hitler's invasion of Russia—an event beyond their control—saved the party from political and moral stagnation.

On the positive side, some of the initial moves of the Eliáš government deserve credit. In the spring of 1939, its policy of "national concentration" helped to unite the people and strengthen their confidence in the leadership. Such unity is a pre-condition, though not a guarantee, of effective national resistance. The Prime Minister's own "double game" helped to maintain the busy underground exchange between Prague and London which provided the Allies with much useful information. But the strategy of the Prague government, tailored to the relatively lenient Neurath regime, proved to be no match for Heydrich. Whatever resistance potential Czech unity entailed, it did not materialize in any form seriously damaging to Nazi power; in particular, the opportunities for effective non-violent resistance and non-compliance remained unexplored. Even under Heydrich's terror, at least individual defiance was still possible. The case of Minister Ježek shows that an individual could resist German pressure for active collaboration without serious punishment.

Despite a few positive signs, the balance of the Czechs' response to Nazi rule was overwhelmingly negative. The people proved singularly defenseless against oppression. This was to a considerable extent a result of specific historical and geographic conditions in Bohemia and Moravia. But further research in the wartime history of Europe may prove that people in other advanced industrial countries, bred in the traditions of democracy, tolerance, and humanism, were surprisingly susceptible to a regime based on the very antitheses of these traditions. Democratic institutions alone, if not sustained by strong civic spirit, are no guarantee against abject submission to force. Furthermore, in societies where too many people have too much to lose, comfort and affluence may become serious obstacles to resistance.

Yet our inquiry into the failure of national resistance need not end on a note of resignation and passivity. We know better than our predecessors in the thirties and forties that modern autocratic regimes, far from being omnipotent, suffer from serious weaknesses. Despite appearances, their power is limited, and against limited power no one is entirely helpless. Even in today's world, men should be prepared for situations where the need for resistance might arise. Still, whatever its techniques, these would always involve risk, humiliation, and suffering, with uncertain results. Thus ultimately the protection is prevention. For any nation lucky enough to be enjoying freedom and independence, its self-respect, faith in its institutions, and readiness to defend them, with the force of arms if necessary, are the best guarantee that its citizens would never have to resist an enemy under conditions of subjugation.

APPENDICES

a specific historical problem in the form of a short paper, approximately 5-10 pages. Subjects must be approved in advance by the instructor. Papers will be due one week before the beginning of final exam week. An informal report to the class may be required.

Graduate students have no extra requirements, except that their research paper needs to be more thorough and properly documented.

Examinations and Grades

There will be a one-hour midterm (October 20) and a two-hour final exam (December 7), consisting of a mixture of essay and objective questions.

Final grades will be based on the paper and the two exams on a 25-25-40 ratio, leaving 10 percent for class attendance and participation.

Office Hours

You are advised to consult with your instructor whenever necessary. Office hours are scheduled as follows, however, you may make an appointment when these hours are not suitable for you.

221N Morris Hall   Monday and Wednesday 10:00-12:00 a.m.
                    Tuesday - 1:00-2:00 p.m.

History 412/512
Fall, 1983

HISTORY OF MODERN GERMANY
A Syllabus

Dr. Johannes Postma
221N Morris Hall

Objectives and Content

The aim of this course is to provide an understanding of the history of the German people, with an emphasis on the past 200 years. The course is designed for history majors, minors, social study majors, and other related fields such as studies in German culture and language, international relations, international business, or anyone who has an interest in Germany as a major world power or the German people.

After a brief introduction on German historical roots, the course focuses on the various German states and culture before the unification, the mid-nineteenth century unification process, the second German Empire, World War I, the Weimar Republic, the Third Reich and World War II, and finally the division and post-war recovery of Germany. The last half of the quarter will deal exclusively with the twentieth century. The textbook will be used as a guide for specific topics, and assignments for text-book reading will be made in class.

Requirements

The textbook, Germany: A Modern History by Marshall Dill, must be read in its entirety. Specific assignments will be made

A. PARTITIONS OF CZECHOSLOVAKIA
IN 1938–1939

Sudetenland
Oct. 1, 1938

Hultschiner Ländchen
to: Administrative District
Oppeln Oct. 1, 1938

Teschen
to: Poland Oct. 10, 1938
to: Administrative District
Katowitz Nov. 20, 1939

Protectorate of
Bohemia

and Moravia
Mar. 16, 1939

Slovakia Mar. 14, 1939

to: Administrative
District Regensburg
Oct. 1, 1938

to: Lower
Danube
Oct. 1, 1938

to: Upper Danube
Oct. 1, 1938

to: Hungary
Nov. 2, 1938

Carpathian Ukraine
to: Hungary
Mar. 16, 1939

B. LOCALITIES IN THE PROTECTORATE AND THE SUDETENLAND

C. GLOSSARY OF GEOGRAPHICAL TERMS

Throughout the text, the following forms have been used for geographical terms:

1. *English*, if it exists (*e.g.*, Prague, Cologne, Carlsbad, Bohemia),
2. *German*, if it is more familiar to an American reader than other forms (*e.g.*, Pilsen, Leitmeritz, Teschen, Stettin),
3. *Native* in all other cases (*e.g.*, Lidice, Hradec Králové, Suwałki).

In the glossary, the form used in the text is listed first. In the second column, the German equivalent is given in roman type, the Czech or Slovak equivalent in italics, and the Polish equivalent in roman type followed by (P).

Aš	Asch
Bavarian Ostmark	Bayerische Ostmark
Bernartice	Bernartitz
Bohemia	*Čechy*; Böhmen
Bratislava	Pressburg
Breslau	Wrocław (P)
Brno	Brünn
Budweis	*České Budějovice*
Carlsbad	*Karlovy Vary*; Karlsbad
Carpathian Ukraine	*Podkarpatská Rus* (before 1945), *Zakarpatská Ukrajina* (after 1945); Ruthenien
Česká Lípa	Böhmisch-Leipa
Chełmno (P)	Kulm
Czechoslovakia	*Československo*; Tschechoslowakei
Ciechanów (P)	Zichenau
Cologne	Köln
Cracow	Kraków (P); Krakau
Danube	Donau; *Dunaj*
Elbe	*Labe*
Frýdek	Friedek
Hradec Králové	Königgrätz
Hultschiner Ländchen	*Hlučínsko*

Jičín	Jitschin
Jihlava	Iglau
Katowitz	Katowice (P)
Kladno	Kladno
Klatovy	Klattau
Kutná Hora	Kuttenberg
Lány	Lana
Leitmeritz	*Litoměřice*
Ležáky	—
Liberec	Reichenberg
Lidice	Liditz
Łódź (P)	Litzmannstadt (1939–1944)
Loket	Elbogen
Lower Danube	Niederdonau
Místek	Mistek
Moravia	*Morava*; Mähren
Munich	München; *Mnichov*
Oder	*Odra*; Odra (P)
Olomouc	Olmütz
Oppeln	Opole (P)
Ostrava	(Mährisch-) Ostrau
Pardubice	Pardubitz
Pilsen	*Plzeň*
Poznań (P)	Posen; *Poznań*
Prague	*Praha*; Prag
Regensburg	*Řezno*
Silesia	*Slezsko*; Śląsk (P); Schlesien
Slaný	Schlan
Slovakia	*Slovensko*; Slowakei
Stettin	Szczecin (P)
Sudetenland	*Sudety* (before 1945), *pohraničí* (after 1945)
Suwałki (P)	Sudauen
Tábor	Tabor
Teschen	*Těšín*; Cieszyn (P)
Theresienstadt	*Terezín*
Troppau	*Opava*
Upper Danube	Oberdonau
Vienna	Wien
Vítkovice	Witkowitz
Vltava	Moldau
Warsaw	Warszawa (P); Warschau
Zdice	Zditz
Žilina	Sillein
Zlín	Zlin; *Gottwaldov* (after 1949)

D. GLOSSARY OF INSTITUTIONAL TERMS

Foreign names of institutions have been used in the original form, if this form is common in English usage (*e.g.*, Gestapo, Führer), or if it is not readily translatable (*e.g.*, *Gauleiter*, *Oberlandrat*). The latter are italicized. All other terms have been translated into English. In the glossary, the form used in this study is given first. In the second column, the German equivalent appears in roman type, the Czech or Slovak equivalent in italics.

Administrative district	Regierungsbezirk
Armament Command	Rüstungskommando
Armament Inspection Board	Rüstungsinspektion
Armed Forces High Command	Oberkommando der Wehrmacht
Armed Forces Plenipotentiary (to the Reich Protector)	Wehrmachtsbevollmächtigter (beim Reichsprotektor)
Army Group	Heeresgruppe
Army High Command	Oberkommando des Heeres
Assistant State Secretary	Unterstaatssekretär
Blood and Soil	Blut und Boden
Board for Youth Education	*Kuratorium pro výchovu mládeže*; Kuratorium für Jugenderziehung
Central Association	*Ústřední svaz*; Zentralverband
Central Leadership of Home Resistance	*Ústřední vedení odboje domácího*
Central National Revolutionary Committee of Czechoslovakia	*Ústřední národně revoluční výbor Československa*
Central Office for Ethnic Germans	Volksdeutsche Mittelstelle
Central Office for Jewish Emigration	Zentralstelle für jüdische Auswanderung
Central Office for Public Contracts	Zentralstelle für öffentliche Aufträge
Central Office for the Protectorate	Zentralstelle zur Durchführung des Führererlasses (über das Protektorat Böhmen und Mähren)
Central Office for the Settlement of the Jewish Question	Zentralstelle für die Regelung der Judenfrage in Böhmen und Mähren
Central State Archives	*Státní ústřední archiv*
Chief of Civil Administration	Chef der Zivilverwaltung

Chief of Staff	Chef des Generalstabs
Commander	Befehlshaber, Kommandant
Commissioner	Kommissar
Commissioner-in-Charge	Kommissarischer Leiter
Communist Party of Czechoslovakia	Komunistická strana Československa
Criminal Police	Kriminalpolizei
Czech National Committee	Český národní výbor
Czechoslovak National Committee	Československý národní výbor
Defense Area	Wehrkreis
Defense Economy Inspection Board	Wehrwirtschaftsinspektion
District	Okres; Bezirk (in the Protectorate), Kreis (in Germany and in NSDAP organization)
District Governor	Okresní hejtman; Bezirkshauptmann
Export Institute	Exportní ústav
Fascist Action Committee	Fašistické akční komité
Fighter Staff	Jägerstab
Foreign Department	(OKW) Ausland
Foreign Office	Auswärtiges Amt
Four Year Plan Authority	Vierjahresplan
General Staff	Generalstab
German Academy of Sciences in Bohemia and Moravia	Deutsche Akademie der Wissenschaften in Böhmen und Mähren
German Association for Welfare and Settlement Assistance	Deutscher Reichsverein für Volkspflege und Siedlungshilfe
German Labor Front	Deutsche Arbeitsfront
Government Force	Vládní vojsko; Regierungstruppe
Hermann Göring Works	Reichswerke Hermann Göring
Heydrich Action	Heydrich-Aktion; Heydrichova akce
Heydrich Foundation	Reinhard Heydrich-Stiftung
Higher SS and Police Leader	Höherer SS- und Polizeiführer
Hitler Youth	Hitlerjugend
Home Defense Department	Abteilung Landesverteidigung, Wehrmachts-Führungsamt (in 1940), Wehrmachts-Führungsstab (after 1940)
Jewish Council	Rada starších židovské náboženské obce; Ältestenrat der Juden
Joy of Work	Radost z práce
Labor Office	Pracovní úřad; Arbeitsamt
Land Office	Pozemkový úřad; Bodenamt

Legal Section	Rechtsabteilung (des Auswärtigen Amtes)
Martial Law	*Stanné právo*; Standrecht
Matricular Contribution	*Matrikulární příspěvek*; Matrikular-beitrag
Ministry of Economics and Labor	*Ministerstvo hospodářství a práce*; Ministerium für Wirtschaft und Arbeit
Ministry of Industry, Commerce and Trade	*Ministerstvo průmyslu, obchodu a živností*; Ministerium für Industrie, Handel und Gewerbe
National Assembly	*Národní shromáždění*
National Bank	*Národní banka*; Nationalbank
National Fascist Community	*Národní obec fašistická*
National Socialist German Workers' Party	Nationalsozialistische Deutsche Arbeiterpartei
National Solidarity Movement	*Národní souručenství*
National Student Union	*Národní svaz studentstva*
National Union of Employees	*Národní odborová ústředna zaměst-nanecká*
Office for Public Enlightenment	*Úřad lidové osvěty*; Amt für Volks-aufklärung
Office of the Reich Protector	Amt des Reichsprotektors
Party Chancery	Parteikanzlei
Party Liaison Office	Parteiverbindungsstelle
People's Court	Volksgerichtshof
Police President	*Policejní president*; Polizeipräsident
Privy Councillor	Regierungsrat
Protective custody	Schutzhaft
Protectorate of Bohemia and Moravia	*Protektorát Čechy a Morava*; Pro-tektorat Böhmen und Mähren
Province	*Země*; Land (in the administration of the Protectorate)
Provincial Government	*Zemský úřad*; Landesbehörde
Provincial President	*Zemský president*; Landespräsident
Race and Settlement Head Office	Rasse- und Siedlungshauptamt
Regular Police	Ordnungspolizei
Reich Attorney General	Oberreichsanwalt
Reich Bank	Reichsbank
Reich Chancellery	Reichskanzlei
Reich Commissioner for the Strengthening of Germandom	Reichskommissar für die Festigung deutschen Volkstums
Reich Group	Reichsgruppe
Reich Labor Service	Reichsarbeitsdienst
Reich Leader of the SS	Reichsführer-SS

Reich Ministry of Armaments and Ammunition	Reichsministerium für Bewaffnung und Munition
Reich Ministry of Economics	Reichswirtschaftsministerium
Reich Ministry of Education	Reichserziehungsministerium
Reich Ministry of Food	Reichsernährungsministerium
Reich Ministry of the Interior	Reichsinnenministerium
Reich Ministry of Justice	Reichsjustizministerium
Reich Ministry for Public Enlightenment and Propaganda	Reichsministerium für Volksaufklärung und Propaganda
Reich Ministry of Transport	Reichsverkehrsministerium
Reich Protector	Reichsprotektor
Reich Security Head Office	Reichssicherheitshauptamt
Representative of the Foreign Office	Vertreter des Auswärtigen Amtes
Secret Cabinet Council	Geheimer Kabinettsrat
Sector	Abschnitt (SS, SD)
Security Police	Sicherheitspolizei
Security Service	Sicherheitsdienst
Slovak National Council	*Slovenská národná rada*
Southeast Europe Company	Südosteuropa-Gesellschaft
Special Court	Sondergericht
SS Body Guard	SS-Leibstandarte
State Council	*Státní rada*
State Prosecutor	Staatsanwalt
State Secretary	Staatssekretär
State Secretary for Special Tasks	Staatssekretär für besondere Aufträge
Strength through Joy	Kraft durch Freude
Sudeten German Party	Sudetendeutsche Partei
Summary Court	Standgericht
Superior Court	Oberlandesgericht
Supreme Administrative Court	*Nejvyšší správní soud*
Svatopluk Guards	*Svatoplukovy gardy*
Technical Emergency squads	Technische Nothilfe
Union for Cooperation with the Germans	(*Český*) *svaz pro spolupráci s Němci*
Union of Manufacturers	*Svaz průmyslníků*; Verband der Industriellen
War Economy and Armaments Board	Wirtschafts- und Rüstungsamt
War Equipment Export Board	Ausführgemeinschaft für Kriegsgerät

BIBLIOGRAPHY

BIBLIOGRAPHY

This listing includes all sources cited, except isolated references to unpublished documents or to news articles in periodicals. Identifying information, for such references, is given in footnotes. Unpublished archival materials are listed here according to place of deposit. Since the Military Archives at Coblenz are at present being reorganized, the identifying codes used here will eventually be replaced by new ones. In all cases, however, source materials can be easily located by referring to the data in the footnotes, although identifying systems vary.

I. ARCHIVAL AND BIBLIOGRAPHICAL AIDS

Benčík, Antonín, and Tvarůžek, Břetislav. "Les sources de l'histoire de la résistance en Tchécoslovaquie et le travail sur ces sources," in *European Resistance Movements, 1939–45* (New York: Macmillan, 1964), Vol. I, pp. 248–55.

Brod, Toman. "Quelques résultats et problèmes de l'historiographie tchécoslovaque sur l'occupation hitlérienne et la résistance antifasciste." Prepared for the 12th International Congress of Historical Sciences, Vienna, 1965. (Mimeographed.)

Guide to Captured German Records in the Custody of the Department of the Army Agencies in the United States. Washington: Department of the Army, 1951. (Mimeographed.)

Guides to German Records Microfilmed at Alexandria, Va. 42 vols. Washington: National Archives, 1958–1964. (Mimeographed.)

Halley, Fred G. *Preliminary Inventory of the Records of the United States Counsel for the Prosecution of Axis Criminality.* Washington: National Archives, 1949. (Mimeographed.)

Křen, Jan. "L'historiographie sur la seconde guerre mondiale et la résistance en Tchécoslovaquie," *Revue d'histoire de la deuxième guerre mondiale*, LII (1963), pp. 79–92.

Lötzke, Helmuth. "Quellen zur tschechoslowakischen Geschichte im Deutschen Zentralarchiv (1867–1945)," in *Aus 500 Jahren deutsch-tschechoslowakischer Geschichte.* Edited by Karl Oberman and Josef Polišenský (East Berlin: Rütten und Löning, 1958) pp. 405–28.

Mikula, Karel, and Schubert, Erich. *Zeitungen und Zeitschriften im Protektorat Böhmen und Mähren.* Prague: Orbis, 1941.

Nývlt, Karel. "Les sources de documentation pour l'histoire de la résistance antinazie en Tchécoslovaquie." Prepared for the 12th

International Congress of Historical Sciences, Vienna, 1965. (Mimeographed).

Šindelářová, Jitka. "Druhá světová válka a protifašistický odboj: Přehled článků uveřejněných v českých časopisech a denících v letech 1964–1965" [World War II and Anti-Fascist Resistance: A Bibliography of Articles Published in Czech Journals and Newspapers in 1964–1965], *Odboj a revoluce*, IV (1966), No. 1, Supplement.

———. *Idem* for the first half of 1966, *ibid.*, IV (1966), No. 5, Supplement.

———. *Idem* for the second half of 1966, *ibid.*, V (1967), No. 1, Supplement.

———. *Idem* for the first half of 1967, *ibid.*, VI (1968), No. 2, Supplement.

———. *Idem* for the second half of 1967, *ibid.*, VI (1968), No. 3, Supplement.

Synnatzschke, Rudolf (ed.). *Europa-Bibliographie.* Part VI: *Grossdeutschland, Reichsgau Sudetenland, Protektorat Böhmen und Mähren.* New series, vol. I (1941–1942), No. 1–3: *Protektorat Böhmen und Mähren.* (With addenda for 1937–1940.) Leipzig: Harrasowitz, 1943.

Weinberg, Gerhard L. *Supplement to the Guide to Captured German Documents.* Washington: National Archives, 1959. (Mimeographed.)

———, *et al. Guide to Captured German Documents.* Maxwell Field, Ala.: Air Force University, 1952. (Mimeographed.)

II. PRIMARY SOURCES

A. ARCHIVAL DOCUMENTS

National Archives, Washington, D.C.

Records of the German Foreign Office (T-120)

Records of the Reich Ministry for Public Enlightenment and Propaganda (T-70)

Records of Headquarters, German Armed Forces High Command (T-77)

Records of Headquarters, German Army High Command (T-78)

Records of German Army Areas (T-79)

Records of German Field Commands (T-501)

Records of the National Socialist German Labor Party (T-81)

Records of the Reich Leader of the SS and Chief of German Police (T-175)

Records of the Deutsches Auslands-Institut, Stuttgart (T-81)

DeWitt C. Poole collection (RG-59)

World War II Records Division, Alexandria, Va.

Deutsche Wirtschaftsbetriebe (DWB)

International Law Library, Columbia University, New York, N.Y.
United States v. Weizsäcker et al. (mimeographed proceedings, defense document books)
United States v. Greifelt et al. (mimeographed proceedings)
Nuremberg documents and staff evidence analyses (mimeographed series PS, NG, NO, NI, NID, NOKW)
Records of the Eichmann Trial (mimeographed proceedings and documents)
Yivo Institute for Jewish Research, New York, N.Y.
Collections Occ. E 7 and G 96
Bundesarchiv, Coblenz
Reich Chancellery (R 43 II)
Reich Ministry of Justice (R 22)
Reich Ministry of Economics and Reich Bureau of Statistics (R 24)
Reich Ministry of Finance (R 2)
Reich Security Head Office (R 58)
Office of the Reich Attorney-General in the People's Court (R 60 II)
Gestapo records concerning deportations from Moravia in 1939 (R 70 Böhmen-Mähren/9)
Deputy of the Führer-Party Chancery (NS 6)
Reich Organization Leader of the NSDAP (NS 22)
Race and Settlement Head Office (NS 2/191)
Brammer collection (Z Sg 101)
Schumacher collection
Military Archives
Armament Inspection Board, Prague
Armament Commands, Prague and Brno
Diary of Ulrich Schröder
Geheimes Staatsarchiv, West Berlin
Reich Ministry of the Interior (320)
Reich Ministry of Finance (306/V)
Reich Ministry of Education (76)
Berlin Document Center, West Berlin
Personal files
Institute für Zeitgeschichte, Munich
Nuremberg documents and staff evidence analyses (series PS, NG, NO, NI, NID, NOKW, EC)
Collection of NSDAP ordinances (Db)
Hitler's daily activities (MA 3(1))
Imperial War Museum, London
Reich Ministry of Armaments and Ammunition
Interrogations of Albert Speer and his collaborators
Wiener Library, London
Collection Nazi Justice

Centre de documentation juive contemporaine, Paris
  Protectorate collections
Yad Vashem, Jerusalem
  Records of the Jewish Religious Community in Prague

B. PERIODICALS

A–Zet Pondělník [A–Z Monday Weekly]. Prague, 1941.
Böhmen und Mähren. Prague, 1940–1942.
Brünner Tageblatt. Brno, 1941.
České slovo [The Czech Word]. Prague, 1939–1942.
Deutsche Justiz. Berlin, 1940–1941.
Keesing's Contemporary Archives. London, 1939.
Lidové noviny [The People's Daily]. Prague, 1938–1939.
Ministerialblatt des Reichs- und Preussischen Ministeriums des Innern.
  Berlin, 1939.
Der Neue Tag. Prague. 1939–1942.
Reichsgesetzblatt. Berlin, 1939–1942.
*Sammlung der Gesetze und Verordnungen des Protektorates Böhmen und
  Mähren.* Prague, 1939–1942.
Der Stürmer. Berlin, 1939.
Verordnungsblatt für Böhmen und Mähren. Berlin, 1939.
Verordnungsblatt des Reichsprotektors in Böhmen und Mähren. Prague,
  1939–1942.
Völkischer Beobachter. Berlin, 1939.

C. EDITIONS OF DOCUMENTS AND MEMOIRS

Amort, Čestmír (ed.). *Heydrichiáda.* Prague: Naše vojsko-Svaz proti-
  fašistických bojovníků, 1965.
——. *Na pomoc československému lidu: Dokumenty o československo-
  sovětském přátelství z let 1938–1945* [To the Aid of the Czechoslovak
  People: Documents on Czechoslovak-Soviet Friendship, 1938–1945].
  Prague: Nakladatelství Československé akademie věd, 1960.
Bareš, Gustav (ed.). "Dokumenty ze zasedání II. ilegálního ústředního
  výboru KSČ v září 1941" [Documents from the Conference of the
  Second Underground Central Committee of the CPC in September
  1941], *Příspěvky k dějinám KSČ*, I (1961), pp. 546–56.
Bareš, Gustav, and Janeček, Oldřich (eds.). "Depeše mezi Prahou a
  Moskvou, 1939–41" [The Radio Messages between Prague and
  Moscow, 1939–41]. *Příspěvky k dějinám KSČ*, VII (1967) pp. 375–
  433.
Beneš, Edvard. *Memoirs of Eduard Beneš: From Munich to New War
  and New Victory.* London: Allen and Unwin, 1954.
——. *Mnichovské dny: Paměti* [The Munich Days: Memoirs]. Prague:
  Svoboda, 1968.

Beran, Rudolf. *Die Tschecho-Slowakei zwischen "München" und Besetzung.* Munich: Sudetendeutsches Archiv, 1965. (Mimeographed.)

Blet, Pierre *et al.* (eds.). *Actes et documents du Saint-Siège rélatifs à la Seconde Guerre Mondiale,* vol. I: *Le Saint-Siège et la guerre en Europe, mars 1939–août 1940.* Rome: Libreria editrice vaticana, 1965.

Boberach, Heinz (ed.). *Meldungen aus dem Reich: Auswahl aus den geheimen Lageberichten des Sicherheitsdienstes der SS, 1939–1944.* Neuwied and West Berlin: Luchterhand, 1965.

Boelcke, W.A. (ed.). *Kriegspropaganda, 1939–1941: Geheime Ministerkonferenzen im Reichspropagandaministerium.* Stuttgart: Deutsche Verlags-Anstalt, 1966.

Český národ soudí K.Ḣ. Franka [The Trial of K. H. Frank by the Czech People]. Prague: Ministerstvo informací, 1947.

I documenti diplomatici italiani. Ninth series. Vols. I, II, and IV. Rome: Libreria dello Stato, 1954–1960.

Documents on British Foreign Policy, 1919–1939. Third series. Vol. IV. London: Her Majesty's Stationery Office, 1951.

Documents on German Foreign Policy, 1918–45. Series D. Vols. I, II, IV, VII, VIII. Washington: United States Government Printing Office, 1949–1958.

Dodd, William E. *Ambassador Dodd's Diary, 1933–1938.* New York: Harcourt, Brace, 1941.

Doležal, Jiří, and Křen, Jan (eds.). *Czechoslovakia's Fight: Documents on the Resistance Movement of the Czechoslovak People, 1938–1945.* Prague: Nakladatelství Československé akademie věd, 1964.

Ďurčanský, Ferdinand. "Mit Tiso bei Hitler." *Politische Studien,* VII (1956), No. 80, pp. 1–10.

Eliášová, Jaroslava, and Pasák Tomáš (eds.). "Poznámky k Benešovým kontaktům s Eliášem ve druhé světové válce" [Beneš's Contacts with Eliáš during World War II]. *Historie a vojenství,* 1967, pp. 108–140.

Feierabend, Ladislav Karel. *Beneš mezi Washingtonem a Moskvou: Vzpomínky z londýnské vlády: Od jara 1943 do jara 1944* [Beneš between Washington and Moscow: Reminiscences of the London Government from Spring 1943 to Spring 1944]. Washington, 1966.

——. *Ve vládách druhé republiky* [In the Cabinets of the Second Republic]. New York: Universum, 1961.

——. *Ve vládě Protektorátu* [In the Protectorate Cabinet]. New York: Universum, 1962.

——. *Ve vládě v exilu* [In the Exile Cabinet]. Vol. II: *Východní vítr nad Londýnem* [East Wind over London]. Washington, 1966.

Foreign Relations of the United States: Diplomatic Papers. 1939. Vol. II. Washington: United States Government Printing Office, 1956.

Fremund, Karel (ed.). "Dokumenty o nacistické vyhlazovací politice" [Documents of the Nazi Extermination Policy]. *Sborník archivních prací*, XIII (1963), No. 2, pp. 3–45.

——. "Heydrichova nadace—důležitý nástroj nacistické vyhlazovací politiky" [The Heydrich Foundation: An Important Instrument of Nazi Extermination Policies]. *Sborník archivních prací*, XIV (1964), No. 1, pp. 3–38.

——. "Z činnosti poradců nacistické okupační moci" [Activities of the Advisers to the Nazi Occupation Regime]. *Sborník archivních prací*, XVI (1966), No. 1, pp. 3–49.

The French Yellow Book: Diplomatic Documents (1938–1939). New York: Reynal and Hitchcock, 1940.

Gisevius, Hans Bernd. *To the Bitter End.* Boston: Houghton Mifflin, 1947.

Goebbels, Josef. *The Goebbels Diaries.* London: Hamilton, 1948.

Halder, Franz. *Kriegstagebuch.* Vol. I. Stuttgart: Kohlhammer, 1962.

Hassell, Ulrich von. *The Von Hassell Diaries, 1938–1944.* Garden City: Doubleday, 1947.

Havelka, Jiří. "Vzpomínka na generála Eliáše" [A Reminiscence of General Eliáš]. *Dějiny a současnost*, VII (1965), No. 3, pp. 40–42.

Henderson, Nevil. *Failure of a Mission: Berlin, 1937–1939.* New York: Putnam, 1940.

Hieke-Stoj, František. "Mé vzpomínky z druhé světové války" [My Reminiscences from World War II]. *Historie a vojenství*, 1968, pp. 581–619.

Hronek, Jiří (ed.). *Černá kniha Heydrichova režimu: Dokumenty a zápisy, září 1941–leden 1942.* [The Black Book of the Heydrich Regime: Documents and Notes, September 1941–January 1942]. London: Čechoslovák, 1942.

Jacobsen, Hans-Adolf (ed.). *Der Zweite Weltkrieg: Grundzüge der Politik und Strategie in Dokumenten.* Frankfurt a. Main: Fischer, 1965.

Jaksch, Wenzel. *Europe's Road to Potsdam.* New York: Praeger, 1963.

Ježek, Josef. "Odchod ministra vnitra z protektorátní vlády" [The Departure of the Minister of the Interior from the Protectorate Cabinet]. *Dějiny a současnost*, X (1968), No. 10, pp. 46–48.

Keitel, Wilhelm. *The Memoirs of Field-Marshal Keitel.* New York: Stein and Day, 1966.

Kennan, George F. *From Prague after Munich: Diplomatic Papers, 1938–1940.* Princeton: Princeton University Press, 1968.

Kersten, Felix. *The Kersten Memoirs: 1940–1945.* London: Hutchinson, 1956.

K. H. Frank, vrah českého národa, před soudem lidu: Proces a rozsudek nad K. H. Frankem [K. H. Frank, the Murderer of the Czech People,

Facing Trial by the People: The Trial and Sentence of K. H. Frank]. Žilina: Pravda, 1946.

Kleist, Peter. *Zwischen Hitler und Stalin.* Bonn: Athäneum, 1950.

Krejčí, Ludvík. "Obranyschopnost ČSR 1938" [Czechoslovakia's Defense Readiness in 1938]. *Odboj a revoluce,* VI (1968), No. 2, pp. 14–41.

Král, Václav (ed.). *Das Abkommen von München 1938.* Prague: Academia, 1968.

——. *Die Deutschen in der Tschechoslowakei, 1933–1947: Dokumentensammlung.* Prague: Nakladatelství Československé akademie věd, 1964.

——. *Die Vergangenheit warnt: Dokumente über die Germanisierungs- und Austilgungspolitik der Naziokkupanten in der Tschechoslowakei.* Prague: Orbis, 1960.

Křen, Jan (ed.). "Nové dokumenty o boji KSČ proti nacistickému panství" [New Documents Concerning the Struggle of the CPC against Nazi Rule]. *Příspěvky k dějinám KSČ,* I (1961), pp. 231–40.

Laštovička, Bohuslav. *V Londýně za války: Zápasy o novou ČSR, 1939–1945* [In London during the War: Struggles for a New Czechoslovakia]. Prague: Státní nakladatelství politické literatury, 1960.

Machát, František. "Vzpomínky na spolupráci a generálem Bílým" [Reminiscences about Collaboration with General Bílý]. *Odboj a revoluce,* V (1967), No. 2, Supplement, pp. 5–20.

Masařík, Hubert. "Poslední měsíce s generálem Eliášem" [The Last Months with General Eliáš]. *Reportér,* III (1968), No. 21, pp. i–vii.

Meissner, Otto. *Staatssekretär unter Ebert, Hindenburg, Hitler: Der Schicksalsweg des deutschen Volkes von 1918–1945, wie ich ihn erlebte.* Hamburg: Hoffman und Campe, 1950.

Mnichov v dokumentech [Munich in Documents]. Vol. II. Prague: Orbis, 1958.

Nazi Conspiracy and Aggression. 8 vols. and supplements A, B. Washington: United States Government Printing Office, 1947.

Nazi-Soviet Relations. Washington: Department of State, 1948.

"Nové dokumenty o Lidicích" [New Documents about Lidice]. *Hlas revoluce,* XVI (1963), No. 5.

Orlík, Josef (ed.). *Opavsko a severní Morava za okupace: Z tajných zpráv okupačních úřadů z let 1940–1943* [The Troppau Country and Northern Moravia during the Occupation: Secret Reports of the Occupation Authorities from 1940–1943]. Ostrava: Krajské nakladatelství, 1961.

Otáhalová, Libuše, and Červinková, Milada (eds.). *Dokumenty z historie československé politiky, 1939–1943* [Documents on the History of Czechoslovak Politics]. 2 vols. Prague: Academia, 1966.

Parliamentary Debates, House of Commons. Vols. 345 and 348. London: His Majesty's Stationery Office, 1939.

Pravdová, Marie (ed.). "Soupis nejvýznamnějších komunistických letáků rozšiřovaných ve středních Čechách v letech 1939–1941" [A List of the Most Important Communist Leaflets Distributed in Central Bohemia in 1939–1941]. In *Středočeské kapitoly z dějin okupace, 1939–1942* (Prague: Krajské osvětové středisko, 1966), pp. 157–94.

Radimský, Jiří (ed.). "Letáky z počátku druhé světové války" [Leaflets from the Beginning of World War II]. *Sborník Matice moravské,* LXXXIV (1965), pp. 258–77.

Rouard de Card, E. (ed.). *Les traités de protectorat conclus par la France en Afrique, 1870–1895.* Paris: Pedone, 1897.

Schellenberg, Walter. *The Schellenberg Memoirs.* London: Deutsch, 1956.

Schmidt, Paul. *Statist auf diplomatischer Bühne, 1923–1945.* Bonn: Athäneum, 1958.

Schubert, Miroslav. "Konec druhé republiky: Vzpomínky na tragické události 15. března 1939" [The End of the Second Republic: Reminiscences of the Tragic Events of March 15, 1939]. *Naše hlasy* (Toronto), March 14, 1964.

Schwerin von Krosigk, Lutz. *Es geschah in Deutschland: Menschenbilder unseres Jahrhunderts.* Tübingen: Wunderlich, 1951.

Statistisches Jahrbuch für das Protektorat Böhmen und Mähren, 1942. Prague: Statistisches Zentralamt, 1942.

Stehlin, Paul. *Témoignage pour l'histoire.* Paris: Laffont, 1964.

Štěpán, František (ed.). "Nové dokumenty o protičeskoslovenských plánech dnešních revanšistů z let 1938–1939" [New Documents Concerning Anti-Czechoslovak Plans of Today's Revanchists in 1938–1939]. *Příspěvky k dějinám KSČ,* I (1961), pp. 726–39.

Strankmüller, Emil. "Československé ofenzívní zpravodajství v letech 1937 do 15. března 1939" [The Czechoslovak Intelligence Service from 1937 to March 15, 1939]. *Odboj a revoluce,* VI (1968), No. 2, pp. 42–73.

Szathmáryová-Vlčková, Věra. *Putování za svobodou, 1938–1945* [Pilgrimage for Freedom]. Prague: Československý kompas, 1946.

Táborský, Eduard. *Pravda zvítězila: Deník druhého zahraničního odboje* [The Truth Has Prevailed: The Diary of the Second Resistance Movement Abroad]. Prague: Družstevní práce, 1947.

Trial of the Major War Criminals. 42 vols. Nuremberg: International Military Tribunal, 1947–1949.

Trials of War Criminals before the Nürnberg Military Tribunals. 15 vols. Washington: United States Government Printing Office, 1949–1954.

Vaněk, Ladislav. "Atentát na Heydricha" [The Attempt on Heydrich's Life]. *Dějiny a současnost,* IV (1962), No. 5, pp. 10–12.

——. "Lidé proti smrti" [The People against Death]. *Lidová demokracie*, October 4, 1963.

Za svobodu: Do nové Československé republiky: Ideový program domácího odbojového hnutí vypracovaný v letech 1939–41 [For Freedom: Into a New Czechoslovak Republic: A Program of the Resistance Movement at Home Prepared in 1939–41]. Prague, 1945.

Za svobodu českého a slovenského národa: Sborník dokumentů k dějinám KSČ v letech 1938–1945 [For the Freedom of the Czech and Slovak Peoples: A Collection of Documents on the History of the CPC in 1938–1945]. Prague: Státní nakladatelství politické literatury, 1956.

Zločiny nacistů za okupace a osvobozenecký boj našeho lidu [Nazi Crimes during the Occupation and the Liberation Struggle of Our People]. Prague: Státní nakladatelství politické literatury, 1961.

Zpověď K. H. Franka: Podle vlastních výpovědí v době vazby u krajského soudu trestního na Pankráci [The Confession of K. H. Frank: From His Own Deposition during Detention at the Circuit Criminal Court at Pankrác]. Prague: A.S. tiskařské a nakladatelské podniky, 1946.

D. OTHER PRIMARY SOURCES

Domarus, Max. *Hitler: Reden und Proklamationen, 1932–1945.* Vol. II (1939–1945). Neustadt a. d. Aisch: Schmidt, 1963.

Ergebnisse der vierteljährlichen Lohnerhebungen für die Monate März, Juni und September 1943. Prague: Statistisches Zentralamt, 1944. (Mimeographed.)

Frank, Karl Hermann. *Ansprache des Staatssekretärs und SS-Gruppenführers Karl Hermann Frank anlässlich der 1. Kundgebung der NSDAP auf dem Altstädter Ring zu Prag am 2. Dezember 1939.* Berlin: Volk und Reich, 1940.

——. "Tschechischer Legionärgeist—oder Friede im Protektorat?" *Böhmen und Mähren*, January 1941, pp. 12–14.

Fučík, Julius. *Milujeme svůj národ: Poslední články a úvahy, 1941–1942* [We Love Our People: The Last Articles and Essays, 1941–1942]. Prague: Svoboda, 1951.

Heydrich, Reinhard. "Nationalsozialistische Führung." *Die Aktion*, III (1942), p. 313.

Hitler, Adolf. *Hitler's Secret Book.* New York: Grove Press, 1961.

——. *Hitler's Table Talk: 1941–1944.* London: Weidenfeld and Nicolson, 1953.

——. *Mein Kampf.* Boston: Houghton Mifflin, 1943.

——. *The Speeches of Adolf Hitler, April 1922–August 1939.* Edited by Norman H. Baynes. Vol. II. London: Oxford University Press, 1942.

Hufnagel, Hermann. "Organisation der Verwaltung im Protektorat Böhmen und Mähren." *Böhmen und Mähren*, 1940, No. 1.

Kehrl, Hans. "Das Protektorat im Grossdeutschen Wirtschaftsraum." *Zeitschrift des Vereins Berliner Kaufleute und Industrieller*, XXII (1941), No. 4, pp. 19–23.

Marschbefehl: Mähren: Mit dem VIII. Ak. ins Protektorat. Berlin: Klinghammer, 1939.

Megerle, Karl. "Deutschland und das Ende der Tschecho-Slowakei." *Monatshefte für auswärtige Politik*, VI (1939), pp. 763–76.

Moravec, Emanuel. *V úloze mouřenína* [In the Moor's Role]. Prague: Orbis, 1940.

Müller, Karl Valentin. "Die Bedeutung des deutschen Blutes im Tschechentum." *Archiv für Bevölkerungswissenschaft und Bevölkerungspolitik*, IX (1939), pp. 325–58, 385–404.

——. "Die Bedeutung des deutschen Leistungserbgutes im tschechischen Volkstum." *Forschungen und Fortschritte*, XVII (1941), pp. 335–37.

——. "Deutschtum und Tschechentum in rassen- und gesellschaftsbiologischer Betrachtung." *Rasse*, VIII (1941), pp. 303–307.

——. "Grundsätzliche Ausführungen über das deutsche und tschechische Volkstum in Böhmen und Mähren." *Raumforschung und Raumordnung*, V (1941), pp. 488–96.

——. "Zur Rassen- und Volksgeschichte des böhmisch-mährischen Raumes," in *Das Böhmen und Mähren-Buch*. Edited by Friedrich Heiss (Prague: Volk und Reich, 1943), pp. 127–34.

——, and Zatschek, Heinz. "Das biologische Schicksal der Premysliden." *Archiv für Rassen- und Gesellschaftsbiologie*, XXXV (1941), pp. 136–52.

Odložilík, Otakar. "Stará nebo nová situace" [An Old or a New Situation?]. *Brázda*, II (1939), pp. 238–40.

Picker, Henry. *Hitlers Tischgespräche im Führerhauptquartier, 1941–42*. Bonn: Athäneum, 1951.

Rauschning, Hermann. *Hitler Speaks: A Series of Political Conversations with Adolf Hitler on His Real Aims*. London: Butterworth, 1939.

Sabeau, Vincent. "Le 15 mars, vu de Prague." *L'Europe nouvelle*, 1939, pp. 465–67.

Schneider, Erich (ed.). *Reinhard Heydrich: Ein Leben der Tat*. Prague: Volk und Reich, 1944.

Schubert, Erich (ed.). *Deutscher Sozialaufbau in Böhmen und Mähren*. Prague: Orbis, 1943.

Stuckart, Wilhelm. *Neues Staatsrecht*. Leipzig: Kohlhammer, 1939.

Tagesziel: Prag: Mit dem IV. Armeekorps nach Prag. Berlin: Klinghammer, 1939.

Thomas, Georg. *Geschichte der deutschen Wehr- und Rüstungswirtschaft (1918–1943/45)*. Boppard: Boldt, 1966.

Thürauf, Ulrich (ed.). *Schulthess' Europäischer Geschichtskalender*. Vol. LXXX (1939). Munich: Beck, 1940.

V hodině dvanácté: Soubor projevů státního presidenta a členů vlády Protektorátu Čechy a Morava po 27. květnu 1942 [At the Eleventh Hour: A Collection of Speeches by the State President and the Members of the Government of the Protectorate of Bohemia and Moravia after May 27, 1942]. Prague: Orbis, 1942.

Wedelstädt, Erich von. "Die wirtschaftliche Eingliederung des Protektorats." *Die deutsche Volkswirtschaft*, IX (1940), pp. 290–93.

Wirth, Hermann. "Löhne, Preise und Kaufkraft im Protektorat." *Böhmen und Mähren*, August 1940.

III. SECONDARY SOURCES

BOOKS AND ARTICLES

Adler, H.G. *Theresienstadt, 1941–1945: Das Antlitz einer Zwangsgemeinschaft. Geschichte, Soziologie, Psychologie*. Tübingen: Mohr, 1960.

Amort, Čestmír. *Partyzáni na Podbrdsku: K historii národně osvobozeneckého boje českého lidu v letech 1939–1945* [Partisans in the Brdy Hills: A Contribution to the History of the Liberation Struggle of the Czech People in 1939–1945]. Prague: Naše vojsko – Svaz protifašistických bojovníků, 1958.

——. "Švýcarsko zůstalo svobodnou zemí" [Switzerland Remained a Free Country]. *Dějiny a současnost*, VIII (1966), No. 12, pp. 10–11.

——. "Z nacistických plánů na zotročení Evropy" [The Nazi Plans for the Enslavement of Europe]. *Mezinárodní politika*, 1962, pp. 572–73.

——, and Jedlička, I.M. *Tajemství vyzvědače A-54: Z neznámých aktů druhého oddělení* [The Secret of Agent A-54: From the Unknown Papers of the Second Department]. Prague: Vydavatelství časopisů MNO, 1965.

Andic, Suphan, and Veverka, Jindřich. "The Growth of Government Expenditure in Germany since the Unification." *Finanzarchiv*, XXIII (1964), pp. 169–278.

Antoš, Zdeněk. "Blut und Boden—ke 'konečnému řešení' národnostní otázky v sudetské župě" [*Blut und Boden*: The "Final Solution" of the Nationality Question in the *Gau* Sudetenland]. *Slezský sborník*, LXIV (1966), pp. 28–59.

——. "Jihotyrolská otázka za II. světové války a naše země" [The South Tyrolian Question during World War II and the Czech Lands]. *Slezský sborník*, LXIV (1966), pp. 390–93.

Arendt, Hannah. *Eichmann in Jerusalem: A Report on the Banality of Evil*. New York: The Viking Press, 1964.

Bareš, Arnošt, and Pasák, Tomáš. "Odbojová organizace Zdeňka Schmoranze" [Zdeněk Schmoranz's Resistance Organization]. *Historie a vojenství*, 1968, pp. 1003–1033.

Bareš, Gustav. *Tři pře Jana Zíky* [Jan Zíka's Three Trials]. Prague: Mladá fronta, 1961.

Batowski, Henryk. *Kryzys dyplomatyczny w Ewropie, jesień 1938–wiosna 1939* [The Diplomatic Crisis in Europe, Fall 1938–Spring 1939]. Warsaw: Wydawnictwo Ministerstwa Obrony Narodowej, 1959.

Baumont, Maurice. *La faillite de la paix*. Vol. I. Paris: Presses universitaires de France, 1960.

Beloff, Max. *The Foreign Policy of Soviet Russia 1929–1941*. Vol. II (1936–1941). London: Oxford University Press, 1952.

Benčík, Antonín, *et al. Partyzánské hnutí v Československu za druhé světové války* [The Partisan Movement in Czechoslovakia during World War II]. Prague: Naše vojsko, 1961.

Bennett, Jeremy. *British Broadcasting and the Danish Resistance Movement 1940–1945: A Study of the Wartime Broadcasts of the B.B.C. Danish Service*. Cambridge: Cambridge University Press, 1966.

Biman, Stanislav. "17. listopad" [November 17]. *Dějiny a současnost*, VIII (1966), No. 11, pp. 17–20.

Bodensieck, Heinrich. "Das Dritte Reich und die Lage der Juden in der Tschecho-Slowakei nach München." *Vierteljahrshefte für Zeitgeschichte*, IX (1961), pp. 249–61.

——. "Der Plan eines 'Freundschaftsvertrages' zwischen dem Reich und der Tschecho-Slowakei im Jahre 1938." *Zeitschrift für Ostforschung*, X (1961), pp. 462–76.

——. "Die Politik der Zweiten Tschecho-Slowakischen Republik (Herbst 1938–Frühjahr 1939)." *Zeitschrift für Ostforschung*, VI (1957), pp. 54–71.

——. "Zur 'Spiegelung' der nach-Münchener tschechoslowakischen Politik in der zeitgenössischen tschechischen Publizistik (Herbst 1938–Frühjahr 1939)." *Zeitschrift für Ostforschung*, XVI (1964), pp. 79–101.

——. "Zur Vorgeschichte des 'Protektorats Böhmen und Mähren.'" *Geschichte in Wissenschaft und Unterricht*, XIX (1968), pp. 713–32.

Bohmann, Alfred. "Die Stellung der Oberlandräte-Inspekteure: Zur deutschen Verwaltungsorganisation im ehemaligen Protektorat Böhmen und Mähren." *Zeitschrift für Ostforschung*, XV (1966), pp. 118–26.

Bosák, František. "Germanisační úloha německých škol na Českobudějovicku za okupace" [The Germanization Task of the German Schools in the Budweis Country during the Occupation]. *Jihočeský sborník historický*, XXXIII (1964), pp. 58–73.

Boss, Otto. "Die Zweite Tschecho-Slowakische Republik im Spiegel zeitgenössischer tschechischer Pressestimmen (Oktober 1938–März

1939)," in *Bohemia: Jahrbuch des Collegium Carolinum*, vol. III (Munich: Lerche, 1962), pp. 402–25.

Brandt, Karl. *Germany's Agricultural and Food Policies in World War II*. Vol. II. Stanford: Stanford University Press, 1953.

Brod, Toman, and Čejka, Eduard. *Na západní frontě: Historie československých vojenských jednotek na Západě v letech druhé světové války* [At the Western Front: A History of the Czechoslovak Military Units in the West during World War II]. Prague: Naše vojsko – Svaz protifašistických bojovníků, 1963.

Broszat, Martin. *Nationalsozialistische Polenpolitik, 1939–45*. Stuttgart: Deutsche Verlags-Anstalt, 1961.

——. "Die Reaktion der Mächte auf den 15. März 1939," in *Bohemia: Jahrbuch des Collegium Carolinum*, vol. VIII (Munich: Lerche, 1967), pp. 253–80.

Bruegel, Johann Wolfgang. *Tschechen und Deutsche, 1918–1938*. Munich: Nymphenburger Verlagshandlung, 1967.

——. "Zur Erinnerung an die Besetzung Prags 1939. Hans Arthur Sager: Ein unbekannter Martyrer." *Deutsche Rundschau*, LXXXV (1959), pp. 220–25.

Buchheit, Gert. *Der deutsche Geheimdienst: Geschichte der militärischen Abwehr*. Munich: List, 1966.

Bullock, Alan. *Hitler: A Study in Tyranny*. London: Odhams, 1964.

Burgess, Alan. *Seven Men at Daybreak*. London: Evans Bros., 1960.

Celovsky, Boris. *Das Münchener Abkommen 1938*. Stuttgart: Deutsche Verlags-Anstalt, 1958.

Černý, Bohumil. *Most k novému životu: Německá emigrace v ČSR v letech 1933–1939* [The Bridge to a New Life: The German Exiles in Czechoslovakia in 1933–1939]. Prague: Lidová demokracie, 1968.

Chmela, Leopold. *Hospodářská okupace Československa, její methody a důsledky: Znalecký posudek v procesu s K. H. Frankem* [The Economic Aspect of the Occupation of Czechoslovakia, Its Methods and Consequences: Expert Opinion in the K. H. Frank Trial]. Prague: Orbis, 1946.

Crkovský, František. "Ostravsko a 15. březen 1939" [The Ostrava Country and March 15, 1939]. *Slezský sborník*, LIX (1961), pp. 475–90.

Cygański, Mirosław. "Zamach na Reinharda Heydricha i tragedia Lidic" [The Attempt on Reinhard Heydrich's Life and the Tragedy of Lidice]. *Wojskowy Przegląd Historyczny*, 1964, pp. 163–85.

Dallin, Alexander. *German Rule in Russia, 1941–1945: A Study of Occupation Policies*. London: Macmillan, 1957.

Deakin, F. W. *The Brutal Friendship: Mussolini, Hitler and the Fall of Italian Fascism*. New York: Harper and Row, 1962.

——. "Great Britain and European Resistance," in *European Resistance Movements*, vol. II (Oxford: Pergamon, 1964), pp. 98–119.

De Jong, Lois. "Zwischen Kollaboration und *Résistance,*" in *Das Dritte Reich: Bericht über die Tagung des Instituts für Zeitgeschichte in Tutzing, Mai 1956* (Munich: Institut für Zeitgeschichte, 1957), pp. 133–52.

Doležal, Jiří. *Jediná cesta* [The Only Way]. Prague: Naše vojsko – Svaz protifašistických bojovníků, 1966.

——, "Diverze a vznik partyzánského hnutí v českých zemích" [Sabotage and the Origins of the Partisan Movement in Bohemia and Moravia], in *Z bojů za svobodu* [The Struggles for Freedom], vol. I (Prague: Nakladatelství politické literatury, 1963), pp. 78–138.

——, and Křen, Jan. "Český odboj a heydrichiáda" [The Czech Resistance and the Heydrich Terror]. *Nová mysl,* 1962, pp. 973–84.

Durica, Milan S. *La Slovacchia e le sue relazioni politiche con la Germania, 1938–1945.* Vol. I. Padua: Marsche, 1964.

Durmanová, Marie. "Řízené hospodářství a správa Ústředního svazu průmyslu za nacistické okupace" [Guided Economy and the Administration of the Central Association of Industry under the Nazi Occupation]. *Sborník archivních prací,* XVI (1966), No. 2, pp. 366–96.

Engel-Janosi, Friedrich. "Remarks on the Austrian Resistance." *Journal of Central European Affairs,* XIII (1953), pp. 105–22.

Erdely, Eugene V. *Germany's First European Protectorate: The Fate of the Czechs and the Slovaks.* London: Hale, 1942.

Feierabend, Ivo Karel. "The Pattern of a Satellite State: Czechoslovakia 1938–1939." Unpublished doctoral dissertation, Department of Political Science, Yale University, 1960.

Fest, Joachim C. *Das Gesicht des Dritten Reiches: Profile einer totalitären Herrschaft.* Munich: Piper, 1963.

Fichelle, Alfred. "La crise interne de la Tchécoslovaquie de la signature des accords de Munich (29 septembre 1938) à l'instauration du Protectorat (15 mars 1939) vue de Prague par des observateurs étrangers." *Revue d'histoire de la deuxième guerre mondiale,* LII (1963), pp. 21–38.

Food, Famine and Relief, 1940–1946. Geneva: League of Nations, 1946.

Friedman, Philip. "Aspects of the Jewish Communal Crisis in the Period of the Nazi Regime in Germany, Austria and Czechoslovakia," in *Essays on Jewish Life and Thought: Presented in Honor of Salo Wittmayer Baron.* Edited by J. L. Blau (New York: Columbia University Press, 1959), pp. 199–230.

Gedye, G. E. R. *Betrayal in Central Europe: Austria and Czechoslovakia: The Fallen Bastions.* New York: Harper, 1939.

Georg, Enno. *Die wirtschaftlichen Unternehmungen der SS.* Stuttgart: Deutsche Verlags-Anstalt, 1963.

Gilbert, Martin, and Gott, Richard. *The Appeasers.* London: Weidenfeld and Nicolson, 1963.

Görtler, Miroslav. "Akce Gitter ve středních Čechách" ["Operation

Bars" in Central Bohemia], in *Středočeské kapitoly z dějin okupace* (Prague: Krajské osvětové středisko, 1966), pp. 7–38.

Grant Duff, Shiela. *A German Protectorate: The Czechs under Nazi Rule*. London: Macmillan, 1942.

Haas, Antonín. "Vyvlastňování české půdy na Českobudějovicku za okupace" [The Expropriation of Czech Land in the Budweis Country during the Occupation]. *Jihočeský sborník historický*, XXXI (1962), pp. 172–77.

Hájek, Miloš. *Od Mnichova k 15. březnu* [From Munich to March 15]. Prague: Státní nakladatelství politické literatury, 1959.

Hamšík, Dušan, and Pražák, Jiří. *Eine Bombe für Heydrich: Historische Reportage*. East Berlin: Der Morgen, 1964.

Healey, Denis (ed.). *The Curtain Falls*. London: Lincolns-Prager, 1951.

Heiber, Helmut. "Zur Justiz im Dritten Reich: Der Fall Eliáš." *Vierteljahrshefte für Zeitgeschichte*, III (1955), pp. 275–96.

Hilberg, Raul. *The Destruction of the European Jews*. Chicago: Quadrangle, 1961.

Hoensch, Jörg K. *Die Slowakei und Hitlers Ostpolitik: Hlinkas Slowakische Volkspartei zwischen Autonomie und Separation, 1938/39*. Cologne: Böhlau, 1966.

——. *Der ungarische Revisionismus und die Zerschlagung der Tschechoslowakei*. Tübingen: Mohr, 1967.

——. "Revize a expanze: Úvahy o cílech, metodách a plánech Hitlerovy československé politiky" [Revision and Expansion: Aims, Methods and Plans in Hitler's Policy toward Czechoslovakia]. *Odboj a revoluce*, VI (1968), No. 3, pp. 49–82.

Ilnytzkyj, Roman. *Deutschland und die Ukraine, 1934–1945*. 2 vols. Munich: Osteuropa-Institut, 1955–1956.

Ivanov, Miroslav. *Nejen černé uniformy: Monology o atentátu na Reinharda Heydricha* [Not Only the Black Uniforms . . .: Monologs about the Attempt on Reinhard Heydrich's Life]. Prague: Naše vojsko, 1965.

Jacobsen, Hans-Adolf. *Fall Gelb*. Wiesbaden: Steiner, 1957.

——. *Nationalsozialistische Aussenpolitik, 1933–1938*. Frankfurt a. M.: Metzner, 1968.

Janáček, František. *Dva smery v začiatkoch národného odboja (október 1938–jún 1940)* [Two Trends at the Beginning of the National Resistance Movement, October 1938–June 1940]. Bratislava: Vydavateľstvo politickej literatúry, 1961.

——. "Linie a ideologie KSČ 1939–1941: Pokus o osvětlení politických souvislostí a ideologických komponentů" [CPC's Line of Policy and Ideology, 1939–1941: An Interpretation of Political Connections and Ideological Factors]. *Odboj a revoluce*, IV (1966), No. 4, pp. 5–64.

Janák, Jan. "Die deutsche Bevölkerung der 'Iglauer Sprachinsel' zwischen München und dem 15. März 1939." *Sborník prací filosofické fakulty Brněnské university*, 1965, C 12, pp. 123–62.

Janeček, Oldřich. "K programové činnosti zahraničního vedení KSČ v první polovině roku 1939" [Programs of the CPC's Foreign Leadership in the First Half of 1939]. *Odboj a revoluce*, IV (1966), No. 4, Supplement, pp. 154–59.

——. "O programu Petičního výboru 'Věrni zůstaneme' z let 1940–1941" [The Program of the Committee of the Petition "We Remain Faithful" in 1940–1941]. *Příspěvky k dějinám KSČ*, VI (1966), pp 481–99.

Jelínek, Jaroslav. *PÚ – Politické ústředí domácího odboje: Vzpomínky a poznámky novináře* [The Political Center of Home Resistance: Memoirs and Comments by a Journalist]. Prague: Kvasnička a Hampl, 1947.

Jelínek, Zdeněk. "Z dějin nacistické okupace a hnutí odporu na Kutnohorsku" [The History of the Nazi Occupation and the Resistance Movement in the Kutná Hora Country], in *Středočeské kapitoly z dějin okupace* (Prague: Krajské osvětové středisko, 1966), pp. 54–99.

Jenks, William A. *Vienna and the Young Hitler*. New York: Columbia University Press, 1960.

Kahan, Vilém. "Úloha a úroveň zpravodajství v nekomunistickém odboji" [The Role and Quality of Intelligence in the Non-Communist Resistance Movement]. *Odboj a revoluce*, V (1967), No. 2, Supplement, pp. 87–112.

Káňa, Otakar, and Michňák, Josef. *Ostravsko v době nacistické okupace* [The Ostrava Country under Nazi Occupation]. Ostrava: Krajské nakladatelství, 1962.

Klapal, Čeněk. "Několik poznámek k působení SD v okupovaném Československu" [The Security Service in Occupied Czechoslovakia]. *Odboj a revoluce*, V (1967), No. 5, pp. 82–96.

Klein, Burton H. *Germany's Economic Preparations for War*. Cambridge, Mass.: Harvard University Press, 1959.

Klimešová, Libuše, and Pekárek, Bohumil. "Ilegální tisk" [The Underground Press]. *Odboj a revoluce*, IV (1966), No. 4, Supplement, pp. 28–40.

Kmoníček, Josef. "Ilegální činnost KSČ na Královéhradecku 1938–1941" [Underground Activities of the CPC in the Hradec Králové Country]. *Odboj a revoluce*, IV (1966), No. 4, Supplement, pp. 41–82.

——. "O některých formách práce nacistického okupačního aparátu proti odboji na Královéhradecku" [The Working Patterns of the Nazi Occupation Machinery Used against Resistance in the Hradec Králové Country]. *Historie a vojenství*, 1965, pp. 755–72.

Koehl, Robert L. *RKFDV: German Resettlement and Population Policy*,

1939–1945: A History of the Reich Commission for the Strengthening of Germandom. Cambridge, Mass.: Harvard University Press, 1957.

Konopka, Vladimír. *Zde stávaly Lidice* [Lidice Used to Stand Here]. Prague: Naše vojsko – Svaz protifašistických bojovníků, 1962.

Korbel, Josef. *The Communist Subversion of Czechoslovakia, 1938–1948: The Failure of Coexistence.* Princeton: Princeton University Press, 1959.

Krajina, Vladimír. "La résistance tchécoslovaque." *Cahiers d'histoire de la guerre,* III (1950), pp. 55–76.

Král, Václav. *Otázky hospodářského a sociálního vývoje v českých zemích v letech 1938–45* [Economic and Social Development in Bohemia and Moravia in 1938–45]. 3 vols. Prague: Nakladatelství Československé akademie věd, 1957–1959.

——. "Kolaborace nebo rezistence?" [Collaboration or Resistance?]. *Dějiny a současnost,* VII (1965), No. 7, pp. 1–7.

——. *Pravda o okupaci* [The Truth about the Occupation]. Prague: Naše vojsko, 1962.

Krausnick, Helmut, *et al. Anatomy of the SS State.* New York: Walker, 1968.

Křen, Jan. *Do emigrace: Buržoazní zahraniční odboj, 1938–1939* [Into Exile: The Bourgeois Resistance Movement Abroad]. Prague: Naše vojsko, 1963.

——. "Dr. Beneš za války" [Dr. Beneš during the War]. *Československý časopis historický,* XIII (1965), pp. 797–826.

——. "Hodža—slovenská otázka v zahraničním odboji" [Hodža and the Slovak Question in the Resistance Movement Abroad]. *Československý časopis historický,* XVI (1968), pp. 193–214.

——. "Vojenský odboj na počátku okupace Československa (1938–1940)" [Military Resistance at the Beginning of the Occupation of Czechoslovakia]. *Historie a vojenství,* 1961, pp. 271–313.

——, and Kural, Václav. "Ke stykům mezi československým odbojem a SSSR v letech 1939–1941" [The Relations between the Czechoslovak Resistance Movement and the USSR in 1939–1941]. *Historie a vojenství,* 1967, pp. 437–71, 731–71.

Kropáč, F., and Louda, V. *Persekuce českého studentstva za okupace* [The Persecution of Czech Students during the Occupation]. Prague: Orbis, 1946.

Kučera, Karel, and Truc, Miroslav. "Poznámky k fašizaci německé university pražské" [The Fascist Transformation of the German University in Prague], in *Historia Universitatis Carolinae Pragensis,* vol. I–II (Prague: Státní pedagogické nakladatelství, 1960), pp. 203–23.

Kulischer, Eugene M. *The Displacement of Population in Europe.* Montreal: International Labour Office, 1943.

Kural, Václav. "Hlavní organizace nekomunistického odboje v letech 1939–1941" [The Principal Organizations of the Non-Communist Resistance Movement in 1939–1941]. *Odboj a revoluce*, V (1967), No. 2, pp. 5–160.

Kvaček, Robert. "Československo-německá jednání v roce 1936" [Czechoslovak-German Negotiations in 1936]. *Historie a vojenství*, 1965, pp. 721–54.

——, and Vinš, Václav. "K německo-československým sondážím ve třicátých letech" [German-Czechoslovak Feelers in the Thirties]. *Československý časopis historický*, XIV (1966), pp. 880–96.

Lagus, Karel, and Polák, Josef. *Město za mřížemi* [A City behind Bars]. Prague: Naše vojsko – Svaz protifašistických bojovníků, 1964.

Latour, Conrad F. *Südtirol und die Achse Berlin-Rom, 1938–1945*. Stuttgart: Deutsche Verlags-Anstalt, 1962.

Lehár, Lubomír. "Vývoj Národní odborové ústředny zaměstnanecké v prvních letech nacistické okupace" [The Development of the National Union of Employees in the First Years of the Nazi Occupation]. *Historie a vojenství*, 1966, pp. 584–619.

Letocha, Josef. "Okupační veřejná správa 1938–1945 ve Východočeském kraji" [The Occupation Administration in East Bohemia in 1938–1945], in *Východní Čechy 1964* (Havlíčkův Brod: Východočeské nakladatelství, 1964), pp. 20–42.

Lukacs, John A. *The Great Powers and Eastern Europe*. New York: American Book Company, 1953.

Lukeš, František. "Dvě tajné cesty Vladimíra Krychtálka do Německa" [Vladimír Krychtálek's Two Secret Trips to Germany]. *Dějiny a současnost*, IV (1962), No. 2, pp. 28–29.

——. "K volbě Emila Háchy presidentem tzv. druhé republiky" [The Election of Emil Hácha as President of the So-Called Second Republic]. *Časopis Národního musea*, Social Science series, CXXXI (1962), pp. 114–20.

——. "Německá politika po Mnichovu a okupace Československa" [German Policy after Munich and the Occupation of Czechoslovakia]. *Odboj a revoluce*, IV (1966), No. 2, pp. 3–18.

——. "Příspěvek k objasnění politiky české a německé buržoazie v předvečer 15. března 1939" [The Policy of the Czech and German Bourgeoisie on the Eve of March 15, 1939]. *Časopis Národního musea*, Social science series, CXXX (1961), pp. 49–74.

Luža, Radomír. *The Transfer of the Sudeten Germans: A Study of Czech-German Relations, 1933–1962*. New York: New York University Press, 1964.

Lvová, Míla. *Mnichov a Edvard Beneš* [Munich and Edvard Beneš]. Prague: Svoboda, 1968.

Mabey, Melvin P. "The Origin and Development of the Communist

Party of Czechoslovakia, 1918–1938." Unpublished doctoral dissertation, St. Antony's College, Oxford University, 1955.

Macek, Jaroslav. "Okupační justice v českém pohraničí a její vývoj (1938–1945)" [The Occupation Judiciary in the Czech Borderland and Its Development (1938–1945)]. *Sborník archivních prací*, XIII (1963), No. 1, pp. 63–118.

Madajczyk, Czesław. "Okupační politika Třetí říše vůči polskému národu" [The Occupation Policy of the Third Reich toward the Polish People], in *Nacistická okupace Evropy*, vol. I, part 1 (Prague: Naše vojsko, 1966), pp. 234–74.

Mastny, Vojtech. "Design or Improvisation: The Origins of the German Protectorate of Bohemia and Moravia in 1939," in *Columbia Essays in International Affairs*. Edited by Andrew W. Cordier (New York: Columbia University Press, 1966), pp. 127–53.

——. "Unfinished Revolution." *The New Leader*, June 23, 1969, pp. 21–24.

Meyer, Henry Cord. *Mitteleuropa in German Thought and Action, 1815–1945*. The Hague: Nijhoff, 1955.

Milward, Alan S. *The German Economy at War*. London: Athlone Press, 1965.

"Nacistický bezpečnostní aparát na Moravě v letech 1939–1945" [The Nazi Security Machine in Moravia in 1939–1945]. *Sborník Matice moravské*, LXXXIV (1965), pp. 232–57.

Nesvadba, František. "Vládní vojsko a jeho odsun do Itálie" [The Government Force and Its Transfer to Italy]. *Historie a vojenství*, 1968, pp. 924–61.

"Neue Veröffentlichung über Globke." *Stuttgarter Zeitung*, February 7, 1961.

Novák, Jaroslav. *Im Zeichen zweier Kreuze*. Prague: Orbis, 1962.

Novotný, Josef. "Činnost KSČ v letech 1938–1941" [CPC's Activities in 1938–1941]. *Odboj a revoluce*, IV (1966), No. 4, pp. 65–114.

Odboj a revoluce, 1938–1945: Nástin dějin československého odboje [Resistance and Revolution, 1938–1945: An Outline of the History of Czechoslovak Resistance]. Prague: Naše vojsko, 1965.

"Options in Czechoslovakia: A Symposium." *Studies in Comparative Communism*, II (1969), No. 2, pp. 74–94.

Orlow, Dietrich. *The Nazis in the Balkans: A Case Study of Totalitarian Politics*. Pittsburgh: University of Pittsburgh Press, 1968.

Pasák, Tomáš. "Aktivističtí novináři a postoj generála Eliáše v roce 1941" [The Activist Newsmen and General Eliáš's Attitude in 1941]. *Československý časopis historický*, XV (1967), pp. 173–92.

——. "Generál Eliáš a problémy kolaborace" [General Eliáš and the Problems of Collaboration]. *Dějiny a současnost*, X (1968), No. 6, pp. 33–37.

258   Bibliography

——. "K činnosti Českého národního výboru na počátku okupace" [The Czech National Committee at the Beginning of the Occupation], in Z českých dějin [From Czech History]. Edited by Zdeněk Fiala and Rostislav Nový. (Prague: Universita Karlova, 1966), pp. 289–315.

——. "Nekomunistický odboj a jeho spolupráce s protektorátní vládou" [The Cooperation of the Non-Communist Resistance Movement with the Protectorate Government]. Odboj a revoluce, V (1967), No. 2, Supplement, pp. 71–83.

——. "Problematika moravského extrémně-pravicového hnutí v roce 1939" [The Extreme Right-Wing Movements in Moravia in 1939]. Slezský sborník, LXVI (1968), pp. 16–27.

——. "Problematika protektorátního tisku a formování tzv. skupiny aktivistických novinářů na počátku okupace" [The Protectorate Press and the Origins of the Group of the So-Called Activist Newsmen]. Příspěvky k dějinám KSČ, VII (1967), pp. 52–80.

——. "Prohlášení generála Aloise Eliáše před německým soudem v roce 1941 a jeho rozpornost" [The Discrepancies in the Declaration of General Alois Eliáš before the German Court in 1941]. Československý časopis historický, XVI (1968), pp. 447–58.

——. "Vývoj Vlajky v období okupace" [Vlajka's Development in the Occupation Period]. Historie a vojenství, 1966, pp. 846–95.

Pěnička, Alois. Kladensko v boji za svobodu [The Kladno Country in the Struggle for Freedom]. Prague: Svoboda, 1953.

Perman, Dagmar. The Shaping of the Czechoslovak State: Diplomatic History of the Boundaries of Czechoslovakia, 1914–1920. Leiden: Brill, 1962.

Polavský, Arnošt. V boj [Into Combat]. Třebechovice pod Orebem: Dědourek, 1946.

Polišenský, Josef. "28. říjen a 15. a 17. listopad 1939, perzekuce českého studentstva" [October 28 and November 15–17: The Persecution of the Czech Students], in Sedmnáctý listopad [The Seventeenth of November]. (Prague: Naše vojsko – Svaz protifašistických bojovníků, 1959), pp. 33–46.

Přikryl, Josef. "Příspěvek k ilegálním přechodům hranic na jihovýchodní Moravě na počátku nacistické okupace" [Illegal Border Crossings in Southeastern Moravia at the Beginning of the Nazi Occupation]. Odboj a revoluce, V (1967), No. 2, Supplement, pp. 137–52.

——. "Vojenská odbojová organizace Obrana národa" [The Military Resistance Organization "Nation's Defense"]. Sborník Matice moravské, LXXXVI (1967), pp. 43–60.

"Proč přišel Heydrich" [Why Heydrich Came]. Hlas revoluce, September 22, 1961.

"Proceedings of a Conference on Britain and European Resistance

1939–45 Organised by St. Antony's College, Oxford, December 10–16, 1962." (Mimeographed.)

Procházka, Václav. "Město zemře za svítání" [The Town Will Die at Dawn]. *Jihočeská pravda*, June 2, 1963.

Průcha, Václav, and Olšovský, Rudolf. "L'occupazione nazista e l'economia cecoslovacca," in *L'occupazione nazista in Europa*. Edited by Enzo Collotti (Rome: Editori Riuniti, 1964), pp. 311–66.

Radimský, Jiří. "Z prvního roku okupace" [From the First Year of the Occupation]. In *Brno v minulosti a dnes*, vol. VII (Brno: Blok, 1965), pp. 183–92.

Rauschning, Hermann. *Makers of Destruction: Meetings and Talks in Revolutionary Germany*. London: Eyre and Spottiswood, 1942.

Reitlinger, Gerald. *The SS: Alibi of a Nation*. London: Heinemann, 1956.

Ripka, Hubert. *Munich: Before and After*. London: Golancz, 1939.

Rossi, Arturo (Tasca, Angelo). *Physiologie du parti communiste français*. Paris: Self, 1948.

Robbins, Keith. *Munich 1938*. London: Cassell, 1968.

Roberts, Adam (ed.). *The Strategy of Civilian Defense*. London: Faber and Faber, 1967.

Robertson, Esmonde Manning. *Hitler's Pre-War Policy and Military Plans, 1933–1939*. London: Longmans, 1963.

Schiefer, Hans. "Deutschland und die Tschechoslowakei von September 1938 bis März 1939." *Zeitschrift für Ostforschung*, IV (1955), pp. 48–66.

Schorske, Carl. "Politics in a New Key: Schönerer," in *The Responsibility of Power*. Edited by Leonard Krieger and Fritz Stern (New York: Doubleday, 1967), pp. 233–51.

Schweitzer, Arthur. *Big Business in the Third Reich*. Bloomington: Indiana University Press, 1964.

Seabury, Paul. *The Wilhelmstrasse: A Study of German Diplomats under the Nazi Regime*. Berkeley and Los Angeles: University of California Press, 1954.

Ševčík, Antonín. "Příspěvek k dějinám okupační správy v Brně v letech 1939–1945" [The History of the Occupation Administration in Brno in 1939–1945]. In *Brno v minulosti a dnes*, VI (Brno: Krajské nakladatelství, 1964), pp. 127–37.

Shirer, William L. *The Rise and Fall of the Third Reich: A History of Nazi Germany*. New York: Simon and Schuster, 1960.

Šíma, Ladislav. *Ležáky: Vražda mužů a žen, odvlečení dětí do ciziny, srovnání osady se zemí* [Ležáky: The Murder of the Men and Women, the Kidnapping of Children Abroad, the Leveling of the Village]. Prague: Ministerstvo vnitra, 1947.

Šimka, Alois. *Od Mnichova k 15. březnu* [From Munich to March 15]. Jihlava: Krajský výbor Svazu protifašistických bojovníků, 1959.

——. "Chronologie odboje na jihozápadní Moravě, 1939–1945" [The Chronology of Resistance in Southwestern Moravia, 1939–1945]. *Odboj a revoluce*, V (1967), No. 3, pp. 169–98.

Šisler, Stanislav. "Příspěvek k vývoji a organizaci okupační správy v českých zemích v letech 1939–1945" [The Development and Organization of the Occupation Administration in Bohemia and Moravia in 1939–1945]. *Sborník archivních prací*, XIII (1963), No. 2, pp. 46–95.

Skilling, H. Gordon. "Communism and Czechoslovak Traditions." *Journal of International Affairs*, XX (1966), No. 1, pp. 118–36.

——. "The Czechoslovak Struggle for National Liberation in World War II." *Slavonic and East European Review*, XXXIX (1960), pp. 174–97.

Sobota, Emil. *Co to byl protektorát* [What the Protectorate Was]. Prague: Kvasnička a Hampl, 1946.

Stahl, Pavel. "Niektoré problémy prechodu KSS do ilegality" [Problems Concerning the Passage of the Communist Party of Slovakia Underground]. *Odboj a revoluce*, V (1967), No. 1, pp. 40–46.

Stein, George. *The Waffen SS: Hitler's Elite Guard at War, 1939–1945*. Ithaca: Cornell University Press, 1966.

Strnadel, Josef. "Marek Frauwirth a 17. listopad" [Marek Frauwirth and November 17]. *Plamen*, V (1963), No. 11, pp. 135–36.

Ströbinger, Rudolf. *A-54: Spion mit drei Gesichtern*. Munich: List, 1966.

Szporluk, Roman. "Masaryk's Idea of Democracy." *Slavonic and East European Review*, XLI (1962), pp. 31–49.

Taborsky, Eduard. "Local Government in Czechoslovakia, 1918–1948." *American Slavic and East European Review*, X (1951), pp. 202–15.

Taylor, A. J. P. *The Origins of the Second World War*. London: Hamilton, 1961.

Tesař, Jan. "'Záchrana národa' a kolaborace" [The "Saving of the Nation" and Collaboration]. *Dějiny a současnost*, X (1968), No. 5, pp. 5–9.

Thomson, S. Harrison. *Czechoslovakia in European History*. Princeton: Princeton University Press, 1953.

Toynbee, Arnold, and Toynbee, Veronica M. (eds.). *Hitler's Europe*. London: Oxford University Press, 1954.

Vávrovský, Emil. "Obrana Čajánkových kasáren ve Frýdku-Místku" [The Defense of the Čajánek Barracks at Frýdek-Místek]. *Těšínsko*, 1959, No. 9, p. 1.

Veselý-Štainer, Karel. *Cestou národního odboje: Bojový vývoj domácího odbojového hnutí v letech 1938–1945* [The Path of National Resistance: The Fighting Development of the Home Resistance Movement in 1938–1945]. Prague: Sfinx, 1947.

Vilinskij, Valerij. "České koncerny za války" [The Czech Concerns during the War]. *Statistický obzor*, 1946, pp. 56–62.

Vital, David. "Czechoslovakia and the Powers, September 1938." *Journal of Contemporary History*, I (1966), No. 4, pp. 37–67.

Vozka, Jaroslav. *Hrdinové domácího odboje* [The Heroes of the Home Resistance]. Prague: Práce, 1946.

Vrabec, Václav. "Petiční výbor 'Věrni zůstaneme'" [The Committee of the Petition "We Remain Faithful"]. *Odboj a revoluce*, V (1967), No. 2, Supplement, pp. 21–37.

Vrbata, Jaroslav. "Přehled vývoje veřejné správy v odtržených českých oblastech v letech 1938–1945" [The Devolopment of the Public Administration in the Separated Czech Territories in 1938–1945]. *Sborník archivních prací*, XII (1962), No. 2, pp. 45–67.

Walter, Eugene V. *Terror and Resistance: A Study in Political Violence.* New York: Oxford University Press, 1969.

Weinberg, Gerhard L. *Germany and the Soviet Union, 1939–1941.* Leiden: Brill, 1954.

——. "Secret Hitler-Beneš Negotiations in 1936–37." *Journal of Central European Affairs*, XIX (1960), pp. 366–74.

Wheeler-Bennett, John W. *Munich: Prologue to Tragedy.* New York: The Viking Press, 1964.

Whiteside, Andrew Gladding. *Austrian National Socialism before 1918.* The Hague: Nijhoff, 1962.

Wighton, Charles. *Heydrich, Hitler's Most Evil Henchman.* London: Odhams, 1962.

Windsor, Philip, and Roberts, Adam. *Czechoslovakia 1968: Reform, Repression and Resistance.* New York: Columbia University Press, 1969.

Wiskemann, Elisabeth. *Czechs and Germans: A Study of the Struggle in the Historic Provinces of Bohemia and Moravia.* London: Oxford University Press, 1938.

Zinner, Paul E. "Czechoslovakia: The Diplomacy of Eduard Beneš," in *The Diplomats, 1919–1939.* Edited by Gordon A. Craig and Felix Gilbert (Princeton: Princeton University Press, 1953), pp. 100–122.

Zipfel, Friedrich. *Kirchenkampf in Deutschland, 1933–1945: Religionsverfolgung und Selbstbehauptung der Kirchen in der nationalsozialistischen Zeit.* West Berlin: De Gruyter, 1965.

INDEX